Le Corbusier
Elements of a Synthesis

Le Corbusier
Elements of a Synthesis

Stanislaus von Moos

The MIT Press
Cambridge, Massachusetts, and London, England

Second printing, July 1980
Copyright © 1979
The Massachusetts Institute of Technology

Originally published in German as
Le Corbusier, Elemente einer Synthese by
Verlag Huber in 1968

This book was set in VIP Palatino by Achorn Graphic Services, Inc.,
and printed and bound by Halliday Lithograph Corp. in the United
States of America.

Library of Congress Cataloging in Publication Data

Moos, Stanislaus von.
   Le Corbusier, elements of a synthesis.

   Translation of Le Corbusier, Elemente einer Synthese.
   Includes bibliographical references.
   1.   Jeanneret-Gris, Charles Édouard, 1887–1965.
I.   Title.
NA1053.J4M613   720′.92′4   78–25940
ISBN 0–262–22023–7

Contents

Preface

The original version of this book was written ten years ago, as part of a series of monographs on famous Swiss-born men and women of science, art, and literature—from Paracelsus to Paul Klee and C. G. Jung. At that time, no comprehensive, critical study on Le Corbusier's work was available, so my plan was to fill this gap. When I started to work on the book, Le Corbusier's personal archives were not accessible; thus my sources of information were primarily the published works of the architect himself, and the eight volumes of the *Oeuvre complète*. Furthermore, I have visited almost all of Le Corbusier's buildings, seen a great many of his paintings, and met many of his former collaborators and friends who agreed to assist me with biographical information.

That a general study compiled a decade ago, before Le Corbusier became a fashionable subject in the architectural academe, should now be submitted to an English and American public is both pleasing and disconcerting. It is pleasing because the book—which, when it first appeared, was given a sympathetic reception by English and American critics—may now become available in a part of the world where the interest in its subject has been by far livelier than in its place of origin. Its contents also bring to mind many good discussions between 1971 and 1977 at places like Harvard University, the Architectural Association in London, the Technische Hogeschool in Delft, and various American schools.

Yet I cannot help that certain parts of the book, seen at the distance of ten years, appear out of date in the light not only of recent studies but also of my own altered views concerning the subject. I have included what appears to be the most important new information available on Le Corbusier's career and work, and have rewritten certain parts to correspond better with my present outlook. A new chapter on the typological and ideological premises of the Unité d'habitation has also been added. Yet on the whole, this remains the translation of a series of essays written between 1967 and 1968, and I have not tried to alter their character, for perhaps what appears as either lack of objectivity or excess of enthusiasm may contribute to their readability as a book.

Had I to write another monograph on the same topic today, I would probably go much further in my attempts to decode the social and ideological contents of Le Corbusier's programs and formal *dimostrazioni*. To the extent that visions of the future are extrapolations of certain aspects of the present, I believe that Le Corbusier is more interesting today as a "visionary" of his own time than as a prophet. If this is true, then it is so thanks to his stature as an artist and the intelligence and complexity of his visual and poetic approach to reality. As far as this aspect of the problem is concerned, much more detailed discussions of his works would be needed than the necessarily brief comments in this book; yet I would still work along the lines of my notes on "Typology" and on the "Elements of a Synthesis" which, it seems to me, have not been superseded by more recent approaches.

The persons and the institutions who were most helpful in the early stages of my involvement with Le Corbusier have been listed in the original edition; I would like to reiterate my thanks although the list of names is far from complete. I am especially indebted to Willy Boesiger (Zurich), editor of the *Oeuvre complète*, for having allowed the use of material from his own archives for the illustrations in this book. The following friends and collaborators of Le Corbusier have offered their help in my search for biographical information: Albert Jeanneret, Le Corbusier's brother (Vevey), Léon Perrin (La Chaux-de-Fonds), J.-P. de Montmollin (Neuchâtel), Tino Nivola (Long Island) and, above all, Pierre A. Emery (Villars S. Ollon, Switzerland).

Many institutions have facilitated access to source material and professional literature: the Bibliothèque de la Ville de La Chaux-de-Fonds, the Bibliothèque du Musée des Arts Décoratifs in Paris, and the Library of the Museum of Modern Art, New York. Maurice Besset, at that time the head of the Fondation Le Corbusier, allowed me to study the collection of paintings and drawings then in the possession of the foundation. Heidi Weber (Zurich) was kind enough to help me out with photographs of works from her collection.

Walter Gropius, José Luis Sert, Eduard F. Sekler (Cambridge, Mass.) and Arthur Drexler from the Museum of Modern Art (New York) agreed to talk to me about Le Corbusier and have thereby contributed to clarifying my ideas on the subject;

various conversations with Alfred Roth (Zurich) were particularly helpful.

My trip to Chandigarh (April 1968) and various excursions to France have been made possible by a grant from the Janggen-Poehn Foundation, St. Gallen (Switzerland).

The greater my distance to these beginnings, the more clear is it to me how much I owe especially to three people whom I was fortunate to have worked with during the sixties: Sigfried Giedion, his wife Carola Giedion-Welcker, and Hans Curjel. I should add that I never actually met Le Corbusier himself.

Many friends have encouraged me in the preparation of the revised text. I am grateful to André Corboz (Montreal) who wrote the most perceptive review of the book's French edition in the *Journal de Genève* (1972); to Peter Serenyi, who included two parts of what he called "the first historical study of Le Corbusier's entire artistic career" in his useful anthology *Le Corbusier in Perspective* (New York, 1974), and to Elizabeth Sussman (Cambridge, Mass.), H. Allen Brooks (Toronto), Alan Colquhoun (London) and Harvey Mendelsohn (Paris) who read parts of the manuscript. The Fondation Le Corbusier in Paris has been helpful in my more recent research efforts and in granting permission for the reproduction of various hitherto unknown documents from the Le Corbusier archives. However, I would never have tackled this translation had I not been invited to teach the History of Architecture for four years in the United States, in a building designed by Le Corbusier—Harvard's Carpenter Center for the Visual Arts; and to students whose critical share of my interests has been a challenge.

The actual translation has been a long and cumbersome affair which involved the competence and the goodwill of many people: in its early stages it was drafted by Beatrice Mock and supervised by Joseph Stein of the MIT Press, and I shall always feel indebted to him for his help and his friendship. The final shape of the text is due to the last-minute help of Maureen Oberli (Vitznau, Switzerland).

Le Corbusier
Elements of a Synthesis

1 Charles-Edouard Jeanneret

La Chaux-de-Fonds, where Le Corbusier was born on October 6, 1887, is a frontier town, situated between two ridges of the Jura, not far from the French border. The valley, austere and remote, 300 feet above sea level, is almost alpine in character; the broad shoulders of the mountains are frequently cut by ravines and gorges which expose the rock. Charles L'Eplattenier's paintings depict this scenery with wide horizons, often hung with clouds, occasionally offering a glimpse southward into the sunnier plains of the Swiss midlands (fig. 1).

Since the twelfth and thirteenth centuries, the time of the Albigensian wars, religious minorities from southern France used to retire into the Jura valleys in order to escape persecution and repression. Protestant refugees from the south and from Burgundy arrived during the Wars of Religion and especially after the Edict of Nantes in the sixteenth century. Today the people of La Chaux-de-Fonds still like to speak of their history as being revolutionary, and they are proud of their democratic tradition. To quote Le Corbusier's own words, "I need not be ashamed of my origins. The mountains of Neuchâtel have witnessed a past of liberty, ingenuity and courage."

He reminisced about the region's struggle for independence from the Prussians who had remained the rulers of Neuchâtel, and thus of La Chaux-de-Fonds, even after 1814 when the county of Neuchâtel had become a Swiss canton: "On March 1, 1848, my grandfather Jeanneret-Rauss went with Fritz Courvoisier, on foot, from La Chaux-de-Fonds to Neuchâtel and captured the castle without shedding a drop of blood. He was one of the leaders of the revolution. My great-grandfather was a revolutionary too, and died as a result of his imprisonment."[1]

Le Corbusier did not, however, always consider his Swiss ancestry to be an advantage. In order to ease his way into the Paris establishment, he claimed to have French ancestors. A group of houses not far from Le Locle, a few miles west of La Chaux-de-Fonds, called "Les Jeannerets" on a seventeenth-century map, substantiated this version of his genealogy. These sixteenth-century stone houses, which were gutted by a fire in 1918, displayed a form of low-pitched roof similar to the vernacular house styles of the Languedoc, a region in southern France.[2]

Whatever the veracity of this evidence of the family's genealogy may be, it indicates the architect's determination to be part of the Mediterranean world. One should not forget that Le Corbusier's emotional links with the Mediterranean were primarily the result of a cultural choice and not of a natural condition; and this choice reflects the experiences of years spent in the Swiss Jura in a landscape where the snow under the trees does not melt for almost six months.

La Chaux-de-Fonds lives by its watchmaking industry, and both Le Corbusier's father and grandfather worked there as enamelers of watch faces. His father, Edouard Jeanneret-Perret served for many years as president of the local Alpine Club and his mother was a piano teacher. The authority she exerted over her two sons—especially the younger one, Charles-Edouard, the future Le Corbusier—can hardly be overestimated. Her Protestant morality and outlook have shaped the architect's own feelings about life, work, and social responsibility. She used to say, "Whatever you do, do it."[3]

Charles L'Eplattenier and the Art School in La Chaux-de-Fonds

For sixteen years (1900–1916) the art school in La Chaux-de-Fonds was the background of Charles-Edouard Jeanneret's education. The director of the school, Charles L'Eplattenier, guided the student's first experiences in the arts and later provided him with his first teaching position (1911). Jeanneret spent three years learning the craft of watch engraving, an exact and demanding skill requiring precision and strict concentration. One false move and an expensive piece of gold or silver is ruined.[4]

The school's atmosphere was characterized by an emphasis on craftsmanship and skill, and, due to the director's own intellectual temperament, a passion for ideas. L'Eplattenier was about twenty-five years old when Jeanneret entered the school. The Ecole d'Art itself was founded in 1870 in order to supply the local watch industry with engravers; but in 1903, when L'Eplattenier took over the directorship, a redefinition of the school's purpose was urgently needed. The preprofessional character of its educational program had become problematic. Watch manufacturing was on the road to industrialization, and the demand for expensive, engraved pocket watches was diminishing while the wrist-watch was beginning to conquer the international markets.

L'Eplattenier realized that the arts and crafts as they had traditionally been taught at the school now had to face a dual challenge: on one hand, it had become necessary to make designers aware of the specific needs and problems of industrial production; on the other hand, new fields had to be opened up for the application of the skills which had been, up to then, almost exclusively directed toward the decoration of watch faces.[5]

In 1905, L'Eplattenier was able to realize the first steps toward a reform of the school by creating a postgraduate program which he called "Cours Supérieur d'Art et de Décoration." He had invited the best graduates of the school to enroll in the new program where they were assigned various, often large projects involving architectural and interior design. Jeanneret was among the first group of students in the "Cours Supérieur" together with Léon Perrin, Georges Aubert, and others who later (after 1910) joined forces to found the "Ateliers d'Arts Réunis."[6]

Art Nouveau, Ruskin, and the Jura Landscape

It must have been L'Eplattenier's intention to create in La Chaux-de-Fonds a counterpart to Victor Prouvé's successful venture in Nancy: an international center of Art Nouveau design. He was very much aware of contemporary efforts in the applied arts, and he shared an interest in organic, especially floral and vegetable, ornament with the international advocates of Art Nouveau architecture. The ornament had in fact become the *mot d'ordre* of the age; it allowed the designers to free themselves from what they considered the suffocating legacy of historic styles, and freed them to tackle the new construction techniques, particularly those involving iron and concrete, with an often ingenious directness. In their individual ways, architects such as Gaudí in Barcelona, Guimard in Paris, or van de Velde in Belgium had reinterpreted architecture as the art of monumental ornamentation, illustrating Julius Meier-Graefe's statement that "one frequently began with the endpaper of a book and ended with the facade."[7]

But for these architects and designers ornament was more than mere formal play, it was a means of symbolizing essential

qualities of life. This was also the view adopted by L'Eplattenier, who tried to develop, together with his pupils, a new,
decorative style characteristic of the Jura region. To this end he
used examples from ancient art in order to demonstrate his
aims. According to L'Eplattenier there were three immortal
periods of architecture: ancient Egyptian, with its lotus leaf,
Greek, with its acanthus, and Gothic, with its flowers, animals,
and chimera. With this in mind, he and his students went out
into the woods to study the fauna and the flora of the Jura region with the intention of establishing a genuine Jura style.

The results were sometimes more surrealistic than monumental. The school of arts and crafts in La Chaux-de-Fonds pre-
serves many curiosities, such as a huge bookcase beautifully
carved with plants, pine cones, branches, and a lizard according to the master's instructions. L'Eplattenier's later projects in
the area of the applied arts often tended toward an almost
Egyptian monumentality, for example, his sculptural decorations for the staircase in the La Chaux-de-Fonds museum
(1924).[8]

Some of Charles-Edouard Jeanneret's early studies give the
clearest insight into L'Eplattenier's educational program. They
illustrate the transition from natural, organic form to abstract,
stylized ornamentation, which was the central theme of the
school's aesthetics. In numerous drawings, the process can be
followed step-by-step (figs. 3, 6). Among the recurring motives
are leaves, frogs, and lizards. Pine trees, too, the symbolic icons
of the Jura forests, were combined into decorative patterns
evoking snow-laden branches, or isolated as simple triangles.
These studies arrive at a degree of geometric abstraction that is
unusual in Art Nouveau design. Some of them come, in turn,
surprisingly close to the superb color plates in Owen Jones's
Grammar of Ornaments (1856), a copy of which was available at
the La Chaux-de-Fonds school. These studies are formal exer-
cises in decoration and geometry while at the same time indicating a more theoretical concern: they seek a common ground
where nature and mathematics meet. In other words, they attempt to make the structural laws of nature visible and to express them in clear and universal geometric patterns.

The preoccupations that emerge from these studies are in

many respects closer to Owen Jones or to John Ruskin than to
any of the contemporary protagonists of Art Nouveau. The cult
of Ruskin's ideals was an aspect of European artistic culture
around 1900, and Le Corbusier later recalled how much L'Eplattenier's school stood under the spell of the great Victorian
moralist:

In our childhood we were exhorted by Ruskin. . . . He spoke
of spirituality. In his *Seven Lamps of Architecture* he evoked the
lamp of sacrifice, the lamp of truth, the lamp of humility. . . .
Ruskin has deeply moved our hearts. . . .
    One realizes that nature as phenomenon is organized, one
opens one's eyes. 1900. Effusion. Beautiful moment, truly![9]

    But it was only possible for Ruskin's gospel to generate
such enthusiasm because it came at the right moment and it
offered answers to the problems of day-to-day existence and
gave meaning to what otherwise would have remained a vague
feeling.
    Outdoor life played a crucial role in Jeanneret's childhood.
His father used to take his sons for long walks, discoursing on
local plants and animals. As president of the town's Alpine
Club, he wrote detailed articles about his experiences as a
mountain climber for the *Bulletin Fédéral du Club Alpin*. Le Corbusier reported that his father's compulsive mountain climbing
ruined the Alps for him,[10] but in later years he liked to recall the
landscape of the Jura with its distant horizons.
    L'Eplattenier's early paintings, such as *Au sommet* ("On the
Summit," 1904), evoke the atmosphere: the dark, humid, shady
valley of La Chaux-de-Fonds to the right, the wide horizons
with Lake Neuchâtel to the left—a remote promise of sunshine
and Mediterranean clarity (fig. 1). In the closing chapter of *L'art
décoratif d'aujourd'hui* (1925), entitled "Confession," Le Corbusier recalls how he and his friends used to escape from the
bustle of the town to a remote barn in order to be closer to nature.[11] Sometimes, with knapsacks on their backs, they would
undertake long treks into the Swiss midlands. A barn or an
apple tree would provide shelter for the night, and in winter
they joined the first groups of skiers in the Bernese Oberland.
    The romantic ethusiasm for nature and open-air life that

inspired L'Eplattenier's students culminated in the idea of a shrine dedicated to nature, symbolically embodying the landscape with its flora and fauna.

On Sundays we often gathered at the summit of the highest mountain. Peaks and gently sloping banks; pastures, herds of large animals, infinite horizons, flights of crows. We prepared the future. "Here," said the master, "we will build a monument dedicated to nature. We will dedicate the ends of our lives to this project. We will leave the town and live in the forests at the foot of the edifice which we will slowly fill with our works. The entire site will become incarnate here. All the fauna, all the flora. Once every year great celebrations will be held. At the four corners of the edifice huge braziers will burn."[12]

"You will be an architect"—Villa Fallet

Jeanneret had decided that he wanted to become a painter. But his teacher insisted, "You will be an architect." At first Jeanneret demurred. But in the school's small library there was a copy of Charles Blanc's *Grammaire des arts du dessin*, one of the best-known textbooks of the period, in which architecture was described as the mother of the arts. Jeanneret must have been fascinated by that book, which is far more than a dry text: it depicts a panorama of history in arresting prose and contains the promise of great things to come. Blanc eloquently opposed the conception of the architect as mere decorator of an engineer's constructions.[13] In the spirit of Viollet-le-Duc and Choisy he proclaimed that the architecture of the future would develop from new construction methods and would be based on a thorough knowledge of the monuments of the past, which had been rediscovered in the nineteenth century. "But the regeneration of our schools can only be accomplished on one condition: if they do not become entrenched in archaeology, in pure imitation of objects, but grasp instead the spirit of things, extracting from the jumble of relics only those great and rare ideas that stand out."[14]

L'Eplattenier contacted the architect René Chapallaz, who had a small office in nearby Tavannes, and asked him to assist his student in the design and execution of a small house. Previously he had persuaded a member of the school board to give the seventeen-year-old Jeanneret the commission to build his villa. It was Jeanneret's first house, the Villa Fallet, situated on the slope of the Jura north of the town (1906) (fig. 2).[15]

Le Corbusier did not include his first building among his *Oeuvre complète*. There are no pictures of it in his publications; all that exists are occasional remarks on a little house executed at the age of eighteen "with extreme care"; a house which is "probably dreadful, yet untouched by architectural routine."[16] Yet this little "chalet" offers important clues for understanding Le Corbusier's background. The living area and the bedrooms are grouped around an open, two-storied hall, an idea which was not unusual in post-Arts-and-Crafts architecture around 1900, and which foreshadows Le Corbusier's obsession with two-story living rooms and galleries. But more surprising is the crust of decorative details that covers the facades and the interior walls.

In very general terms, the villa, with its raw, rusticated base and exposed timber and half-hipped gable, shows a preference for a neomedieval (rather than Art Nouveau) type of suburban residence. And it shares an aura of national romanticism with some of the great Swiss hotels of the period. But the detailing goes beyond eclectic medievalism. These decorations display a highly self-conscious iconography: most decorative forms are derived from the firs of the Jura—the wrought iron knocker on the front door, the iron balustrades of the two balconies, the reliefs on the interior paneling, the multicolored graffito pattern on the facade (fig. 4). Even the timberwork (Jeanneret worked out the details together with his comrades on the building site) obeys the iconography; the timber of the roof as well as the crossbars of the windows are geometric derivations of Jura pines (fig. 5). It is a conglomerate of ideas distilled from L'Eplattenier's Cours Supérieur, executed with enormous care, yet controlled by taste.

Florence; Vienna and Joseph Hoffmann

When in September 1907 with his first architect's fee in his pocket, Jeanneret traveled to Florence, he was in fact embarking on a discovery of Italy through Ruskin's eyes. Together with Perrin, who had preceded him, he rented a room opposite the Log-

gia dei Lanzi and visited Tuscany. Many drawings, especially
from Florence and Siena, survive.[17] The Middle Ages were
more attractive to him than the Renaissance; in the museums
it was the fourteenth-century "primitives" that caught his attention. His sketches of architecture reveal a passion for the
chromatic subleties of surface patterns and articulations, and
some of them, especially those of the interior of S. Croce in
Florence, display a concern with problems of structure and
architectural space.

When in the fall of the same year the two friends headed for
Vienna, they passed through Vicenza. Perrin recalls that Palladio's buildings there were not considered a sufficient pretext
for interrupting the journey. Palladio epitomized academic
classicism, so he was ignored. They did, however, visit
Ravenna; its mosaics had already made a strong impression on
Jeanneret at school.

On their way eastward the two travelers visited Trieste and
Budapest, but Vienna was where they decided to stay. They
were probably aware of the city's fame as one of the European
centers for modern arts and crafts. Otto Wagner, Vienna's
Stadtbaumeister since 1894, had been a well-known protagonist
of a "functional" approach to architecture since at least 1895,
when his little book *Moderne Architektur* was published. But he
was not only famous as a writer and as the architect of the stations of the "Wiener Stadtbahn." Wagner also counted among
his disciples two of the most famous avant-garde designers of
the time: Josef Maria Olbrich and Joseph Hoffmann. These
men were both much less interested in giving form to the
new realities of industrialization than was their master Otto
Wagner, whose concern with this matter made him a forerun-
ner of the International Style. Instead, they concentrated their
efforts upon a reform of the decorative arts through a refined
concept of design. Olbrich had been called to Darmstadt in 1899
by the Grand Duke Ernst Ludwig. But Hoffmann had remained
in Vienna and opened the "Wiener Werkstätte" in 1903, which
for the next three decades remained a center of modern handicrafts.

When Jeanneret arrived in Vienna, the Opera, the Phil-
harmonic, and the Kunsthistorisches Museum were of the
greatest interest to him, as were the exhibitions of the "Sezes-

sion" and the "Hagenbund," which displayed the works of the Viennese avant-garde. He seems to have been interested by Hoffmann's achievements and the Wiener Werkstätte. It is unlikely, however, that he was particularly impressed by Wagner or even familiar with Hoffmann's "rival" Adolf Loos and his famous article "Ornament and Crime" that appeared in 1906. For a long time Jeanneret seems to have hesitated to ask Hoffmann for a job, yet when he finally submitted his Italian sketches to the Austrian master he was hired immediately. As it turned out, however, it was too late. Jeanneret had seen a performance of Puccini's *La Bohème* a few days earlier, and as he later recalled, the representation of the gay life of Paris made him decide to leave for Paris at once.[18]

Jeanneret and Perrin left Vienna in March of 1908. In Munich, Jeanneret met with Chapallaz to discuss the construction of two houses he had designed in Vienna. The villas Jaquemet and Stotzer (figs. 10, 11) were to be built by Chapallaz next to the earlier villa Fallet in La Chaux-de-Fonds.[19] They are larger variations of the Fallet theme, less pedantic in their decorative detailing and in a way reminiscent of some slightly earlier designs by Olbrich, such as "Das Blaue Haus" or the "Haus in Rosen" in Darmstadt—although a direct influence is unlikely. Whereas the Fallet villa is organized around a central hall, the Jaquemet house is divided into two separate apartments. The Villa Stotzer in turn, a one-family house still owned by the Stotzer family and therefore in an excellent state of preservation, is served by a narrow staircase. These villas may lack the spatial complexity and elegance of Olbrich's, yet their rusticated bases, their mixed use of concrete and masonry, their timberwork, and the paneling of the interiors are full of imaginative details.

Paris, 1908: Perret and Nietzsche

Unlike Brussels with Victor Horta, Amsterdam with H. P. Berlage, or Vienna with Wagner and Hoffmann, the Paris of 1908 lacked an establishment of radically modern designers capable of neutralizing the cultural hegemony of the Ecole des Beaux-Arts and its academicism. There were, of course, the great iron structures of Labrouste, Eiffel, Boileau, and others of the

nineteenth century, which were to be so important for the definition of the Modern Movement's own ambitions. Furthermore,
no architect interested in structural innovation could ignore
Guimard's genius and Hennebique's pragmatism in the use of
reinforced concrete. The Perret brothers had already realized
some of their important works, such as the apartment house
at 25 bis, rue Franklin (1902). The recent addition to the
"Samaritaine" department stores by Frantz Jourdain was a
landmark in the history of iron and glass structures, although
its decorative fretwork partially obscured its boldness. Still
more important perhaps, was Henri Sauvage who by 1908 was
known for his competent Art Nouveau designs as well as for his
involvement in the reform of working class housing.[20]

On the road from Munich, Jeanneret stopped briefly in
Nuremberg, Strasbourg, and Nancy, and arrived in Paris later
in the spring. At that point he was an architect trying to find
work as a draftsman. He contacted Eugène Grasset, a graphic
designer and handicraftsman whose important book on ornamental composition had made his name familiar to the La
Chaux-de-Fonds group.[21] Grasset suggested that he look up
Perret, who was delighted with Jeanneret's drawings and offered him a part-time job. Perrin found a position with Hector
Guimard, the designer of the Paris Métro stations (1889–1904).
"A folder filled with my drawings from Italy. I knock at the door
at rue Franklin," Le Corbusier later recalled, "and find, as
though they had stepped out of a picture frame in the Pavillon
de Marsan, the two male figures from the *Déjeuner sur l'herbe*,
Auguste and Gustave Perret."[22]

The contacts with the Perret firm seem to have opened a
new chapter in Jeanneret's career as an architect by putting
him in contact with problems of structure and contemporary
means of resolving them.[23] The apartment house at 25 bis, rue
Franklin, where the Perrets' office was located, had been an almost revolutionary statement in this respect. With its U-shaped
plan opening up a maximum of the facade to·the sun and the
panorama of Paris, and with its seemingly fragile, exposed, yet
decorated, concrete frame, it seemed a hazardous experiment. It
had in fact been realized only because the architects were their
own contractors; no bank had been willing to grant a mortgage,
since imminent collapse had been predicted.[24]

    While working part-time for the Perrets, Jeanneret at-
tended history classes at the Ecole des Beaux-Arts and studied
at the museums, spending Sundays with the masterpieces in
the Louvre, and weekdays with applied art in the Musée de
l'Homme or the Trocadéro.[25] He also studied Notre Dame in
detail, in the footsteps of Viollet-le-Duc, fascinated by the logic
of its construction and confused by the wildness and fragmentation of its form. He spent the evenings studying the works of
Letarouilly, Choisy, Viollet-le-Duc, and others; but this was not
enough. He wanted to have a total grasp of the subject. Perret
advised him to study mathematics and statics.
    These months in Paris seem to have brought about a crys-
tallization of his ideas and feelings about architecture and especially about his mission as an architect on the threshold of a
new age. His master in La Chaux-de-Fonds had taught him to
consider the arts as a great idealist enterprise, and to consider
himself, the artist, as a servant of a moral regeneration of mankind. He had read books like Henri Provensal's *L'art de demain*
(1904) and Edouard Schuré's *Les grands initiés* (1907). And now
in Paris he devoured Nietzsche's *Thus Spake Zarathustra*. As
Paul Turner has shown in his fascinating study on Le Corbusier's education, these books played a fundamental role in
determining Jeanneret's self-awareness as an artist.[26] They
shaped his ideas and left their mark on his writing for the
rest of his career. Art and architecture as a "harmonious expression of thought" (Provensal), and thus as a mirror of eternal
laws, and the artist as a prophet leading his people toward a
spiritual purification and rejuvenation were (in simplest
terms) the beliefs which Jeanneret seems to have acquired from
these early readings. It need not be emphasized that the values
of Puritanism and charity he was brought up with were a fertile
basis for the development of such idealistic and spiritualistic
concepts. Nietzsche's image of the lonely superman, whose
tragic destiny it was to be sacrificed for the sake of mankind,
seems to have become a key to Jeanneret's understanding of his
own role as an artist in society.[27]
    Seen in this perspective, Jeanneret's earlier involvement in
the reform of the arts and crafts appears as a modest step toward
a real confrontation with the world. In November of 1908, Jeanneret sent a letter to L'Eplattenier, announcing his impending

visit to La Chaux-de-Fonds. It conveys a strong conviction and a defiant determination to suffer:

Today, childish dreams are over, those dreams of success like that achieved by one or two German schools: Vienna, Darmstadt. This is too easy, and I want to wrestle with truth itself. . . . It is from our thoughts that today . . . or tomorrow, the new art will emerge. Thoughts are naked and one has to wrestle with them. And in order to meet them so that the struggle can take place, one needs solitude.

As for myself, I say: all this petty success is premature; ruin is at hand. One does not build on sand.[28]

To Germany: Behrens and the AEG

After returning from Paris late in 1909, Jeanneret spent only a few months in La Chaux-de-Fonds. It was long enough, however, to get the work of the "Ateliers d'Art Réunis" underway.[29] In April 1910, he left his town again, this time for Germany. In Munich he looked up Theodor Fischer, who recommended him to a number of German architects, designers, and museum people. In the next few months Jeanneret made contact with the key figures in the German Werkbund. He met Peter Behrens, Hermann Muthesius, Karl Ernst Osthaus, Bruno Paul, Wolf Dohrn, and Heinrich Tessenow.

For five months he worked as a draftsman for Peter Behrens. He admired Behrens's professional competence, but he had mixed feelings about the man, "An ill-tempered bear, crabbed and choleric without reason, and this goes on from morning till evening."[30]

Rumor has it that Jeanneret worked there side by side with Gropius and Mies. The fact is that Gropius, who had long been the first draftsman in Behrens's studio, had left to go into business for himself a few months before Jeanneret arrived in Berlin. Mies van der Rohe in turn later recalled having met a certain Jeanneret on the doorstep of Behrens's office. At the time, in May 1911, Jeanneret was at the point of leaving for Dresden, whereas Mies joined the office as Behrens's new collaborator.[31]

Two months after his arrival in Germany, in June 1910, Jeanneret received a letter from the La Chaux-de-Fonds Art School asking him to prepare a report on the state of German crafts, on "methods of instruction, on design and on the manufacture and sale of art products." The report was later published as a book,[32] but it did not really get the attention it deserved, especially in France, for obvious political reasons.

Jeanneret describes the situation in the context of the political, intellectual, and artistic conditions in Germany and France. Germany was driven by a stubborn will to build, a grandiloquence that smacked of the 1870s. France was resting securely on a rich artistic heritage and so was unproductive. Individual personalities are characterized only briefly, but with an acute instinct for the specific character and the general significance of their contributions. Art Nouveau, which had been the overriding influence in Jeanneret's youth, is now viewed from a distance. Much space is in turn devoted to the problems of industrial design and, above all, to Peter Behrens's crucial role as chief designer of the AEG (*Allgemeine Elektrizitäts-Gesellschaft*) in Berlin.

Behrens, who had started his career as a painter, not only supervised the design of the new parts of the AEG factory itself, he designed virtually everything that the AEG produced—kitchenware, radiators, lamps, etc.—down to its letterheads. This attempt to create a corporate image not only of the AEG, but of German industrialism, if not of the Machine Age *tout court*, was of the greatest interest to Jeanneret.

At the end of his report he declares, "Germany is a book of topical interest. If Paris is the focus of the arts, Germany remains the great center of production."[33]

Voyage d'Orient

In May 1911, Jeanneret decided to visit Budapest and Bucharest, together with his friend from Berne, August Klipstein, who was then writing a thesis on El Greco and later became a well-known art dealer. They planned a short journey; it became a pilgramage to the East. At various stages of the trip Jeanneret wrote detailed reports for the *Feuille d'Avis*, the local newspaper of La Chaux-de-Fonds, that took the form of letters to his friends from the Ateliers d'Art Réunis.[34] The rhapsodic tone of these travel notes is disappointing to anyone who expects precise architectural observations: "I travel on foot, on horseback, by boat, by car, finding in the diversity of races the fundamental unity of human nature."[35]

This "Grand Tour" was not just a professional study trip, but a total experience, providing the raw material for Jeanneret's beautiful journal. "This trip to the East, far removed from the confused architecture of the north is a response to the persistent call of the sun, the blue seas, and the great white walls of the temples," Jeanneret declares. But then: "The impressions, I confess, were staggering, unexpected. Slowly they began to seize me. . . ."[36] His visits to Constantinople, Athos, and the Acropolis in Athens marked the climax of the trip.

He had formed his image of Istanbul long before he arrived there: "Under the white light I want a totally white city; only the green cypresses may punctuate it. And the blue of the sea will echo the blue of the sky." When he arrived it was a great disappointment. "The lead of the sky was allowed to pollute the water, making the sea gray. The Golden Horn was muddy and its rivers uncertain, like those in a swamp. The mosques, as dirty as old walls, were like blemishes on the somber wooden houses ranged in tiers among numerous trees"[37] (fig. 8). He decided that old Byzantium, "impérialement dissolue," Istanbul, Bera, and Scutari—that bazaar of activity and dirt—left him cold. It took him three weeks to appreciate the mosques. It was only when he began to understand the Eastern approach to life that he "saw" them. He describes their interiors as "lofty so that the prayers can breathe."[38] Here he started to grasp the meaning of a religion that does not instill the fear of death, that is both boundless and smiling. So Istanbul was yet another confirmation of deep spiritualistic convictions. He did not neglect the bazaars and the folklore, and he was fascinated by the city's center that seemed to be in constant danger of fire because of its wooden frame houses. He admired the vernacular architecture of Istanbul and wrote in his journal, "The wooden Turkish house, the konak, is an architectural masterpiece."[39]

Mount Athos brought still another confrontation with a way of life organized in a metaphysical perspective. It was a tumultuous confrontation and Jeanneret left Athos after a stay of 18 days, exclaiming in his journal, "Oh, to fight, to live, to shout, to create."[40]

In Athens, Jeanneret claims to have visited the Acropolis every day during four weeks, regardless of the weather. The northern colonnade of the Parthenon was not yet rebuilt. The drums of the columns laid there as they had fallen in 1687, when the powder stored inside the cella exploded as the result of a Turkish bombardment, "flung down, like a man who is hit full in the face."[41]

With his eyes and hands Jeanneret explored the sculptural relief of this architecture. He took it for granted that the Acropolis was the criterion for all art and all architecture. The problem for him was now to substitute experience for what had been up to then mere cultural baggage. At times he wavered between amazement and discouragement. "Admiration, adoration, then defeat," he notes in a frustrated effort to put the Parthenon in relation to the necessities of the present. And again his tone becomes almost Nietzschean. "This is an art which one cannot escape. Glacial, like an immense and unchanging truth. But when I see in my notebook a sketch of Stamboul, the fire in my heart is rekindled!"[42]

He saw the architecture together with the landscape: "The temples are the reason for the countryside."[43] His sketches were drawn as if he was in a state of feverish excitement. They are Romantic, almost Wagnerian, and they evoke the buildings as part of a landscape with wide horizons—horizons like those he had experienced on the Jura heights (fig. 9). Curiously, the few hasty scenographic impressions are all that seem to remain from these examinations on the Acropolis which, if Jeanneret was correct, occupied him for no less than four weeks.

The Nouvelle Section de l'Ecole d'Art

In retrospect, Le Corbusier spoke of the *Voyage d'Orient* as the closing chapter of his youth and the first stirrings of a radically fresh start. In 1925, he summarized, "Return. Digestion. A conviction: one must start all over again. One must state the problem."[44]

Things appear more complicated if one follows Jeanneret's career closely. In Istanbul, by chance he had run into Perret, who seems to have offered him a job in connection with the design for the Théâtre des Champs Elysées.[45] But Jeanneret had

other plans. He wanted to return to La Chaux-de-Fonds, for
while traveling he had been appointed a professor to the
Nouvelle Section de l'Ecole d'Art, a new department of the
school that had grown out of the Cours Supérieur.[46] L'Eplattenier had previously taught the Cours Supérieur alone; now,
however, he invited the three most advanced graduates to join
him: Jeanneret, the architect; Léon Perrin, the sculptor, and
Georges Aubert, the interior designer.

The story of the Nouvelle Section was one of frustrations,
like that of many other comparable ventures. The old school,
dominated by a conservative faculty, tried hard to rid itself of
the new appendage. Among other measures there was a requirement that the teachers of the Nouvelle Section had to obtain cantonal certificates as master draftsmen. In December
1913, Jeanneret announced that he was in possession of the
necessary diploma—the only one he ever acquired.

But the days of the Nouvelle Section were numbered.
Many socialists considered the new department a luxury, destined to produce "experts" for whom society had no jobs, and
the local craftsmen feared competition from the "designers."
Thus it was decided to present the curriculum of the Nouvelle
Section within the framework of the school's traditional program. This in effect amounted to dissolving the course. But the
Nouvelle Section did not submit meekly to its fate. Jeanneret, as
secretary of the Ateliers d'Art Réunis, was quite experienced in
the art of bombarding sluggish authorities and commissions
with letters. While the Nouvelle Section was in the process of
closing its doors, he drafted a small treatise that makes an impressive epitaph for the experiment. Experts from all over
Europe were asked for their opinion of the Nouvelle Section;
Eugène Grasset (Paris), Karl Ernst Osthaus (Essen), Peter
Behrens (Berlin), Theodor Fischer (Munich), Alfred Roller
(Vienna), and Hector Guimard (Paris), all responded with
enthusiastic praise and applause. But it was too late.[47]

L'Eplattenier resigned in March 1914; Jeanneret, Aubert,
and Perrin also refused to teach under the terms. Only Léon
Perrin later changed his mind; he remained loyal to the art
school in La Chaux-de-Fonds throughout his life. In contrast,
Jeanneret maintained that he had no desire to teach engravers
and jewelers.[48]

Thus the art school of La Chaux-de-Fonds returned to
where it had been in 1903: it was again a professional school for
engravers and jewelers serving the needs of the local watch
industry.

Buildings and Projects after 1911: The Influence of Behrens and Hoffmann

In 1908 Jeanneret had decided that he had to "wrestle with
truth" in order to help "the new art" emerge. At first sight the
elegant suburban residences for Swiss watchmakers built after
1911 may seem to fall short of this vow. Yet it was in its reestablishment of order, proportion, and neoclassical severity that
Jeanneret's generation took its revenge against the indi-
vidualism of Art Nouveau and the "petty success" of Vienna
and Darmstadt.

Jeanneret did not live solely by teaching following his return
from the East. He had a series of interesting commissions that
allowed him to inaugurate what one might call the second pre-
Corbusian phase of his early work. It is characterized by a shift
away from Art Nouveau toward a neoclassicism of German origin. In 1912 he designed a villa for his parents on the rue de la
Montagne near the Villa Fallet (figs. 12, 13). It is a middle-class
residence, with sizable pretensions of elegance.[49] The rooms
are grouped around a large music room where Madame Jeanneret gave her piano lessons. A large window opens toward the
south. On the side facing the garden an apsidal wing protrudes.
The windows on the second floor are aligned in a horizontal
band, in order to let light flood in; a solution that is somewhat reminiscent of some designs by Peter Behrens, such as the
Villa Schröder at Eppenhausen, near Hagen (1908–1909)
(fig. 14).

More interesting, however, is the Villa Favre-Jacot, built
in the same year, 1912, in nearby Le Locle for a well-known
watch manufacturer (figs. 15, 19, 20). It is a curious compilation
from Behrens, Ostendorf, and other, more remote academic
sources.[50] The *Rundbagenstil* windows of the first floor, the
strip window on the piano nobile, the form and proportion of
the hip roof, and even the small portico with its gable (which,
in Le Locle, appears on the rear facade on the second floor) are

taken from Behrens's almost contemporary Villa Goedecke in
Eppenhausen (1911–1912) (fig. 16). The entrance, with its
asymmetrically arranged flanking wings, is a variation on the
old theme of the cour d'honneur. It is a cour d'honneur curiously squeezed and stretched in order to fit into the reality of
the site, and the entrance facade is the most brilliant result of
Jeanneret's will to accommodate classical symmetry and grand
design to the intricacies of the site and the demands of a modern, functional house plan. The semicircular porch, answering
the concave movement of the low flanking wings, is a sort of
joke—possibly inspired by Behrens (compare the cylindrical
stairwell of his house for Dr. Cuno in Hagen-Eppenhausen (fig.
18) 1909–1910), but it has classical seventeenth-century French
precedents as well, such as the porch of the Hôtel de Beauvais in
Paris.

A closer inspection of the decorative details reveals an updated, classicized version of the earlier Jura flora and fauna imagery. Yet, while developing a taste for an elegant life style,
Jeanneret was also studying the possibilities of concrete construction, partly encouraged by his friend Max Dubois, an expert in concrete engineering.[51] He had not forgotten his former
collaboration with Perret, and was waiting for an occasion to
display his experience in the field of concrete engineering. This
occasion presented itself in September 1914.

Domino

Reports of war damage in Flanders filled the papers. This news
seemed to indicate that the war was about to end and that the
time for rebuilding had arrived. Jeanneret designed a system
based on two horizontal concrete slabs supported by columns
and connected by stairs (fig. 22). In plan these slabs look like
dominoes—hence their label. He believed that the elements
of this simple system could be easily mass-produced. Once
erected in war-ravaged areas it would be up to the individual
owner to supply the missing parts of the bare skeleton; prefabricated window and wall sections would be made available in
order to permit completion of every unit according to the needs
of each dweller.

In its utter simplicity, the Domino principle went beyond
the concrete frame imagery as it had been established by Hennebique and Perret. The ceiling slabs were left without sup-

porting beams: they were thought of as homogeneous surfaces combining tensile and compressive strength. Furthermore, the vertical supports were recessed with respect to the outer walls, thus allowing the facade to become structurally independent. Windows could easily go around corners as some of Jeanneret's sketches suggest. .

Numerous variations of the Domino house drawn between 1914 and 1915 (fig. 21) show that Jeanneret was familiar with Tony Garnier's projects for Lyons. He must have visited Garnier's office in Lyons in 1915, for there are letters proving Jeanneret's familiarity with the *Cité Industrielle*, which at this moment had not yet been published.[52] But neither in Flanders nor in Sicily, where some members of Parliament had shown interest, were the Domino houses built. Significantly, the idea first found application in an extremely elegant villa for a local industrialist.

The Villa Schwob

In contrast to the earlier house designs that Le Corbusier rarely mentioned, he pointed with pride to the Villa Schwob and even published it in detail in *L'Esprit Nouveau*—although not in the *Oeuvre complète*.[53] There is no doubt that it is the most successful of his early designs (figs. 24, 26). Its use of a concrete frame has secured the "maison turque" (as the villa is still called today) a safe place in the history of the modern movement as one of the first concrete frame villas in Europe—together with van t'Hoff's villa in Huis ter Heide.[54]

Even in the Villa Schwob, however, the originality of the solution lies less in the invention of new forms than in the bold transformation of existing ones—and in the careful detailing throughout. The large center window and the apsidal wings on each side are developed from the earlier Villa Jeanneret-Perret. These wings are enlarged and arranged symmetrically on two sides, and the center window is stretched over two stories. It is as if this was done in order to let the interior space expand and breathe. The main room is two stories high; the second floor, which contains the master bedrooms, has a gallery that opens toward the living room.

This "corps du logis," two stories high, is organized symmetrically around a lateral and a longitudinal axis. An additional part of the building, three stories high and containing the stairwell and the lobby, is attached to the lower "corps du logis" and oriented toward the street. Seen from the side (fig. 24), the villa seems to result from the collision of two design concepts; various elements, such as the massive cornice, can no doubt partly be understood as attempts to unify, at all costs, a composition that seems in danger of breaking apart.

The idea of the "corps du logis" consisting essentially of a hearth that extends in different directions and adjoins the bedrooms and the utility rooms recalls Frank Lloyd Wright. It is well known that Wright, following the publication of his drawings in the Wasmuth edition in 1910, exerted an enormous influence, primarily on the Dutch and German architects of the time. That Jeanneret, who was in Berlin in 1910, saw that famous portfolio volume is improbable, but he certainly did see a reprint of a lecture by H. P. Berlage on new American architecture, which appeared in the *Schweizerische Bauzeitung* some time later.[55] In that lecture, Berlage gave a comprehensive survey of Wright's early houses, and the illustrations seem to have helped Jeanneret to organize the plan of the Villa Schwob.[56] But where Wright liked to suggest a flow of space across the screens that separate inside and out, Jeanneret stressed the role of walls as solid envelopes. His Villa Schwob is a self-contained, bilaterally symmetrical volume, cramped and massive. Its facades are organized like Beaux-Arts compositions with regulating lines determining the size and proportion of their elements. To press a massive cornice onto a broken volume is an idea that recalls once again Behrens's house for Dr. Cuno, if not Paul Thiersch's Landhaus Syla (1914); yet the form of the cornice as such is reminiscent of Joseph Hoffmann's slightly earlier solutions for the Villa Ast (1910–1911) or the "Villenkolonie" in Vienna-Kaasgraben (1912–1913) (fig. 23).[57]

1. Charles L'Eplattenier, *Au sommet* ("On the summit"), oil on canvas, 1904 (Musée des Beaux-Arts, La Chaux-de-Fonds)

2. Charles-Edouard Jeanneret, Villa Fallet in La Chaux-de-Fonds, 1905–1906 (photo: author)

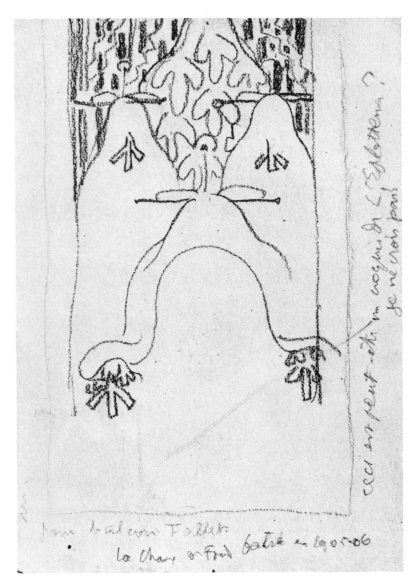

3. Ch.-E. Jeanneret, study
for the balcony of the Villa
Fallet, La Chaux-de-Fonds,
ca. 1905–1906 (Fondation Le
Corbusier, Paris)

4. Villa Fallet, La Chaux-
de-Fonds; detail of main
facade (photo: author)

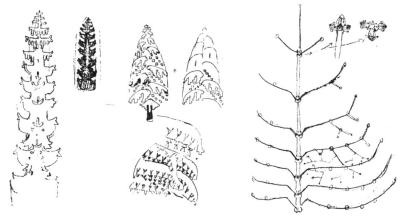

5. Villa Fallet. Detail of roof
(photo: author)

6. Ch.-E. Jeanneret, decorative studies of Jura firs,
ca. 1905 (from *Creation is a
Patient Search*)

7. Ch.-E. Jeanneret, view of Paris, with Sacré Coeur, ca. 1908 (Fondation Le Corbusier, Paris)

8. Ch.-E. Jeanneret, view of Istanbul, 1911 (Fondation Le Corbusier, Paris)

9. Ch.-E. Jeanneret, the
Acropolis in Athens, drawing, 1911 (from *Le Corbusier lui-même*)

11. Ch.-E. Jeanneret, Villa
Jaquemet, La Chaux-de-
Fonds, 1908 (from *Le Cor-
busier lui-même*)

10. Ch.-E. Jeanneret, Villa
Stotzer, La Chaux-de-
Fonds, 1908; elevation
(from *Le Corbusier lui-même*)

12. Ch.-E. Jeanneret, Villa
Jeanneret-Perret, La
Chaux-de-Fonds, 1912
(photo: author)

13. Elevation of the Villa
Jeanneret-Perret (from *Le
Corbusier lui-même*)

14. Peter Behrens,
Schroeder residence in Ep-
penhausen near Hagen,
Germany, 1908–1909 (from
Hoeger, *P. Behrens*)

15. Ch.-E. Jeanneret, Villa Favre-Jacot, Le Locle, 1912; elevation (from *Le Corbusier lui-même*)

16. Peter Behrens, Goedecke residence near Hagen, Westphalia, 1911–1912 (from Hoeger, *P. Behrens*)

17. Ch.-E. Jeanneret, project
for a department store in La
Chaux-de-Fonds, ca. 1912
(La Chaux-de-Fonds, ar-
chives of the Bibliothèque
de la Ville)

18. Peter Behrens, Cuno
residence, 1909–1910 (street
facade) and Schroeder residence (back facade) in Eppenhausen, near Hagen,
Germany (from Hoeger, *P.
Behrens*)

19. Ch.-E. Jeanneret, Villa
Favre-Jacot, Le Locle.
Sketch, 1911(?) (Fondation
Le Corbusier, Paris)

20. Villa Favre-Jacot. Entrance facade (photo: F. Perret, La Chaux-de-Fonds)

21. Ch.-E. Jeanneret. Project
for an application of the
Domino principle, ca. 1915
(from *Oeuvre complète*)

22. Ch.-E. Jeanneret,
Domino—prototype of con-
crete building principle,
1914 (from *Oeuvre complète*)

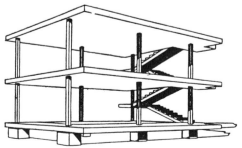

23. Joseph Hoffmann, colony of villas in Kaasgraben, Vienna, 1912–1914 (photo archives: Eduard F. Sekler)

24. Ch.-E. Jeanneret, Villa Schwob, La Chaux-de-Fonds; view of side wing (from *L'Esprit Nouveau*)

25. Frank Lloyd Wright,
Willits residence, Highland
Park, Ill., 1902; ground plan
(from Zevi, *Storia dell'architettura moderna*)

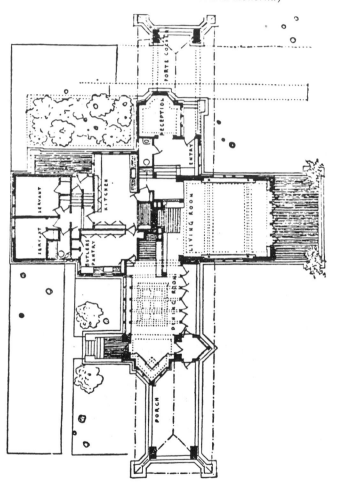

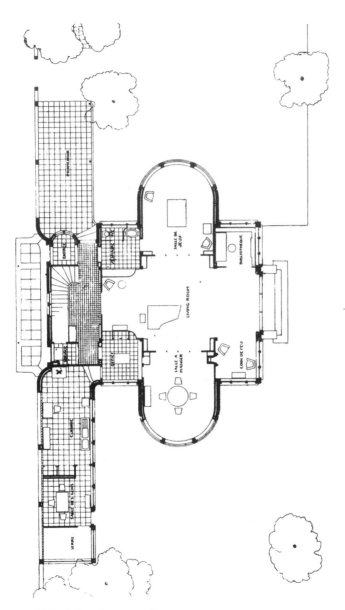

26. Villa Schwob, ground
plan (from *L'Esprit
Nouveau*)

Jeanneret's move to Paris in 1916 was first and foremost an escape from the intrigues of his small town. But getting started in wartime France was no easy matter for a foreigner. Jeanneret rented a servant's room not far from St. Germain-des-Prés, at 20, rue Jacob,[1] opened a studio at 13, rue de Belzume, and started work as a consulting architect for a construction firm engaged in national defense projects (SABA, Société d'application du béton armé). Among other projects, he designed a super-technological slaughterhouse: an exercise in industrial vernacular, with an emphasis on access routes and an axially arranged, visually dramatized conveying system (fig. 27). A little later (1917) he founded his own small enterprise, the "Société d'études industrielles et techniques," which ran a small brick factory at Fonteville, near Paris. The "Briqueterie" seems to have been an extremely modest affair. Once a year it was flooded by the Seine, as Le Corbusier later recalled, and at times the bricks turned into dust and rubble during transport to the building site. Despite the modest scope and success of this enterprise, it nevertheless introduced the young architect to the problems of industrial production and management, and even to "Taylorism, the horrible and inevitable life of the future," as he put it.[2] Although all this was of obvious importance for his later outlook as an architect and planner, it did not provide him with a sufficient income, and it was painting that kept his head above water, both in terms of morale and money.

Amédée Ozenfant and *Après le Cubisme*

It was the painter Amédée Ozenfant who encouraged Jeanneret to paint regularly and thus to realize his old, hitherto frustrated desire to become a painter. In May 1918, Auguste Perret had introduced Jeanneret to Ozenfant at a dinner for the "Art et Liberté" group. Ozenfant owned a small fashion shop that catered to the Parisian haut monde, and what was more important, he had already acquired a solid reputation in Paris as a painter and critic.[3] Ozenfant's versatile and artistically sophisticated style and wide range of interests—he read Plato and Bergson as intensively as the contemporary, outstanding motor magazine *Omnia*—must have held an extraordinary fascination for Jeanneret, who, although knee-deep in business difficulties,

shared his Olympian belief in mechanics and humanism. In
June 1918, he wrote to Ozenfant: "In my confusion I try to
evoke your tranquil, sensitive, clear will. I feel that I am at the
threshold of discoveries, while you are concerned with their
realization."[4]

The meeting with Ozenfant gave a new, clear direction
to Jeanneret's aims and outlook. In September 1918, the two
friends joined forces to revise the introduction to the catalog for
their first joint exhibition to be held at the Galerie Thomas in
the fall of the same year. Ozenfant probably completed the
major portion of the text before he took Jeanneret on as a partner, for the latter took care to have his name printed second
despite his alphabetical priority. It turned out to be a major manifesto, comparable in genre and importance to Gleizes's and
Metzinger's *Du Cubisme* of 1912. The title, *Après le cubisme*
("after cubism," or, better, "beyond cubism") indicated the
authors' intention of establishing a tradition within the avant-
garde; at the same time, it suggested a critical attitude toward
cubism, the leading movement in modern French art.

It is worth noting that the criticism of cubist theory went
far beyond the arguments that had already been advanced by
other Parisian avant-garde groups such as the "Groupe de
Puteaux" or the "Section d'Or." *Après le cubisme* was not concerned solely with the decorative excesses of cubism (that is, of
what Corbusier later called "cu-cubisme"), for the arguments
aimed at a revision of the principles of cubism itself. The authors dispute the cubists' claim that their work was the fruit of
intensive efforts to add new dimensions to the perception of reality and conceded only that it was an attractive but basically
esoteric game with ornamental forms. They characterize the
cubists' interests in African sculpture as an elitist escape into
primitivism.[5] They also categorically reject the method of dis-
membering physical objects and rearranging their outlines in a
new, two-dimensional composition—or in other words, of
simultaneously superpositioning different aspects of a single
object. To quote the authors, "A face is, after all, a plastic continuum."[6] Bearing this in mind, it is not surprising that the
authors rule out the cubist rhetoric about a "fourth dimension
in art," and even consider it to be no more than a "gratuitous
hypothesis by the theorists of cubism."[7] In short, "Present-day

art is created by people living outside their age or by people
who only touch it in passing."[8]

There are, however, a few aspects of cubism that the authors consider worthy of serious attention and the first of these
is its emphasis on rational logic in composition. On the other
hand, they call for works that would "stimulate the intellect to
react."[9] This seems possible to the authors only if the elements
of the artistic vocabulary represent specific, universally un-
derstandable concepts. Bottles, glasses, plates, guitars, and
pipes—the objects of still lifes—are therefore given back their
physical integrity and weight. Not only for abstract aesthetic
reasons, for these "objets types" are regarded as symbols for the
virtues of the new industrial world: its order, its anonymity,
and its purity—in short, its "purism."

This purism became the key concept advanced by Ozenfant
and Jeanneret.[10] The term was intended to convey more than
just a new approach to painting; it stands for the distinctive
characteristics of modern thought.[11] To a certain extent, it
represents a synthesis of French enlightenment and German
Werkbund pragmatism. In the purist world engineers occupy
the center of the stage and the rational discipline of their
skills—insofar as it manifests itself in the static beauty of their
creations—is a constant subject for praise for Ozenfant and
Jeanneret. On the basis of their enthusiasm for the moral and
aesthetic virtues of modern engineering, the two authors develop a kind of rationalist cosmology in which they describe
nature as a logical machine whose adherence to physical laws is
the very reason for its beauty. Within the framework of this
grandiose Neoplatonic perspective, painting serves as the
medium through which eternal reality and the universal striv-
ing for harmony are reconciled on a physiological level.

The return to logic, clarity, and simplicity and a reconcilia-
tion with the great, "eternal" values of the French tradition are
the leitmotivs of purism. In the visual arts, the trend toward a
return to the "plastic continuum" of things was not entirely
new. The rehabilitation of the object in its integral form is an
aspect of the synthetic cubism of Juan Gris's and Marcoussis's
work. "Realistic" studies of everyday objects also appear in
Picasso's drawings even during his cubist phase, although they
never became the focus of a program. The theoretical rationali-

zation of this return to reality only became possible after the war, and the purist manifesto was in fact the first articulate manifestation of a major shift in taste toward an updated form of classicism.[12]

This shift of taste was not a purely French phenomenon. While Ozenfant and Jeanneret were celebrating the aesthetic preciousness of plates, glasses, bottles, or guitars, Oskar Schlemmer and Willy Baumeister in Stuttgart were busy redefining the human body in the somewhat similar terms of a new industrial anonymity and monumentality, and in Italy, Carlo Carrà was rediscovering the "valori plastici" of Giotto.[13] Most important of all, however, was Fernand Léger: uninhibited by the straitjacket of Neoplatonic idealism, his paintings of around 1920 provide the most forceful and immediate evidence of the period's new interest in the commonplace and day-to-day aspects of modern life. In 1920, the first issue of the magazine *L'Esprit Nouveau* reproduced a painting by the neo-impressionist Georges Seurat in full color on the frontispiece, followed by a detailed article about Seurat by the painter Roger Bissière. This symbolic patronage by Seurat (in later issues, Bissière reviewed other grand old men like Corot and Ingres) is as revealing about the outlook of the magazine's editors (Le Corbusier and Ozenfant) as is their own work.

Purism, in short, was an avant-garde movement only in the broadest sense of the word. Its outlook was idealistic and restorative. It glorified order, logic, culture, and technological progress—the very values that Dadaism, and later, surrealism were so eager to undermine. In this way, it hoped to reach larger portions of the bourgeoisie than those already conquered by the previous, more bohemian and esoteric avant-garde movements. Cubism was defeated, Guillaume Appolinaire, its great literary protagonist, dead: the time had come for a new era of postwar reconstruction in all fields, based upon reason and idealism.

Early Paintings

The 1918 exhibition in the small Galerie Thomas contained only two paintings by Jeanneret, compared to a far larger number of works by Ozenfant. These elegant and straightforward paintings show no evidence whatsoever of the dubist revolution. The white die reflected on the marble ledge and the books that appear in what Le Corbusier later called his first painting, *La Cheminée* (1918), are at the same time an echo from Greece and an anticipation of later architectonic concepts. There is scarcely anything comparable to be found in the Parisian art scene of the time, although some works by Jeanneret do recall the decors of Adolpe Appia, the Swiss pioneer of modern stage design. [14]

The months following this first exhibition were devoted to painting. The two friends worked in Ozenfant's studio in the rue Godot-de-Mauroy, a small street off the Boulevard des Italiens, not far from the Madeleine, and Ozenfant's description of their collaboration would appear to be somewhat subjective. "It was truly joint labor: I sounded the tone and he was the echo that occasionally reinforced it." [15]

There can be little doubt that Ozenfant was the driving force at the time, and he also did his best to ensure that posterity would be aware of this. [16] A comparison between purist paintings by Jeanneret and Ozenfant reveals barely perceptible yet decisive differences. Whereas Ozenfant exhibits a slightly frivolous delight in the delicate shading of colors, the perfumed atmosphere of elegant interiors, and the tender outlines of objects, Jeanneret shows a more pointed interest in the sculptural effects of his "objects," accentuated through sharp shadow effects; at the same time, these "objects" are more forcefully incorporated into the picture's overall composition. This unification is accomplished through a "marriage of contours"—as he called it—and through a rigorous limitation of the color palette of either warm or cold tones.

It is interesting to follow the different directions taken by Jeanneret and Ozenfant after they once more began to work independently of one another. Until the end of his life, Ozenfant remained loyal to the credo drawn up in *Après le cubisme*, and in 1965 (after Le Corbusier's death) his attitude toward cubism and toward Guillaume Appolinaire and his "jarryisme dadaiste" was still full of condescension. [17] Le Corbusier's later opinion of *Après le cubisme* was more detached: "It contains both good and bad, subtle shadings and pretentiousness—the wagging finger of the schoolteacher." [18]

In *Towards a New Architecture* (1922), the architect speaks of the "vital change brought about by cubism." [19] In 1925, while revising the book *Peinture moderne* with Ozenfant, he requested that the purist theses concerning neo-impressionism, fauvism and cubism be represented as "personal ideas." [20] For Le Corbusier the painter, purism represented the first stage of an adventure that branched out into quite different directions. [21]

Raoul La Roche and the Kahnweiler Auctions

In 1918, at a Swiss dinner in Paris, Jeanneret was introduced to Raoul La Roche, a banker from Basel. La Roche liked his work and supported him by purchasing paintings from him regularly. In the years 1921, 1922, and 1923, Jeanneret often bid on behalf of La Roche at the Kahnweiler auctions, where outstanding works of cubism came under the hammer, including pictures by Picasso, Braque and Léger. These became the nucleus of the La Roche collection, most of which was ultimately donated to the Basel Kunstmuseum. [22]

Jeanneret's contact with cubism as a result of this activity did not fail to have an effect on his own painting. A comparison between his *Nature morte à la pile d'assiettes*, [23] dated 1920 (fig. 32), and his *Nature morte au Pavillon de l'Esprit Nouveau*, dated 1924 (fig. 33), may suffice as proof. In the painting of 1920, the objects are still clearly identified as such and juxtaposed as distinct elements, whereas in the later work they become parts of a complex, half-transparent surface pattern. The pen-and-pencil drawings from those years illustrate this step-by-step shift of interest. The influence of cubism is clearly mirrored here: the objects gradually lose their bodily presence; they become more and more transparent. Significantly, although the "objects" are now depicted simultaneously from various viewpoints, the viewpoint changes only in a vertical direction. [24] Whereas the cubists circle around their objects in order to unfold the various aspects on a single plane, Le Corbusier—an architect after all—is only concerned with plan and elevation. But in order to approach the cubist ideal of a transparent relief while at the same time relying entirely upon plan and elevation, he has to multiply the components of his still lifes, almost to the point of creating an effect of dizziness: hence the frequent title "Nature morte aux nombreux objets" [still life of numerous objects].

In these paintings the gray (or brown) tones of cubism and the thickly applied, usually dark colors of his earlier paintings are superseded by glowing light blues, pinks, ochres, bottle greens, and browns. But the further we get from the early purist still lifes the clearer the emergence of surprising shapes from the intricate bodily penetrations and intersections of the superimposed contours becomes, and their emphasis by vivid colors is more definite. In the paintings from around 1928, the outlines of the objects serve only as the starting point for an autonomous architecture of contours and surfaces. In short, Jeanneret started working with a powerful synthesis of form around 1918–1920. Later, this synthesis was gradually dissolved into what might be called an analytical approach to the pictorial media: an analysis that questions the identity of the objects more and more radically, to the point where only fantastic puzzles of contours and surfaces reminiscent of the objects remain. The cubists had worked in exactly the opposite way.

So it was not until about 1922 and 1923—fifteen years after Picasso's *Demoiselles d'Avignon*—that cubism started to act as a direct stimulus on the painter Jeanneret—and the architect Le Corbusier. Whatever the impact of cubism upon architecture may have been, it was only after modern painting returned to classical discipline that it could enter into a close dialogue with progressive architecture, as it did later on in the works of Le Corbusier.[25]

L'Esprit Nouveau

It is not surprising that the authors of *Après le cubisme* should want to publish a periodical that would reflect their broad interest in contemporary culture and broadcast their views on art and modern life. By 1919, the editorial—if not the economic—conditions for such an undertaking had been created. Fernand Divoire, a literary critic of *L'Intransigeant*, a leading Paris newspaper, had talked to the two artists about the poet Paul Dermée and his project of a new literary magazine.[26] A meeting followed, and it was decided to give the venture the title of *L'Esprit Nouveau* ("The New Spirit").

With the help of some Swiss friends who had contacts in the world of finance, Jeanneret secured the necessary capital in

Paris and contacted various advertisers. The resulting monthly
publication (a total of twenty-eight issues, some of them extremely bulky, were issued) was more than just another art
magazine: it was a cultural organ with a primary, but by no
means exclusive, interest in the visual arts. In certain respects,
L'Esprit Nouveau was comparable to the *Werkbund-Jahrbuch*
which was published in Germany in the previous decade as a
means of awakening the public to the need for a new style appropriate to the machine age. Not unlike its German precedent,
L'Esprit Nouveau functioned as a sort of marketing agent for the
"New Life Style Inc"—of which Le Corbusier became the
designer-in-chief.

There is little doubt that the immediate inspiration for the
magazine's name came from Guillaume Apollinaire, for on
November 26, 1917, Apollinaire delivered a lecture bearing this
title at the Théâtre du Vieux-Colombier. He died less than one
year later, and on December 1, 1918, *Mercure de France* published the manuscript of this lecture, entitled *L'esprit nouveau
et les poètes* ("The New Spirit and the Poets").[27] Paul Dermée,
who was working with André Breton and Paul Reverdy for the
periodical *Nord-Sud* at the time (1917), must have been familiar
with this important literary testament by Apollinaire, his
friend.

In many respects, the text of this lecture corresponds to
Ozenfant's and Jeanneret's own endeavors. It summarizes the
poet's vision of a new synthesis of the arts in which all visual
and acoustic phenomena of the modern world were to be combined. Furthermore—and this must have made it attractive to
"rationalists" like Ozenfant and Jeanneret—it makes a strong
claim for "clarity" as being peculiar to French intellect and turns
violently against the exaggerations of Wagnerian or Rousseau-
inspired romanticism, as well as against the "parole in libertà"
of the Italian futurists.

The first issue of *L'Esprit Nouveau* appeared in October
1920 (fig. 28). The verso of the title proclaims, *"L'Esprit Nouveau*
is the first magazine in the world truly dedicated to living
aesthetics."

The editors had no reason to be ashamed of their contributors. The first six issues include articles by André Salmon
on Picasso, a portion of the De Stijl manifesto by Theo van

Doesburg, a commentary on Apollinaire's *Calligrammes* by
Louis Aragon, an article "Ornament und Verbrechen" by Adolf
Loos that had already appeared in French in *Cahiers d'aujourd'hui* some years previously (1913), and an article by Céline
Arnauld on Lautréamont's *Les chants de Maldoror*. Maurice
Raynal, Jean Cocteau, and Auguste Lumière, the inventor of
color film, are also among the magazine's contributors. The
writings of Charles Henry, director of the Laboratoire de la
Psychologie de la Perception at the Ecole des Beaux-Arts, much
of whose work appeared in the magazine, had the greatest influence on Le Corbusier's theories.

An article by A. Ozenfant and Ch.-E. Jeanneret entitled
"Sur la Plastique" appears in the first issue.[28] Later in the issue,
the title "Trois rappels à MM. LES ARCHITECTES" [Three re-
minders to architects], appears under the photograph of an
American grain silo.[29] The first sentence proclaims, "L'architecture n'a rien à voir avec les 'styles'. Les Louis XV, XVI,
XIV ou le gothique sont à l'architecture ce qu'est une plume sur
la tête d'une femme; c'est parfois joli, mais pas toujours et rien
de plus." [Architecture has nothing to do with 'styles.' The styles
of Louis XV, XVI, XIV or Gothic are to architecture what a
feather is to a woman's hat; it is sometimes, though not always
pretty, and nothing more.]

The article ended with the following declaration: "Here are
American silos and factories, magnificent BEGINNINGS of a
new age, AMERICAN ENGINEERS DESTROYING A DYING
ARCHITECTURE WITH THEIR CALCULATIONS." It was
signed: LE CORBUSIER–SAUGNIER.

Jeanneret and Ozenfant had decided to adopt pseudonyms
for their writings on architecture. Ozenfant chose his mother's
maiden name: Saugnier. Jeanneret would have done the same,
but the matter was complicated by the fact that his mother's
name happened to be Perret. He then remembered the name of
one branch of his family that no longer existed, Lecorbésier.
Ozenfant suggested, "All right, you can revive the name, but
you will be known as Le Corbusier, in two words, for that
sounds more impressive!"[30]

French antecedents from the time of the Sun King come to
mind: Le Brun, Le Nôtre, Le Nain, Corneille . . . , but there is
also an association with cubism or *corbeau*, "the raven," with

whom "Père Corbu" later cultivated an ironical friendship
based on the similarity of their names. Jeanneret the architect
was known henceforth as Le Corbusier but he continued to sign
his paintings with his family name until 1928.[31]

Towards a New Architecture

It was the book *Vers une Architecture*, published in English
under the inaccurately translated title of *Towards a New Architecture*, that was to bring Le Corbusier's message before an
international public (figs. 34, 37). With the exception of the final
chapter, the book is composed of reprints of the articles by Le
Corbusier–Saugnier that had appeared in *L'Esprit Nouveau* in
1920 and 1921.[32] Although Ozenfant was undoubtedly responsible for parts of its content, it was Le Corbusier who took the
responsibility for the whole. The broad outlook of the book and
the mixture of straightforward rational discourse, missionary
zeal, and declamatory salesmanship that characterizes its style
resulted in its becoming the most influential architectural
textbook of the twenties, and possibly of the first half of this
century. The most superficial reader can easily recognize the
salient points, aided by a wide variety of illustrations.

The book is divided into seven chapters. The first deals
with a theme reminiscent of *Après le cubisme*, "THE ENGI-
NEER'S AESTHETICS AND ARCHITECTURE: Two
things that march together and follow from one another—the
one at its full height, the other in poor state of retrogression."[33]
According to the author, the engineers were at the forefront of
development, whereas the major national schools of architecture were doing no more than feeding their students the leftovers of past styles, teaching them the "tricks of the trade." Le
Corbusier's opinion was that the true architecture of the era was
being created on the engineer's drawing boards, not only because their work was useful, but because it conveyed the impression of harmony, since it was in tune with the laws of
nature.

Then follows the famous "Trois rappels à MM. les Architectes: I, le Volume; II, la Surface; III, le Plan."

A series of American grain silos is shown in the section on
"le Volume" (figs. 34a and b). Some of these had already been

published in 1913 by Walter Gropius in the *Werkbund-Jahrbuch* (figs. 35, 36).[34] In Le Corbusier's book they serve as a background for his famous definition of architecture: "Architecture is the masterly, correct and magnificent play of volumes brought together in light."[35] After a few explanatory remarks the author continues: "Egyptian, Greek or Roman architecture is an architecture of prisms, cubes and cylinders, pyramids, or spheres: the Pyramids, the Temple of Luxor, the Parthenon, the Colosseum, Hadrian's Villa." Gothic architecture, in turn, is another matter: "The cathedral is not a plastic work; it is a drama; the fight against the force of gravity, which is a sensation of sentimental nature."[36]

In the section on "la Surface," Le Corbusier shows American factories and warehouses as a further proof that the major projects of the new age found their resolution in the language of geometry.[37] In the following chapter, "le Plan," he uses axonometric drawings from Choisy's *Histoire de l'architecture* to demonstrate that the secret of good architecture lies in the ground plan. His argument proceeds in a wide sweep, touching on Tony Garnier's *Cité Industrielle* and ending with his own concepts of town planning.

The next part is devoted to the "Tracés régulateurs," or "regulating lines," in which Le Corbusier delves once more into history. He announces, "The primordial physical laws are simple and few in number. The moral laws are simple and few in number,"[38] and he includes these regulating lines, which ensure proportion and order in architectural composition, in these primordial laws. This is a takeover from the French Beaux-Arts tradition. Marcel Dieulafoy and Auguste Choisy had used similar regulating lines in their attempts at reconstructing the laws of composition used in the architecture of the past.[39] But Le Corbusier went back even farther: he quotes the description of the Porte Saint-Denis from Jacques François Blondel's *Cours d'architecture* (1675–1683). More examples of the successful use of proportional rules follow, including the Petit Trianon in Versailles and finally Le Corbusier's own Villa Schwob in La Chaux-de-Fonds.

Almost all Le Corbusier's major arguments are presented here as the inevitable result of a correct understanding of past monumental architecture. So despite its title, which is deliberately turned toward the future, *Vers une architecture* is a book on history. Yet in what former period would it have been possible to call at the same time upon the Parthenon, the Hagia Sophia, St. Peter's, and the Trianon in Versailles as witnesses and guides to a new architecture? In order to arrive at such a panoramic view of history, it was necessary to be familiar with, and also detached from, the past. The ideas that "a great epoch had just begun," and the new cycle of architectural history would be as grandiose as the entire past are leitmotivs of the book.

"Eyes that do not see" is the title of a section in which a number of landmarks of the new age are sandwiched between the key monuments of the academic pantheon. "A serious architect, possessing the eyes of an architect (i.e., a creator of organisms) will find in an ocean liner the liberation from an age-old enslavement," and "The ocean liner is the first stage in the realization of a world organized according to the new spirit."[40]

Pictures of huge liners cut out of travel advertisements illustrate the point. But airplanes also fascinated him, not to mention automobiles (figs. 132–135). The lesson of the automobile, he maintains, is standardization and formation of prototypes. Compared somewhat surprisingly to Doric temples, Le Corbusier's automobiles suggest that an analogous development took place between the Humbert-Cabriolet of 1907 and the Delage Grand Sport of 1921 on the one hand, and the sixth century B.C. Basilica in Paestum and the Parthenon in Athens on the other. The lesson is that "one has to establish *standards* in order to cope with the problem of perfection."[41] It must have escaped his attention that both the Humbert-Cabriolet and the Delage Grand Sport could hardly serve as examples of the logic of mass production, since they were never produced industrially—quite apart from the fact that the Parthenon in Athens represents anything but the "standard" of Doric style.

Mechanization and elementary geometry

Despite its prophetic and declamatory tone, the book is anything but unequivocal, and it is not without its contradictions. While the engineer is held up as the hero of the new civilization, there is an insistence upon the ultimate supremacy of the architect over the technician. While the text insists on rational

methods of design, it also emphasizes that functionalism is
not enough. This is even more clearly suggested by the illustrations: they were selected according to criteria of pure form.
Ultimately, the point of view that emerges is Neoplatonic and
idealist. Technology, engineering, and function are not really
the points. In accordance with its own rules, technology seemed
to have found its way to the primary forms; cubes, cones,
spheres, cylinders, and pyramids, and that was proof enough
that it was in agreement not only with the "lesson of Rome,"
(fig. 38)[42] but also with the beauty of the elementary forms referred to by Plato in *Philebos*. A pseudo-Darwinian law of mechanical selection seemed to have brought about the premises
of a new harmony in the sphere of man-made forms. The ideals
of classical discipline seemed to have come unexpectedly close
to the agencies of mechanization.

It was the reassuring assumption of an inner analogy or
equivalence between classicism and mechanics, "this rediscovery of the old in the new, this justification of the revolutionary by the familiar,"[43] that earned the book its enormous
readership and influence. But the theme as such was not new,
for it was really the updated German Werkbund philosophy
from around 1910. It was no coincidence that some of the most
unusual illustrations were taken from the *Werkbund-Jahrbuch* of
1913. Peter Behrens—Le Corbusier's employer of 1910—had
worked in the same direction following Muthesius's theory of
"types" and "pure form" as the basis of the regeneration of
German industry and trade. The idea that the concepts of art
and form are primordial and basically independent of function
and material quality is very explicit in Muthesius's and
Behrens's thinking.

The return to the classical tradition had been a basic theme
in Behrens's work as the chief designer of the AEG (General
Electric Company) after 1907. Yet both Muthesius and Behrens
had been preceded by another architect and polemist whose
thinking and writing is fundamentally important in understanding Le Corbusier's background: Adolf Loos. If we substitute "engineer" for "bricklayer," we could easily take Loos's
famous dictum that "the architect is a bricklayer who has
learned Latin" for one of Le Corbusier's own slogans. The "return to the great Latin tradition" is beautifully illustrated by the

typographic design of his publications. As early as 1903, Adolf
Loos had set the periodical *Das Andere* in Antiqua type to mark
his radical opposition to the fanciful Art Nouveau characters of
the Sezession and to underline the magazine's leitmotiv that
was unequivocally indicated in the subtitle *Einführung abend-
ländischer Kultur in Oesterreich* [Introduction of European culture
into Austria]. The young Jeanneret had admired the straightforward classical typography that characterized Behrens's
advertisements and trademarks for the AEG.[44] Therefore, it
is not surprising that Le Corbusier's own public relations apparatus, especially *L'Esprit Nouveau*, was designed in a similar
classical style (fig. 28).

   One of the central ideas of *Vers une architecture* was the assumption that an elementary Platonic geometry is inherent in
the nature of mechanical design and that "the wholesome spirit
of the engineer" leads quite automatically to a new classic
beauty and to forms that possess an objective, immutable
character.[45] Yet the development of cars, liners or airplanes
since 1920 proves that technology was anything but on the
verge of "formules définitives." What mattered to Le Corbusier
was that engineering was able to proffer a formal vocabulary at
a moment when architecture seemed to have exhausted its resources and that this vocabulary responded to the architect's
hunger for classical discipline.[46] Furthermore, for those who
shared the confidence in the engineer as a "noble savage," this
vocabulary was loaded with a moral quality of straightforwardness and truth which no architectural style practiced around
1920 could claim to possess.

   In short, it was the imagery and supposed morality of the
machine world, rather than the actual principles of engineering
and advanced technology, that were evoked as the basis of the
new architecture. In an important article published in 1926
in a special issue of the *Journal de Psychologie Normale et de
Pathologie*, Le Corbusier tries to liquidate the inherent conflict
between his concepts of "engineering" and "form." In order to
substantiate his belief in the necessity of formal "permanence,"
he turns to the psychology of perception. While on the one
hand he admits that technology must develop with no regard to
convention, he insists on the other that the constants of sensa-

tion present in the nature of perception require a conformity in the world of man-made shapes.[47]

The "machine for living in" and the dilemma of functionalism
The concept of the "machine for living in" (*machine à habiter*) emerges only peripherally in *Vers une architecture*,[48] although clearly enough to become a subject of controversy. As a definition of the house, this concept must have been rejected by virtually everyone. For conservative critics, it provided proof of Le Corbusier's attempt to reduce architecture to the level of simple mechanics. Among others, Hans Sedlmayr attacked Le Corbusier on these grounds, rightly assigning him to a tradition of thought that began in the eighteenth century. It was in fact the French "revolutionary" architecture of around 1800 that first claimed the equal status of all building tasks, an aspect that was to become a primary symptom in nineteenth-century building. According to Sedlmayr, the nineteenth century's chief concern was with "upward assimilation," for example, the museum was fashioned after the model of a feudal or royal place, or as in Ledoux, the charcoal kiln was made to resemble a pharaoh's grave. Stock exchanges and hotels draped themselves with colonnades reminiscent of temples and palaces. In the twentieth century, however, assimilation proceeded "downward": the house now became a "machine for living in," and the church degenerated into a "soul silo." Sedlmayr bemoans "A lower-placed idol than the machine can hardly be imagined."[49]

In terms of Le Corbusier's own outlook, and indeed in terms of the whole tradition of French rationalism, this is an absurd statement to which neither Pascal nor Descartes, Spinoza nor Leibniz would have agreed—neither could Voltaire, who insisted, "man is so much a machine"; or Béranger, who spoke of "watching the machine of the universe," or Lamettrie with his "homme machine." In France from the eighteenth century onward the machine represented a cosmological and philosophical metaphor of supreme dignity. For Le Corbusier, the concept of the "machine" was far from synonymous with pure "mechanics" and mere utilitarian function. It evoked a spiritual rather than a material order. Thus there is no contradiction between his constant reference to the machine and his polemical refusal of mere functionalism and utilitarianism.

His idealistic obsession with the machine did not preclude him
from criticizing mere utilitarian rationality in building:

One works with stone, or cement; with them one builds
houses, palaces; that is construction. Ingenuity is at work. But
suddenly you touch my heart, you make me feel well, I am
happy, I say: that's beautiful. This is architecture. Now we have
art. My house is practical. That's fine, just as railroads and tele-
phones are fine. But you have not touched my heart.[50]

Le Corbusier did not want to be thought of as a "functionalist" and there can be little doubt that historicism seemed
nonsensical to him. Nevertheless, unlike his dogmatically functionalist contemporaries, he accepted the driving force that had
brought historicism to the fore as a basic requirement for
architecture: the need to elevate construction from a purely
utilitarian to a poetic level. He criticized his functionalist colleagues saying, "If I would discover my hand is dirty . . . I
would prefer washing it to cutting it off."[51] In 1931, he replied
to Alberto Sartoris, who had asked him to write a preface on
"rational architecture," "For me, the term 'architecture' denotes
something more magic than either rationalism or functionalism, something that dominates, predominates, and
imposes."[52]

The Problem of Interior Decoration

As we shall see later, machine aesthetics and industrial production were the declared basis for Le Corbusier's architectural
principles and style. But while in architecture standardization
and mass production remained abstract concepts (because the
transition from traditional methods of planning and execution
to full industrialization occurred, if at all, at a slower rate than
in any other area of production), there already existed in the
twenties a long tradition of mass-produced patent furniture
and household equipment.

Interior decoration had been a fundamental concern in the
history and prehistory of modern design. Yet ever since the
time of the English Arts and Crafts movement, progress in this
area was considered synonymous with improved craftsmanship.
This belief was largely shared in France around 1925, as the
"International Exhibition of Arts and Crafts" in Paris (1925)

proved. Most designers involved in the preparation of this
spectacular show paid eloquent lip service to social needs and
industrial production as the basis of a new style, while at the
same time reaffirming the traditional arts and crafts concept of
the individually designed piece of furniture or suite. Le Corbusier did not follow this path.

The Exposition Internationale des Arts Décoratifs was organized by the French Ministry of Industry and Commerce. Its
purpose was primarily to create a market for French arts and
crafts and to fend off the overpowering influx of foreign products. The idea went back to 1907, but the war postponed its
realization until 1925. The exhibition grounds extended from
the Dome des Invalides to the Petit-Palais on the opposite bank
of the Seine. There were exhibits from a number of foreign
countries and French cities, as well as from French department
stores and publishing houses.[53] The editor of *L'Esprit Nouveau*
was asked to build an "architect's house," but he demurred:
"Why an architect's house? My house is everyone's, anyone's
house; it is the house of a gentleman living in our times."[54]

The concept of this standard dwelling and its equipment
turned out to be an elegant but straightforward protest against
the very concept of handicrafts and interior decoration that the
show was intended to reaffirm (fig. 39). Le Corbusier wanted to
demonstrate that the field of architecture encompassed everything from the smallest household item to the entire city. In this
he was already in agreement with most of his colleagues. This
had been Joseph Hoffmann's dream around the turn of the
century, and it was recreated here by Mallet-Stevens, Ruhlmann,
and other designers of Art Deco furniture who were directly inspired by the Wiener Werkstätte. However, Le Corbusier went
farther, for he wanted to show that industry was now capable of
supplying the apartment and the entire household with mass-
produced furniture.

The "Pavillon de L'Esprit Nouveau" became a manifesto of
modernity:

Instead of "designed" vases of glass or ceramics, there were
laboratory jars, forms purified by use and function. Instead of
elaborate cut-crystal, there were the simple wine glasses of any
French café, objects whose form never ceased to refresh the
fantasy of the Cubist painters. Instead of the carpets of interior

decoration were the vigorously woven Berber carpets from
North Africa with their simple abstract patterns. Instead of
teardrop chandeliers were stage floodlights or store window illumination. Instead of the knickknacks of arts and crafts were
the mother-of-pearl spirals of a seashell; and on the balustrade
of the upper floor, a free-standing sculpture by Jacques
Lipschitz.[55]

It was here that the inexpensive Thonet chair, in production
since 1859, appeared in a modern living room for the first time.
"We have introduced the humble Thonet chair of steamed
wood, certainly the most common as well as the least costly of
chairs. And we believe that this chair, of which millions of
representatives are in use on the Continent and in the two
Americas, possesses nobility."[56]

Together with the tubular staircase that resembled a bicycle
frame, this chair became a symbol of purified form resulting
from an industrial process. There were some luxury items as
well, such as a travel kit for toilet articles made of leather, crystal, and gilded silver that had been lent by Innovation, an elegant Parisian department store. On the cream-colored walls
hung paintings by Léger, Ozenfant, and Le Corbusier.

In short, the "Pavillon de l'Esprit Nouveau" was launched
as the antithesis to the Art Deco interior. The grand, total, uniform design of interiors or whole suites was substituted by an
open, flexible and ironic juxtaposition of partly mass-produced
furniture and objects whose only common characteristic was a
sense of straightforwardness and mechanistic purity. The
anonymous furniture came directly from a hotel or restaurant
supply store: it was not designed in the arts-and-crafts sense
(with the exception of the simple armchairs). It was only a few
years later, in 1928, that Le Corbusier himself ventured into the
field of furniture design when, together with Charlotte Perriand, he produced a series of prototypes that made full use of
the new materials and techniques. No doubt certain anonymous models of patent furniture then available on the French
market served as an inspiration (figs. 40, 41).

L'Art Décoratif d'Aujourd'hui [The Decorative Arts Today]

In 1925, the year of the international arts and crafts exhibition,
Le Corbusier published a lavishly illustrated book in which he

settled accounts with the official tradition of interior decoration: *L'Art décoratif d'aujourd'hui*. [57] It was no easy matter. He knew only too well that his own roots lay in the Arts and Crafts movement of around 1900. To some extent, the book was a rejection of the masters Ruskin, Hoffmann, Guimard, and Grasset; its 218 pages acknowledge debts and declare rebellion, and memories of the past clash with visions of the future. It also expresses the pain of a rift that had long been deferred but could not be postponed any longer.

Over twenty years before, another prophet of modernity had shown the way: Adolf Loos in Vienna. From 1923 to 1928 Loos lived in Paris where he quickly became a center of attraction in the circle that gathered around Tristan Tzara and where he also came into contact with the *Esprit Nouveau* group. It seems that it was only then that his polemic writings started to exert an influence on Le Corbusier, and there is no doubt that they played a major role in the latter's break with the handicrafts.

As early as 1896, when he returned from a three-year stay in the United States, Loos had proclaimed the beauty of the anonymous products of modern industry. He was fascinated by English men's fashions and indulged in memories of the humble Austrian artifacts which, submerged in a flood of bric-a-brac, had been shown at the International Exhibit in Chicago in 1893: "purses, cigars and cigarette cases . . . , writing implements, suitcases, bags, riding whips, canes, silver objects, canteens, everything unadorned." [58] In 1921, Crès (the Paris publisher who later was to bring out the "Collection de l'Esprit Nouveau") issued a collection of old articles in German by Adolf Loos: *Ins Leere gesprochen* [Words without Echo]. Although the title had been suitable enough when it was written in 1900, it was much less appropriate in the twenties. It is very likely that Loos watched with a mixture of approval and anger as Le Corbusier took over the ideas he had championed for a quarter of a century with no great success, and efficiently put them into circulation. Le Corbusier actually brought Loos's historical mission to an end. His success can be credited to the fact that he substituted Loos's delight in anonymous craftsmanship for an absolute belief in mechanization. Modern industry, he announced, was the premise for the overdue purification of

the house and its decor. This gave his argument a social and
economic vitality, with a widespread effect that could not
be compared with Loos's struggle against the bastions of the
Sezession and the Wiener Werkstätte—quite apart from the fact
that Loos's argument functioned at an often questionable level
of seriousness.

The Pavillon de l'Esprit Nouveau was not the only piece of
radically modern design shown at the 1925 Exhibition. In the
Austrian pavilion, Friedrich Kiesler presented his "City in
Space," a spatial adaptation of ideas that had been elaborated
on a few years earlier by the Dutch De Stijl movement. The
pavilion itself was the work of Joseph Hoffmann, and its facade
with its heavy decoration was quite out of line with the in-
novative efforts shown within. But the Russian pavilion by
Melnikov, and the "Information Tower" by Mallet-Stevens
were certainly compatible with Le Corbusier's exhibit. Nevertheless, compared to the vast mass of pavilions and furnishings
(some of them only having recently regained the attention of
collectors and connoisseurs), these were isolated ventures into
the future of the International Style. As early as 1925, one critic
wrote:

The Exposition opened five years too soon. I cannot say
whether Frantz Jourdain, Chareau, Le Corbusier or Mallet-
Stevens would have occupied the first place five years later.
Such questions of precedence are decided by temperament, bu-
reaucratic or financial considerations, and intrigue. But their
ideas, even if applied by others, will be triumphant by 1930.[59]

27. Ch.-E. Jeanneret,
project for an industrial
slaughterhouse in Challuy,
France 1917 (Fondation Le
Corbusier, Paris)

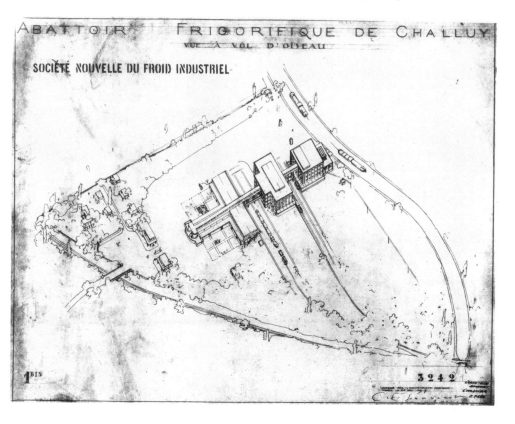

28. *L'Esprit Nouveau*, cover
of the magazine's first
issue, 1920

29. "Le Ronéodex," letter-
head of a firm producing
metal furniture in France
and placing ads in *L'Esprit
Nouveau* (Fondation Le
Corbusier, Paris)

LE RONEODEX

FICHES   VISIBLES

C.^{IE} DU RONEO   27 B.^D DES ITALIENS

PARIS   TÉL. GUT. 22-15
                                               —   —   35-78
                                          -   CENT. 11-15

30 JUILLET 1924

L' ESPRIT NOUVEAU
3 Rue du Cherche Midi
PARIS

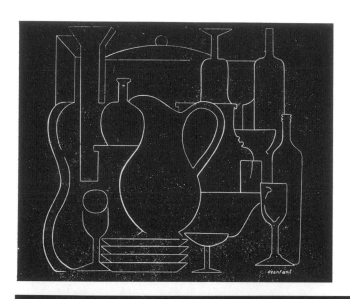

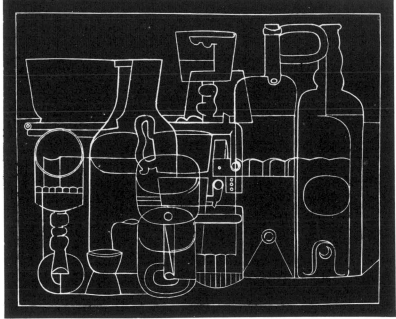

30. Amédée Ozenfant,
purist still life, drawing, ca.
1922 (from S. Giedion,
*Mechanization Takes Com-
mand*)

31. Ch.-E. Jeanneret, purist
still life, drawing, ca. 1922
(Foundation Heidi Weber,
Zurich)

32. Ch.-E. Jeanneret, *Still life with pile of plates*, oil on canvas, 81 × 100 cm, 1920 (Kunstmuseum, Basel)

33. Ch.-E. Jeanneret, *Bottles, carafe and glass*, oil on canvas, 81 × 100 cm, 1926 (Centre Le Corbusier, Zurich)

34 a and b. Pages from *Vers une architecture*, 1923

35 a and b. Industrial architecture, from an article by W. Gropius in *Werkbund Jahrbuch*, 1913

36 a and b. Industrial architecture, from *Vers une architecture*, 1923

PAESTUM, de 600 à 550 av. J.-C.

Le Parthénon est un produit de sélection appliquée à un standart établi. Depuis un siècle déjà, le temple grec était organisé dans tous ses éléments.

Lorsqu'un standart est établi, le jeu de la concurrence immédiate et violente s'exerce. C'est le match; pour gagner, il faut

Cliché de *La Vie Automobile*.   HUMBERT, 1907.

Cliché Albert Morancé.   PARTHÉNON, de 447 à 434 av. J. C.

faire mieux que l'adversaire *dans toutes les parties*, dans la ligne d'ensemble et dans tous les détails. C'est alors l'étude poussée des parties. Progrès.

Le standart est une nécessité d'ordre apporté dans le travail humain.

Le standart s'établit sur des bases certaines, non pas arbi-

DELAGE, Grand-Sport 1921.

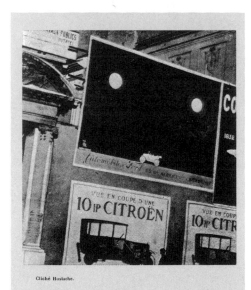

Cliché Hostache.

MAISONS EN SÉRIE

37 a–d. Pages from *Vers une Architecture*, 1923

38. Le Corbusier, "The Lesson of Rome," from *L'Esprit Nouveau*

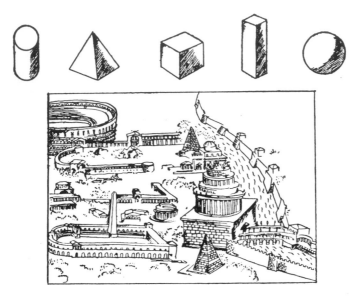

Il y a des formes simples déclancheuses de sensations constantes.

Des modifications interviennent, dérivées, et conduisent la sensation première (de l'ordre majeur au mineur), avec toute la gamme intermédiaire des combinaisons. Exemples:

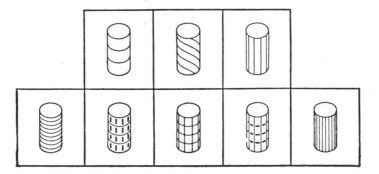

39. Le Corbusier and Pierre
Jeanneret, "Pavillon de
l'Esprit Nouveau" at the
International Arts and
Crafts Exhibition, Paris,
1925 (photo: Musée des Arts
Décoratifs, Paris)

...le "SURREPOS"

du Docteur PASCAUD (Breveté France et Étranger)

Croquis comparatifs illustrant les avantages du SURREPOS par rapport à la chaise longue :

Ici :

Tassement de tout le corps sur le siège bien vite endolori.

Extension des genoux : rapide fatigue.

Glissement de tout le corps : les reins ne sont pas soutenus et en souffrent.

La tête elle-même ne se maintient que grâce à un effort musculaire.

Là :

Répartition du poids du corps sur le dossier et le siège : aucune souffrance.

Flexion légère des genoux : relâchement et bien-être articulaires.

Stabilité du corps assurant aux reins un soutien permanent.

L'inclinaison du dossier fait reposer la tête sur son coussin sans le moindre effort.

Pour toutes ces raisons, auxquelles nous ajouterons l'élévation des membres inférieurs (qui active la circulation de retour) et l'inclinaison du dossier (qui maintient en bonne place les organes intérieurs), le " Surrepos " assure, avec la détente complète de tout l'organisme, un bien-être dont on ne peut réellement se rendre compte qu'après l'avoir éprouvé soi-même.

40. "Le surrepos." Commercial folder of a reclining chair, ca. 1922 (from the archives of *L'Esprit Nouveau*; Fondation Le Corbusier, Paris)

41. Le Corbusier and Charlotte Perriand, "Chaise-longue à règlage continu" (reclining chair for continuous regulation), 1928 (from Maurizio di Puolo and others, *La machine à s'asseoir*)

Concrete, it might seem, is less likely to determine architectural form than any other building material. Its early use in nineteenth-century building had little impact upon style; it merely supplied architects and the building industry with a universally applicable means of crystallizing and multiplying existing formal vocabularies. Being malleable, it provided carte blanche for any sort of eclecticism.

Yet, parallel to the use of concrete as a tectonically neutral "plastic" mass, the nineteenth century discovered other possibilities inherent in the new material. Once applied under the conditions of strict economy, reinforced concrete proved capable of producing better structural results with less material bulk than any previously known material with the exception of the steel frame. Only in combination with economy, that is, the principle of achieving maximum results with a minimum of work, could concrete become the starting point for an architectural renewal. This is what happened in the works of the French pioneers of concrete building—François Hennebique, A. de Baudot, the Perrets, Tony Garnier, and others—and it was from here that Le Corbusier and some of his contemporaries proceeded in their attempts at translating the possibilities of concrete construction into a new architectural vocabulary (fig. 42).[1]

The Five Points of a New Architecture

Since the invention of the Domino system (1915), the use of reinforced concrete had served as a basis for Le Corbusier's architectural speculations (figs. 21, 22). Around 1920, he could claim justifiably to be an expert in this field, and from 1922 onward his technical expertise had the support of a very competent professional: Pierre Jeanneret, his cousin from Geneva, who had worked with Perret from 1920 to 1922. There is no doubt that the close partnership of the two architects (which lasted until 1940) accounts for the structural as well as the aesthetic qualities of much that was to come.[2]

It is no mere coincidence that the first clear-cut, succinct, and programmatic manifesto of the new architecture issued by Le Corbusier, the "five points of a new architecture," is based on a structural argument. It suggests that the new, universally applicable style is nothing but the passive result of a correct

and efficient use of the concrete frame. The immediate pretext for this proclamation was a small book prepared at the
Werkbund-Siedlung "Weissenhof" (1927) by Alfred Roth. It
was an introduction to the two houses in Stuttgart built by Le
Corbusier and Pierre Jeanneret. Its purpose was not philosophical but promotional: the "five points" were intended
to familiarize a large, international public with the ideas underlying the new architecture. Here is a summary of Le Corbusier's manifesto:

1. *The pilotis.* Assiduous research finally achieved results that
opened new perspectives in architecture and urbanism, and
contributed something toward the solution of the great sickness
of the cities . . . [figs. 43, 44]. Previously, the house had been
buried in the earth and the rooms were often dark and damp.
Reinforced concrete gave us the pilotis; the house in the air, far
from the soil, with gardens stretching beneath the house as well
as on the roof.

2. *The roof garden.* For centuries, the traditional saddleback had
been the normal way of keeping out the winter and its snow,
while the interior was heated by stoves. The installation of central heating made the saddleback obsolete. It was now possible
for the roof to be flat rather than inclined and the water drainage occurred in the center of the building instead of down the
outside walls, thus avoiding the danger of freezing in cold climates. Reinforced concrete made the structurally homogenous
roof possible . . . [fig. 45]. Reasons of technique, economy,
and comfort, and a touch of sentimentality lead to the adoption
of the roof terrace and roof garden.

3. *The free plan.* In the past, the plan had been the slave of the
structural walls that started from the basement and were built
up to constitute the first, second, and third floors, etc. Reinforced concrete brought the innovation of the free plan in which
the interiors were no longer rigidly determined by the structural walls. They had become free. . . .

4. *The elongated window.* The window is one of the essential
characteristics of the house, and progress brought liberation
here too. Reinforced concrete revolutionized the window. It
was now possible to place windows along the whole facade
from corner to corner. The window became the standardized
mechanical element ("l'élément méchanique-type") of the
house for all private dwellings, villas, workers' houses, and
apartment blocks . . . [fig. 47].

5. *The free facade.* The pillars retreated from the facades to the

inside of the house. . . . The facades became no more than light membranes consisting of isolating walls or windows. The facade was now free and the windows could extend without interruption from one end to the other.[3]

Although they do not provide a complete explanation of the new architecture, the five points nevertheless indicate some of its outstanding characteristics and so they deserve a brief discussion.

The pilotis

Significantly, the idea seems to have originated in the context or urbanistic proposals. Around 1915, Le Corbusier had developed a project for a town supported on a lattice grillwork twelve to sixteen feet above ground.[4] Later, when applied to individual houses such as the Villa Savoye in Poissy (1929), the pilotis usually served as an element of dramatization and visual isolation (fig. 46). Not only do they emphasize a building's "organic" links with the urban traffic pattern, they also dramatize the individual house as an autonomous, absolute form independent of the soil on which it rests, universally applicable anywhere on the surface of the earth. Thus the Citrohan house exhibited at the Salon d'Automne in 1922 has pillars supporting the box-shaped "corps du logis" like the legs of a piece of furniture. Among the numerous graphic representations of this type is one that suggests a location on a beach, practically in the water. In fact it is not surprising that Le Corbusier's obsession with the absolute and self-sustained building resulted in various projects of houses on water.[5]

But the pilotis also suggest a functional stratification of the house that helps to define it as something ordered and controlled: a machine. As if proclaiming an irrefutable law of nature, Le Corbusier states that in architecture the ground is to be reserved for vegetation and moving objects—in particular, traffic; stationary activities such as working and living belong on the upper floors (1929).[6] The Villa Savoye (fig. 76) is a clear example of this principle: its ground floor is reserved for the cars entering and leaving beneath the suspended box, and the radius of the lobby's semicircular plan is determined by the minimum space required by a turning car.

Thus the pilotis helped to redefine the house as a matter of form, function, and machine-age symbolism. They also made a

historical point; a protest against the surviving Beaux-Arts
practices, which for Le Corbusier were epitomized by heavy
masonry buildings anchored to the soil by massive, rusticated
walls.

The roof garden

Here too, practical considerations were advanced in order to
lend "scientific" weight to the postulate of the flat roof. These
considerations are not all new. The flat cement roof as a feasible
solution to the problem of snow drainage had already been
promoted by technical literature, for example, by the manual of
the American Portland Cement Association (1912) which Le
Corbusier owned. In addition, the flat roof of his Villa Schwob
in La Chaux-de-Fonds (1916) had also received a good deal of
praise from functionalist architects like Hans Schmidt as a remarkable piece of environmental engineering (fig. 24).[7] Underlying these considerations, however, were the innumerable flat
roofs and terraces of vernacular buildings Le Corbusier had
seen and drawn during his Oriental and Mediterranean travels
of 1911—an architectural heritage that had already impressed
Joseph Hoffmann, Adolf Loos, and many others. Hanging gardens with trees and plants were to become a recurring theme in
Jeanneret's architectural sketches from around 1915 and 1916,
and an early monumental version can be seen in the project of a
seashore villa for Paul Poiret, the famous fashion designer.[8]

There is probably no other single feature of Le Corbusier's
architecture that summarizes and symbolizes the determining
point of his philosophy with equal clarity: his belief in moral
and physical regeneration through hygiene and exposure of the
body to the sun. The roof garden, often equipped for sports,
emulates the "conditions of nature" in the human habitat. The
first realization of the idea (in the small house that the architect
built for his parents on Lake Geneva, 1923) is described in a
hymnal tone: "To go up onto the roof! What a delight, like that
experience by other civilizations in other times. . . ."[9] Interestingly enough, the experience of the small roof garden on
Lake Geneva not only recalls the delights of preindustrial,
Mediterranean life, but also the pleasures of traveling on a luxury liner: "Leaning against the deck railing of the vessel. . . .
Leaning against the edge of the roof. . . ."[10]

Once again, a form that seemingly originates from practical needs is charged with a symbolism which takes its meaning both from history and the contemporary "good life." The technology of reinforced concrete, the memory of Mediterranean folk architecture, and the obsession with the ocean liner are the themes that are blended into the visual drama of the numerous roof decks and solaria from the Villa Stein in Garches to the palaces of Chandigarh. Although he describes the phenomenon in terms of pure form and ignores the symbolism, Sigfried Giedion's perception is accurate. "Frank Lloyd Wright's houses demand that we go around them if we wish to understand their formation. Now a house can be looked at from above or below; in a sense it presents a surface that opens on the sky."[11]

The free floor plan

The idea that concrete frame buildings allow a free arrangement of floor plans has been a recurring topic in modern architectural debate long before the turn of the century. In Paris, the principle had been beautifully demonstrated by the Perret's apartment house at 25 bis, rue Franklin. In some sketches for Domino houses (1914–1915), Le Corbusier suggests a complete independence of structural support and architectural "infill"—the latter was to be supplied by the individual tenant according to his needs (figs. 21, 22).[12] Later, Le Corbusier occasionally suggested that wall partitions should be moveable: in one of the two "Weissenhof" houses (Stuttgart, 1927) he used sliding walls that divided the living room into three bedrooms at night.[13] Later projects also demonstrate similar ideas, but on the whole the free floor plan was more important as a basis of architectural poetic license than as an invitation to the occupant to participate in the design process. Some of Le Corbusier's "free" arrangements left the tenant with significantly less freedom than he would have had in a traditional house, the plan of which is supposedly "the slave of the structural walls." In one of the Weissenhof houses plastered brick closets, concrete tables and beds are anchored in the building for eternity, producing an "openness" that is of a purely sculptural nature.

The elongated window

This idea, too, was already present as a possibility in the Domino concept. But it was a factory built by Gropius (1914) that seems to have ignited Le Corbusier's obsession with the form of the facade-long window that is totally independent of structure.[14] There is an element of factory symbolism in the early domestic applications of the form; for example, on an intimate scale on the upper floor of the villa in Vaucresson (1922) (fig. 56) and in the Jeanneret house on Lake Geneva. And it comes as no surprise that the architect once again produces a scientific demonstration in order to prove the superiority of the new window type: he quotes a photographer's handout advising photographers to use one-quarter the exposure time in a room with an elongated window than would be necessary in a room with "normal" openings. "The sensitive film has spoken. Ergo!" (fig. 47).[15]

The free facade

In the context of the previous postulates, this point is redundant since it is an automatic consequence of the structural principles referred to above and since it is clearly implied in the idea of the elongated window. The real motivation for it was probably Le Corbusier's urge to bring his Olympian statements to the number of five, since the classical orders with which he was at odds were also five.

Much of Le Corbusier's formal language can be (and has been) understood in terms of this basic set of architectural principles. But the five points are an insufficient premise for any attempt at reconstructing the framework of his architectural language. They do isolate a few factors of architectural form—those that seemed, at the time, best suited to the promotion of a universal style based upon objective and scientific "facts." However, as one looks more closely at the individual buildings that incorporate these facts, one becomes aware that the five points are didactic abstractions from a body of architectural thought and style which, at the time they were coined, had already grown so complex that it was impossible to express them adequately in terms of a simple, handy theory.

The House as a Box

One of the basic—though implicit rather than explicit—themes of Le Corbusier's architecture is the box. The iconic character of it has left its imprint on what has since been accepted universally as "modern architecture." The box entered Le Corbusier's vocabulary as the formal solution to a number of problems with which he had been occupied for years. It received its first clearcut articulation in a project for a standardized dwelling unit ("Maison Citrohan") in 1920–1922 (fig. 49). The form was based not only on the newly available construction methods, but also on the architect's Platonic preference for elementary forms and complex housing designs composed of split-level units. In the Villa Schwob, Jeanneret had arranged the bedrooms and service rooms around the three sides of a large, two-story living area. This idea of focusing the family life around a large "foyer" seems to have roots in traditional French rural dwellings—a subject which Le Corbusier had studied around 1914–1915.[16] But now, in the Citrohan-house, the "foyer" was redefined in terms of purist aesthetics. This definition remained the basis for almost all his later proposals for housing units, right up to the "Unité d'habitation" (fig. 48).

The Citrohan-type

One of the sources for the Citrohan idea was the Parisian artist's studio and workshop: a type of building that had vernacular origins—as Banham has shown—and that has received a number of sophisticated modern reinterpretations by architects such as François Lecoeur, Auguste Perret, and later, André Lurçat (fig. 50).[17] The type is simple: a long, often split-level studio-space lit by a large picture window.

There was, however, another and possibly more important source. A small tavern, the bistro "Legendre" opposite Ozenfant's studio on the rue Godot-de-Mauroy, seems to have played a decisive role. The bistro was a regular haunt of Le Corbusier and Ozenfant, and the former wrote about it as follows:

We used to have lunch in a little restaurant frequented by coachmen in the heart of Paris. It had a serving counter, and the kitchen was at the back; halfway up to the ceiling there was a balcony, and the front opened onto the street. One fine day we discovered this and realized that there were all the elements needed for an architectural mechanism corresponding to the organization of a house.[18]

The idea of building the prototype of such a house some-
where in the country occupied Le Corbusier for some time.
He planned to place a large window in the front extending
over both stories and serving as the only source of light for the
interior. There were to be walls on both sides, made of indige-
nous materials—fieldstone, brick or agglomerate furnished by a
local mason. The upstairs floor opening onto the central hall,
the floor of the roof terrace, and the stairs were all to be made of
prefabricated elements. In 1922, at the Salon d'Automne a small
model of the "Citrohan-house" appeared next to the grandiose
project for a City for Three Million Inhabitants. The similarity of
its trade name "Citrohan" with that of "Citroën" was by no
means coincidental, for the name was intended to suggest mass
production—a house capable of being designed, produced, and
distributed like a bus, a ship's cabin, or a car.

In contrast to the first version, the 1922 prototype stood on
"pilotis," thus combining the "box"-type with the principle of
independence from the soil. More variations on the theme appeared in rapid sequence,[19] but the first full-scale realization of
a detached villa was not constructed until 1927 at the Werkbund
exhibit in Stuttgart (fig. 54). In the meantime, the potential of
the type for urban use was explored and developed, and the
Citrohan-box evolved into a dwelling unit for use in large multistory apartment blocks. Of interest is the fact that the box
shape with an open front and back and blind (or almost blind)
sides reappeared in buildings where it was not necessary to restrict the "corps du logis" to only two facades. There is a whole
galaxy of projects of variations on this theme of the supreme
monumental box—including the elegant project for a villa for
Madame Meyer (not built; 1925), a curious small house for the
painter Guiette in Antwerp (1926),[20] and, of course, the Villa
Stein in Garches, and the Supreme Court in Chandigarh
(1952–1956) (figs. 52, 59–61). Interestingly enough, the purest
realization of the Citrohan "container" is in a building that has
nothing to do with housing and that appears as a lavish display
of an architectural vocabulary for its own sake. The Millowners
Association Building in Ahmedabad (1956–1957), headquarters
of the local cotton industry, has only two facades dramatically
articulated by huge sunbreakers, and the brick side walls are
blind except for a single window.

The Weissenhof Development (1927)

The five points plus the box were the formal themes of the two houses realized by Le Corbusier and Pierre Jeanneret at the Werkbund exhibit in Stuttgart (fig. 54). These were first and foremost exhibition buildings: primarily intended to demonstrate architectural principles.[21] Designed for "modern man" per se and not for individual clients with individual wishes, they represent two Corbusian prototypes: the Citrohan-box, almost identical with the 1922 model discussed above, and the stretched and elevated slab with the long corner-to-corner window lighting the interior. The context of the Weissenhof campaign explains the abstract, model-like character of Le Corbusier's contribution: after all, the "Weissenhof" *was* an exhibit. Its purpose was not to cure the housing shortage in Stuttgart, but to demonstrate the endeavors of the modern movement to establish new functional and aesthetic standards in housing. The institution organizing the experiment was the German Werkbund which, at the time, was able not only to muster all the leading innovational forces of the time but was also capable of establishing the necessary contacts with industry. The general plan of the Weissenhof exhibition was laid out by Ludwig Mies van der Rohe, and Le Corbusier was granted the privilege of choosing the site for his two houses. In contrast to the prototypes by Gropius, Mart Stam, and J. J. P. Oud that could be seen in the vicinity, Le Corbusier's two buildings however offered little in the way of "minimal housing": they had—and still have—an almost frivolous *haut goût* of Parisian chic, and they were, in terms of cubic footage, by far the most expensive buildings on the whole estate.

Symmetry and Precarious Equipoise: Dialogue with the Beaux-Arts Heritage

A suburban house in Vaucresson

The box is not the be-all and end-all. In fact, neither of Le Corbusier's first two Parisian realizations—Ozenfant's studio at Avenue Reille (fig. 68) and the small villa in Vaucresson (fig. 56)—have much in common with the Citrohan theme, and measured against the "five points" they are anything but "up-to-date."

The villa in Vaucresson was commissioned by a visitor to
the Salon d'Automne in 1922 who had been impressed by the
Citrohan model and the diorama of a "City for Three Million
Inhabitants." What he got was a small house, surprisingly traditional in character.[22] Among the buildings shown in the first
volume of the *Bauhausbücher* (1925), buildings by Walter Gropius, J. J. P. Oud, Hilbersheimer, Luckhardt, and others, the
little house at Vaucresson looks something like a neoclassical
"revenant."[23] The symmetrically ordered garden facade recalls
the elevation of the Villa Schwob in La Chaux-de-Fonds, and
there is even a small roof cornice terminating the facade in good
classical fashion. Small brackets are situated on both sides of
the large window—almost as if they were waiting to receive
busts or vases—eighteenth-century features purified into the
language of the machine age. On a domestic scale, these brackets are to the Vaucresson house what the axes, obelisks, and
triumphal arches are to the plan of a City for Three Million
Inhabitants done in the same year (fig. 144): they bring the architecture back into the neighborhood of the Beaux-Arts tradition. This is, in fact, a modern middle-class version of the "Petit
Trianon" at Versailles (fig. 55).

The street front with its small bow window projecting from
the facade is reminiscent of the severe symmetry of Le Corbusier's early purist paintings. In those paintings the axis of the
symmetry is often indicated by a small element such as a pipe or
a glass, and the two sides are arranged to create a subtle tension
that generates an optical equivalence (figs. 32, 33). Here in the
Vaucresson house, it is the placement of the windows that generates tension and prevents the symmetrical street front of the
building from becoming lifeless and dull. The staircase is to the
left of the "corps du logis" and separated from, yet loosely attached to, the facade by a vertical window strip. And it is here,
squeezed between the staircase and the main part of the building that the entrance is located.

Whatever the success of the project, the way in which it
combines the need for classical severity on the outside and
functional comfort within is both complex and contradictory; it
is also typical of Le Corbusier's later work and of his understanding of the delicate dialogue between architectural form
and domestic function.

The Villa Stein in Garches (1926–1928)
In 1926 Le Corbusier started work on a large villa in Garches, an elegant Parisian suburb.[24] At the time, increasingly important attempts were being made in Paris to build "modern" and "rich" residences for the affluent and avant-garde-oriented elite. In 1925, Robert Mallet-Stevens had realized a series of private houses in Auteuil, on the cul-de-sac bearing his name; houses where, in Giedion's terms, "Le Corbusier's freshness was turned into opulent elegance."[25] But, whereas Mallet-Stevens's houses evidence a simplified, though basically romantic version of Wiener Werkstätte opulence (Joseph Hoffmann's Palais Stoclet in Brussels had had a powerful influence on his whole work), Le Corbusier aimed at a formal severity that is both classical in character and rich in industrial, machine-age overtones. The materials used are light, white surfaces, and large glass panels wrapped around a fragile concrete frame—industrial, not domestic in their imagery (figs. 59–63).

The house is a variation on the box theme in that it has only two facades: the street and the garden elevations. These two facades are organized by complex proportional rules. The supports divide the plan and the elevations into a basic rhythm of 2:1:2:1:2. Although this is not clearly expressed on the facades—as usual, the "pilotis" stand behind the screens of the outer surfaces—it determines their visual organization. Yet the formal unity of the whole is accomplished with the help of a more academic device; the "tracés régulateurs" (regulating lines). The way in which the diagonal regulating lines and the rhythm of the supports are attuned to each other can be illustrated by this example: the angle of the railing running from the terrace to the garden is parallel to the overall diagonal of the building. At the same time, the steps begin at the exact point determined by the vertical rhythm of the supports. In the end, in order to respect both the regulating lines and the vertical supports, the architect had to create a small, barely noticeable mound that raises the level of the garden to the geometrically correct point for the beginning of the steps. Le Corbusier's commentary sounds Palladian: "In this case, mathematics provide some comforting truths: one leaves one's work with the certitude that the exact result has been reached."[26]

It was Colin Rowe who first compared in his brilliant essay the villa in Garches with Palladio's Villa Foscari, "La Malcontenta," near Venice. In fact, the idea of organizing the ground plan and elevation of a house according to harmonic laws is reminiscent of the architecture of humanism.[27] Both houses evince a sense of intricate formal complexity arising from an obsession with the simultaneity of conflicting geometric orders struggling for primacy within the composition. At Garches, the rhythmic pattern of 2:1:2:1:2 does not—as in the Palladian example where the spatial order is defined by structural walls —determine the interior spaces of the house, but it does generate an overlay of axial symmetries within the facades.

The street elevation, for example, is symmetrically dominated by a loggia on the solarium level, which dramatizes the ritual of the visitor's arrival and departure. The overall symmetry, however, is broken for the approach does not lead to the center of the facade, but to the service entrance, which (although subtly moved towards the right) turns out to be the focus of a secondary symmetrical system *within* the primary system.[28]

Such "symmetries within the symmetry" are equally important in the garden facade: the three axes (2:1:2) to the right of the covered terrace are loosely drawn together by a knob-shaped roof structure.[29] Any suggestion of formality and severe classical order in this building thus has to fit in with the intricate and picturesque requirements of the "functional" plan. The formal result is not so much a simple, overall order, but a combination of order and improvisation due to functional accommodation.

The Villa Stein in Garches is not the only building of this type. The street facade of the Villa Planex, built in the same year on the boulevard Masséna in Paris (1927), is also symmetrically controlled (fig. 57).[30] On the second floor, the living room projects out into the street in the form of a cube. Above it is a niche with the balcony door opening into the artist's studio. The lateral windows—recalling those of Vaucresson—are of different dimensions while still giving the impression of visual equilibrium.

It is not purely chance that similar features can be found in

Tristan Tzara's house in Montmartre, which Adolf Loos had completed in 1926. Here, too, the central axis is sculpturally accentuated by indentations and by an enormous balcony recess on the upper floor.[31] The Planex house lacks the granite severity and forceful proportions of Loos's structure; the Tzara house is and remains the house of a "mason who has studied Latin" (to quote Loos's phrase), whereas Le Corbusier translated the scheme into the language of an airy, stilt-supported "machine à habiter." It seems that Loos was aware of the interpretation provided here by Le Corbusier because the Planex facade reappears in a Viennese house of 1928 (fig. 58)—this time, however, in cold, funereal marble.[32]

But it is not only the organization, that is, the symmetry, of its facade that makes the Maison Planex interesting; it also illuminates the elements of Le Corbusier's formal vocabulary. For example, the oriel is like a loggia in reverse. Projecting like a shield, it gives the impression of being independent of the rest of the facade. Basically, it fulfills two purposes: it emphasizes the midpoint and thus the symmetry of the composition, and it articulates space by stratifying parallel surfaces—an effect frequently sought by Le Corbusier the painter.[33]

But it was only in the project for the Palace of the League of Nations that the full monumental and rhetorical potential of such symmetrical arrangements became explicit. So explicit, in fact, that the jury was able to agree on the merits of Le Corbusier's project even though they must have considered its "functional" character undesirable for so solemn a purpose. The facade of the Assembly Hall facing the lake, the monumental grouping of the two receding wings, and above all the small curved-front structure of the Presidential Pavilion all helped to emphasize the commanding and basically Beaux-Arts characteristics of the scheme (fig. 171).

Le Corbusier never ceased working with traditional organizing patterns, and his monumental schemes conceived after World War II are powerfully controlled by "secret" symmetries and hierarchies of form. How could it be otherwise? For however much Le Corbusier tried to promote himself and his work as an alternative to the Beaux-Arts heritage, he nevertheless continued to be under its spell. Even at Chandigarh—as we will see later—the position of the Palaces in the Capitol is determined by the central axis of the city, although a strict symmetry is no longer followed.

The Impact of De Stijl

It is interesting to note the embarrassment of a critic like Giedion with respect to the classicizing aspects of Le Corbusier's early style.[34] For him, it was the unequivocally modern aspects of this architecture that secured its place in the "new tradition": its use of modern building techniques, "cheap" industrial materials, and avant-garde features, such as the free plan and the dynamic handling of space. The villa at Garches is, obviously, a spectacular example of all this, even if its neoclassical aura should not be overlooked. Closer inspection reveals that the organization of its facades is not limited to a two-dimensional arrangement of its surfaces.

While the desire for a facade organized visually according to surface-rhythms and symmetry is preponderant on the street front, the garden side shows an "explosion of the facade" into vertical and horizontal screens (fig. 61).[35] These screens, delimiting the space of the vast terrace, are reminiscent of the De Stijl aesthetics and particularly of the Schröder house, built in 1924 in Utrecht by Gerrit Rietveld.

Theo van Doesburg, the leading theorist of the De Stijl movement, had defined the house as an object that must be viewed from all sides in order to be understood.[36] In Garches, Le Corbusier incorporated this idea into the terrace without, however, allowing it to determine the spatial organization of the building as a whole.

It was not the first time that the De Stijl movement had brought about a modification of his outlook. He had acknowledged the endeavors of the movement many years previously, he was familiar with the *De Stijl* magazine, and he visited the exhibition of work by van Doesburg and his Dutch friends in Léonce Rosenberg's gallery in 1923.[37] The Dutch ideas partly confirmed his own theses, for both the freeing of the house from the ground and the concept of the roof garden were part of the De Stijl aesthetics. But on the other hand, the Dutch architects by no means restricted themselves to a specific cubic form—such as the box shape of the Citrohan-type—nor had they any leanings toward axial symmetry.[38] In fact, any comparison with the free and dynamic unfolding of volumes in space, which is typical of the efforts of the Dutch neoplasticists, makes Le Corbusier's formal vocabulary look closed, classical, and orthodox (figs. 53, 54).

In addition, there was De Stijl's obsession with color. Le Corbusier must have been especially interested in one of the designs shown in the De Stijl exhibition: an axonometric perspective drawing by van Doesburg and van Eesteren in which the primary colors—red, blue, and yellow—and various shadings of gray were shown decorating the surfaces of a house. This seems to have influenced the polychromy of the interior of the La Roche house which was nearing completion just at that time.

Even the polychromy of Pessac seems to owe more to De Stijl than the elegant warm purist color scheme would suggest. Giedion, who visited Pessac shortly after its completion, saw it in the light of De Stijl aesthetics:

Le Corbusier's houses are neither purely spatial nor purely sculptural: air circulates throughout! Air becomes a constitutant factor! Therefore, neither space nor volume are important, only RELATIONSHIP and PENETRATION. There is only one, single space; it cannot be subdivided. The shells between indoors and outdoors have disappeared.[39]

Serving and Served Spaces

In connection with his design for the Villa Meyer, Le Corbusier states that "the stairs have become free organs, etc. . . . . Throughout, such elements have become distinct, and free with respect to one another."[40] A few years previously, commenting on the villa in Vaucresson, Le Corbusier described in detail how he had arrived at the final arrangement of the stairwell. After first envisioning a rounded segment placed at right angles to the main facade, he finally decided (on the way home from a bicycle race, as he recalls) to locate the stairwell in line with the facade.[41] The interesting point here is that he thought of the stair-housing as an autonomous building ele-

ment. In the Vaucresson house, for example, it is separated
from the "corps du logis" by a vertical strip of window (fig. 62).

Such functional and visual treatment of a stairwell as an independent body cannot be found in any of the early houses by
Oud, Loos, or Gropius, nor even in the later ones by Rietveld or
Mendelsohn.[42] In order to find an analogous conceptual differentiation of building parts one has to take a closer look at the
imagery of 1920 engineering that is so forcefully present in Le
Corbusier's early articles and books.

Among other products of industry, Le Corbusier used to
celebrate automobiles as models for the visual organization of
functional "objets." A 1920 automobile is an assemblage of
clearly articulated, independent forms: the conical prism of the
hood adheres closely to the outlines of the engine, the hemi-
spheric headlights are placed on either side of it, the diagonally
arranged fenders, and the cabin also are tending toward prismatic simplicity. All these parts retain their integrity of form.
Le Corbusier must have been delighted with such functional
and formal purity, and most of the early photographs of his villas include cars, if not actually his own "Voisin." Indeed, it is
often unclear in these images whether it is the car or the house
that supplies the context for an advertisement of the contemporary good life (figs. 59, 65).

The sharply articulated stairwell or ramp remained a leitmotiv for Le Corbusier from the early villas up to Chandigarh.
In one of his two houses in Stuttgart (1927) (fig. 54), the addition of service rooms made it possible to increase the cubical
stair-containers to the size of actual wings; in contrast, in the
design for the Villa Meyer the oval spiral ramp at the rear resembles the knob of a rubber hand stamp.[43] In the Villa
Church in Ville-d'Avray, which was destroyed in the sixties,
the detached stairwell-housing took the form of a semicircular
tower.[44] It recalled a Palladian prototype—see the courtyard of
the Palazzo Chiericati in Vicenza (fig. 64)—and foreshadowed
the bold arrangement of the "servicing spaces" in the workers'
housing project in Zurich that was, however, never built (fig.
123).[45]

But it was at the Swiss Pavilion of the Cité Universitaire
in Paris that the idea was first implemented on a grand scale
(1930–1932). The dramatic juxtaposition of the concave curve of

the stair tower and the austere box of the building itself later reappears in the massive ramps of the Secretariat in Chandigarh (1952–1958), where the ramps are attached to the main facade like handles on a gigantic tool (figs. 64, 66, 191).[46]

In another series of projects where the stairs and ramps appear as independent elements instead of being encased in closed forms, the functional links between levels and spaces are even more clearly emphasized. At the studio of his friend Amédée Ozenfant (1922),[47] the spiral staircase in front of the otherwise sober house seems to drop from the second-floor balcony to the street level like lemon peels in Dutch still lifes, dangling in curls from the edges of lavishly decked tables (fig. 68). In later years, the spiral staircase was more frequently used indoors, for example in the interior of the penthouse built for Charles de Beistégui on the Champs-Elysées (1930–1931), where the staircase was delicately suspended without touching the floor (fig. 220).[48] The "liberated" exterior staircase like the one in the garden of the Planex house is a somewhat "geometrized" spiral organized on both sides of a concrete slab (fig. 69).[49] Decades later, it served as a prototype for the fire escape of the Unité d'Habitation in Marseilles (fig. 70), and it also appears in front of the Millowners building in Ahmedabad, as well as at the Carpenter Center in Cambridge, Massachusetts.

Le Corbusier's desire to dramatize communication within the house and between houses must be the "raison d'être" of those "passerelles" which are often introduced in order to connect various parts of building complexes. The project for a weekend house in Rambouillet (1924) is an example of this.[50] The twin houses "Miestschaninoff" and "Lipschitz" in Boulogne-sur-Seine (1924), with their connecting footbridge make the same point, in this case with strong naval overtones.[51] Once again, however, it was only in the later works that these themes were realized on a monumental scale. The bridge connecting the Secretariat and the Parliament Buildings in Chandigarh (completed around 1958) uses the idea of the twin houses at Boulogne-sur-Seine and their passerelle on a much larger scale, and the lavishly displayed ramps of both the Millowners' buildings in Ahmedabad and Harvard's Visual Arts Center establish dramatic links between the houses and their environments (fig. 75). In all these cases, the ramp is both a matter of pure form and, less explicitly, a metaphor of mechanical transportation; it has, in short, symbolic implications relating to the architect's vision of the machine age. This will be explored further in the context of the Villa Savoye.

The Expanding Box

Le Corbusier's architecture of the twenties was an architecture of rectangles and cubes—but this was not all. Curved partitions accompany, paraphrase, and contradict the rectilinear geometries, charging them with tension. Occasionally, the volume of a box may be expanded and form a rounded body of its own accord offset against the "straight" box to which it belongs. This first occurred in the twin house La Roche/Albert Jeanneret in Auteuil (1923–1924) (figs. 71, 73).[52]

Unlike the isolated Villa Savoye, the La Roche house—or "La Rocca," as the architect called it[53]—is oriented toward the north, and stands on a difficult site in the midst of existing apartment blocks and old trees. These intricacies called for an experienced practitioner, not an Olympian theorist, and Le Corbusier handled them with brilliance and a subtle sense for spatial drama on a domestic scale. La Roche's apartment is arranged around a high, three-storied hall. The stairs in the corners, a landing platform projecting into the room like a pulpit, and the banker's working area stretching across the hall like a commando bridge all contribute to the creation of a broken, yet singularly tense, unified space (fig. 71). Giedion commented, "the manner in which the cool concrete walls are divided, cut up, and distributed here . . . in order to allow space to penetrate from all sides, this we have seen in only some baroque chapels."[54]

More recently, the same hall caused Vincent Scully to wonder if Le Corbusier was familiar (through publications) at the time with American houses like Arthur Little's "Shingleside" in Massachusetts (1881; fig. 72).[55] It is quite possible that the American Shingle Style should have left its imprint here, possibly via Adolf Loos, and a comparison of plans seems to confirm it. But the La Roche house incorporates a number of other elements that indicate a divergence from the "five points": for example, the gallery wing—the shorter limb of the house's L-

shaped plan—introduces the form of the expanding box belly-
ing out toward the garden, and it was here that La Roche's outstanding collection of cubist painting was housed. That which,
in plan, looks like a glazed bow front is in fact a blind wall—
something like the side of a guitar (and guitars appeared frequently in Le Corbusier's painting). From this time on, curved
walls encased between horizontal floor and ceiling slabs became established elements of the Corbusian vocabulary. These
walls usually define small rooms and spaces either on roof gardens (as in Garches and Poissy) or on street level (as in the
"Clarté" flats in Geneva and the "Cité du Refuge") (figs. 78,
126). They are sculptural articulations set off against the straight
and radiant geometry of the main body of the building.

In some cases, however, the "guitar-motif" constitutes the
very essence of the project. This applies to the gallery wing of
the La Roche house and also, forty years later, to Harvard's Carpenter Center (1961–1964) with its large studio spaces arranged
on the two sides of the central ramp (fig. 75). Seen either in
plan or from above, these massive volumes are reminiscent of
the form of a resonance chamber of a musical instrument or, as
students like to put it, of two grand pianos making love.[56]

The La Roche gallery wing introduces yet another feature:
the ramp that in this case leads down from the library along the
curved wall of the exhibition space. From this time on, ramps
became Le Corbusier's obsession. In 1929, for example, he insisted that the different levels of the Palace of the International
Conferences at the Mundaneum (Geneva) be served "by ele-
vators and ramps, but not by stairs."[57] He established and
acted upon exactly the same postulate thirty years later in the
Parliament in Chandigarh.[58] Ramps, however, were not restricted to interiors.

The Villa Savoye and the Symbolism of the Ramp

The Villa Savoye in Poissy is situated on a smoothly sloping
hilltop in the midst of a field, with a splendid view of the Seine
Valley.[59] The house's ground plan is a perfect square. Pilotis
raise the "corps du logis" one story above the ground, and the
ground level is defined as the zone of motion—of traffic. The arrival and departure of guests takes place here protected by the

building itself. The minimum turning radius of an automobile determined the radius of the semicircular ground floor that contains an elegant reception hall, garages, and the servants' quarters. The traffic solution of the Villa Savoye with its curved driveway (recurring, decades later, on a larger scale in American bus terminals) is the most straightforward application of Le Corbusier's definition of the ground level as the area of motion versus the upper stories as the area of the motionless (living and working).[60]

From the hall a two-stage ramp leads up into the living area. The generously dimensioned rooms are arranged in an L-shape along two of the four sides of the "corps du logis." About one-third of the surface area is occupied by an open terrace enclosed by the walls of the house. The corner-to-corner slits of the elongated windows afford views of the distant landscape, and the ramp then leads upward under the open sky to the solarium (fig. 74).

On the solarium level, straight and curved screens form a geometric landscape of surfaces and volumes in space. The immediately surrounding landscape is blocked off; one is left face to face with the sky. Perhaps the most striking feature of the Villa is the ramp, which lends a simple walk on the roof terrace the aura of a ceremonial ascent (fig. 74). What is the origin and meaning of the motif? The articulation of the arrival-zones in terms of solemnly exposed ascents has been a major theme of "high architecture" from Palladio up to the great châteaus of the seventeenth and eighteenth centuries. In Le Corbusier's case, however, the form appears to have industrial, that is, machine age, overtones recalling motorized traffic with its roadways in the forms of bridges, ramps, and loops.[61] In *Towards a New Architecture* he had published a photograph of the Fiat test track on the roof of their factory in Turin (fig. 153),[62] and in Paris, large elevated access ramps for taxis were outstanding architectural elements at the old Gare Montparnasse and the Gare de Lyon.[63] All this must have interested Le Corbusier and there is little doubt that ramps in his houses reflect something of the thrill of fast, motorized circulation within the modern city.

This idea found other, more obvious realizations in later years. The most spectacular is Harvard's Carpenter Center (fig.

75): its ramps are a sort of miniature version of Boston's South-east Expressway running through the structure in a bold S-shaped curve, piercing it like a tunnel, and inviting the pedestrians to take a metaphorical stroll through Corbusier's ideal "ville radieuse."

So much for the implicit machine-age symbolism. But the ramp is also a spectacle of pure form and space, and it has been praised as such by Giedion who insisted that it is impossible to "comprehend the Villa Savoye by a view from a single point; quite literally, it is a construction in space-time."[64] Le Corbusier's own comments on space-time are more straightforward: "It is by moving about . . . that one can see the orders of architecture developing."[65] And once again, as he had done earlier in connection with the Villa La Roche,[66] the architect speaks of "promenade architecturale," and the vernacular architecture of North Africa as sources of inspiration.

Absolute Architecture?

Around 1930, the airiness of the Villa Savoye, which stands in its field "like a landed space ship on stilts,"[67] seemed like a revolutionary antithesis to the massively walled and securely based structures of the past. In this building, architecture seems to have reached a quality of absolute, abstract form: pure, weightless geometry. It might be argued that the interpretations of the Villa Savoye as "hovering box" are based on the photographs published in the *Oeuvre complète*; the actual entrance facade (where the whitewashed cube of the "corps du logis" is brought down to the street level) hardly suggests a spaceship on stilts. Later projects confirm that the search for "weightlessness" was not a matter of primary importance to this architect. In the Swiss pavilion (and even more strikingly in the postwar "Unité d'Habitation") the slender pilotis of the Savoye house were replaced by massive, sculpturally compact posts that visually bear the whole weight of the main body of the building. In these buildings, the sense of weight is therefore not abolished but articulated tectonically in a way basically different from the classical imagery of load and support.

Sedlmayr's observation concerning the "landed space ship on stilts" nevertheless points to an important aspect of Le Cor-

busier's architecture: it is "absolute" in the sense that many of
its forms are independent of the building's location. These
boxes on pilotis—and this is true of almost all the forms invented by Le Corbusier—could be set up anywhere. Early in the
twenties, he suggested a series of locations for the Citrohan
house: at the water's edge, in the water, or—why not?—in the
middle of a Paris suburb. With the plans for his parents' house
in his pocket, he embarked on a search for a good site on Lake
Geneva during 1922–1923.[68] And in a lecture in Buenos Aires
on October 11, 1929, he asserted that the Villa Savoye, then
under construction, was designed in such a way that identical
specimens could be erected in any desired quantity in Argentina (fig. 76).[69] Later, in 1949, while working on the design of a
house on Lake Constance for Professor Fueter he wrote, "This
type of architecture permits building on any terrain whatsoever, level or sloping; there is no need to restrict the gardening area to the surrounding land—you may grow your cabbages
wherever you please."[70] For Le Corbusier, the machine to live
in either as an individual house or as a housing unit was intended to function anywhere in the world, just like a turbine
or an automobile.

Glass and Metal: "Neutralizing Walls"

It is not clear at what point Le Corbusier first considered the use
of a naked steel skeleton. He had probably been preoccupied
with the idea for some time for he admired the iron structures
by Labrouste, Eiffel, and Boileau, of the previous century, and
it was he who encouraged Giedion to make detailed studies on
the subject. In any case, he set to work enthusiastically as soon
as he recognized that the use of the steel frame—instead of reinforced concrete—might help to get some of his ideas realized.

In 1928, Le Corbusier was approached by the Genevan
industrialist Edmond Wanner, who had devised a system of
cold-insulating fiber tiles but was also interested in the problem
of dry-wall construction.[71] Le Corbusier reworked his earlier
"immeuble-villas" for Wanner and eventually developed the
plans for the "Maison Clarté," which was built in Geneva between 1930 and 1932 (fig. 78). At about the same time, the

French Minister of Labor created the "Loucheur law" (1929), whose purpose was to promote public housing and to help the steel industry out of the slump that had been brought about ten years earlier by the termination of war contracts. Le Corbusier's rapid response to this promising situation was the development of the "Loucheur houses" that were to be built entirely out of metal.

Thus, by the end of the twenties, the office at the rue de Sèvres had accumulated some experience, at least theoretically, in glass and metal construction. This came to fruition in a series of large structures realized soon after 1930: the "Cité du Refuge" (Paris), the "Maison Clarté" (Geneva), the "Fondation Suisse" (Paris), the administration building of the Centrosoyus (Moscow), and finally, the apartment house at the Porte Molitor (Paris), where Le Corbusier himself moved in 1934.[72] The problem of dry-wall construction came up again later in the sixties when the architect came into contact with the Renault Company to discuss a large housing project for Meaux; which was, however, never realized.[73]

Around 1928–1930, while Le Corbusier was working on the system of dry-wall construction for Edmond Wanner, a small but significant project was under construction in Paris's Quartier St. Germain. A well-known physician, Dr. Dalsace, had commissioned Pierre Chareau, a Parisian designer and interior decorator, to make alterations to his small house at 31 rue Saint-Guillaume. Up until then, Chareau had had little to do with the endeavors of the modern movement, and his earlier furniture was pure Art Deco. But the design and completion of Dr. Dalsace's house, which he undertook in conjunction with the Dutch architect Bernard Bijvoet (a former collaborator of Johannes Duiker), put him into the forefront of the International Style (fig. 77).[74]

Chareau, one of the co-founders of the CIAM (Congrès Internationaux d'Architecture Moderne) in 1928, and also of the UAM (Union des Artistes Modernes) in 1929, knew Le Corbusier and was probably familiar with his "five points." Nowhere else is the idea of a free ground plan more imaginatively translated into mechanical refinement. Almost all the rooms in Chareau's house are loosely separated by movable rolling or folding walls. In short, this "machine to live in" looks more like a machine than anything Le Corbusier had built up to then and even the smallest details of the furnishings, doors, windows, and closets were a tribute to machine aesthetics.

As early as 1903, Auguste Perret had used glass bricks on the stairwell of the house on the rue Franklin because the neighbors objected to windows being placed there. Bruno Taut had done the same in his glass pavilion at the Werkbund show in Cologne (1914). In the "Maison de Verre," however, Chareau used unframed glass bricks, thus creating a new type of wall that was not transparent but translucent, and massive at the same time. After having consulted Chareau's plans Saint-Gobain, the French glass monopoly, refused to guarantee the solidity of the glass walls. But both the architect and his client were courageous enough to carry out the idea all the same, and it was—as the present totally undamaged condition can prove—a complete success.[75]

The house was finished shortly before Le Corbusier's Clarté flats in Geneva after two years of work. The "Cité du Refuge" and the apartments at the Porte Molitor were under construction at the time. While the "Maison de Verre" was nearing completion, Madame Dalsace's maid observed a man in a black coat and derby hat making sketches on the building site in the evenings, and one evening Madame Dalsace identified the secret visitor as Le Corbusier himself.[76] One is tempted to attribute Le Corbusier's handling of glass brick in combination with metal frame in the Clarté flats, as well as in the apartment house at the Porte Molitor and in the other large structures from those years, to the influence of the Maison de Verre.

Around 1930, glass and steel were also used in a number of other places. Le Corbusier must have been aware of the Gropius-designed and Breuer-furnished "social rooms of a residential hotel" at the Paris Exposition of the German Werkbund in 1930, and a few months later, in 1931, he praised the completely transparent tobacco factory designed by Van der Vlught and Brinkman in Rotterdam (1928–1930) as "the most beautiful spectacle of our modern age, that I know. . . ."[77]

The large glazed surfaces that Le Corbusier started to use at that time led him to redefine the concept of the window. Its function was to bring light into the house; for air, mechanical equipment could be installed. This implied windows that could not be opened—in short, mechanical air conditioning. Gustave Lyon had already created the concept of *l'air ponctuel* in France a few years previously.[78] Thus, for the League of Nations Palace, Le Corbusier envisaged a heating system that would blow warm air between the inner and outer glass walls of the assembly hall. Complete thermal insulation by means of "neutralizing walls" was realized for the first time in the Centrosoyus Palace (fig. 79). But the funds were lacking for the establishment of the necessary mechanical devices and, as might be expected, it was hot inside the Centrosoyus in the summer and cold in winter.

The principle was applied with more success at the Cité du Refuge (1933). The inauguration was scheduled for December 1933, and Le Corbusier recalled that everybody involved was sceptical about the chances of achieving a suitable temperature inside the glass structure for the opening ceremonies; however, the heating functioned perfectly.[79] Nevertheless, *fenêtres d'illusion* ("illusionary windows") had to be cut into the glass wall two years later, for although the heating was sufficient to combat the December cold, funds were lacking for the installation of efficient ventilation during the summer.

Behind the matter-of-factness of simple "neutralizing walls," however, lay a larger and more solemn concept. A well-designed house, Le Corbusier maintained, should function efficiently anywhere, like a machine, independent of local climatic conditions: "At this time of general interpenetration of international scientific techniques, I propose one single house for all countries, all climates: a house with exact respiration."[80]

But the neutralizing walls were not Le Corbusier's last word on the subject of heat control. After his brief enthusiasm for "international scientific techniques" as premises of a truly international architecture, he seems to have quickly returned to the more elementary techniques of environmental control—a choice that became urgent in Algeria. Now, under the heat of the southern sun, he considered that architecture itself should provide the solution where complicated mechanical devices seemed to fail or were not available.

Sunbreakers[81]

In the Villa Bézeult in Carthage, near Tunis (1928),[82] the problem received an elegant solution: the rooms were placed so far
in the interior of the "corps du logis" that the projecting floor
and ceiling slabs took on the function of shade-giving umbrellas (fig. 80). In 1933, Le Corbusier planned something similar
for a worker's housing development in Barcelona; finally, a
sculptured grid of sunbreakers—now independent of the building's structural frame—appeared in the glazed surfaces of a
projected apartment house in Algiers the same year.

But it was not until 1936 that the idea was realized on a
grand scale. At the instigation of Lucio Costa, Le Corbusier was
appointed consultant for a building for the Ministry of Education in Rio. Oddly enough, the glass-walled skyscraper that he
came up with was oriented exactly toward the north; in other
words, it faced into the glaring sun. "Never mind," he declared, "we shall install sunbreakers!"[83]

After World War II there was barely a building planned by
the architects from the rue de Sèvres which did not have some
kind of sunbreaker, and Le Corbusier was eager to have these
arranged "scientifically," that is, according to the needs of the
site. He demanded that they be calculated exactly according to
the position of the sun and then poured in concrete. To build
movable sunbreakers as Costa, Niemeyer, and Reidy had
done at the Education Ministry at Rio (and as Richard Neutra
was to propose later on) was, in his eyes, a sign of weakness:
the acceptance of the incapacity to produce an exact design.
Hence the bulky gridwork set at sophisticated angles to the
facades of Le Corbusier's Indian buildings, the Parliament
buildings in Chandigarh, the Millowners' building in
Ahmedabad, and others.[84]

The idea, plausible in southern or tropical climates, was to
create a sort of architectural casing to be superimposed over the
glass facades to protect them from the inconveniences of strong,
direct radiation without loss of light and air. At low sun elevations, the building was to receive as much light and warmth as
possible, while in the summer when the sun is high it was to be
protected from heat and glare. But in places where sunshine is
only a minor factor of temperature inside a house, the sun-

breakers quickly became an element of style and expression rather than of efficient environmental management. Their back-to-nature symbolism and their sculptural strength helped the sunbreakers to become icons of the later Corbusian vernacular. Furthermore, the architect knew how to give them a visual function comparable to that of the windows, pillars, balustrades, cornices, and loggias in earlier architecture; they were a means of making a building's dimensions recognizable even at a distance.[85] In short, like the earlier principles of Corbusian design—free plan, free facade, etc.—the new device soon transcended its utilitarian roots and became an instrument of sculptural dramatization.[86]

The Undulating Roof

The Citrohan project is the prototype of pure, abstract, cubic form, isolated from and unrelated to the soil upon which it stands: reason's answer to nature. This remained a basic image. There were, however, other themes closer to the soil and earthly sensuality. The "Maisons Monol," small row houses with undulating roofs, date from 1919 (fig. 85). They recall Le Corbusier's description of architecture in terms of the sexes: "female architecture" as opposed to "male architecture."[87] The smoothly undulating roofs of the Monol houses may resemble the curved outlines of the bottles and glasses that appear in Le Corbusier's early paintings, but there is a more direct source. In 1915, Auguste Perret covered the docks in Casablanca with barrel-vaulted "egg-shell" roofs only 7 cm thick (fig. 83), and Le Corbusier, who had worked on the plans for an Algerian project in Perret's studio in 1908 and 1909 was no doubt familiar with this important construction.[88]

Low barrel vaults of varied thicknesses remained one of the recurring themes in Le Corbusier's vocabulary. The roof of his own studio on top of the apartment house at the Porte Molitor took this form, and the roof structure on the project for the "Rentenanstalt" in Zurich (1933) was a variation of it,[89] as was the prototype of a barn for an agricultural settlement developed according to a nationwide "agrarian reorganization" that never took place.[90] When it was first built, the undulating roof changed from the light shell proposed in the earlier projects into

a massive concrete body contrasting with heavy ashlar masonry
walls. This occurred in the elegant bachelor's weekend retreat at
Celle Saint-Cloud (1935),[91] a miniature prototype for such later
landmarks as the villa of the industrialist Sarabhai in Ahmedabad or the Jaoul house in Neuilly (both 1954–1956). The
principle is simple and consists of a sequence of parallel naves
of different lengths, the widths of which are determined by the
module of the "Catalan" vault.

Those who have seen the Villa Sarabhai will agree that it is
on one of the most successful of Le Corbusier's residential designs.[92] If ever he came close to the idea of the *ur*-shelter directly planted in the midst of nature, then it was in this luxurious pavilion orchestrated by rustic materials and strong colors
and embedded in a tropical garden populated with monkeys
and peacocks. The Jaoul house in Neuilly is a highly complex
and rich two-storied version of the same theme.[93] Here, vaulted
ceilings of differing width covered with tiles provide the basic
module of the building, while plain brick and concrete mass
make up the walls (fig. 82).

These are luxury houses. They are indicative of the evolution of Le Corbusier's style and they have become the point of
reference for a whole generation's work.[94] But the potential of
the undulating Monol roof goes much further. The structural
and functional advantages of a parallel arrangement of barrel
vaults have already been fully explored by the builders of Republican Rome (as the Porticus Aemilia shows). Combined to
form large patterns, barrel vaults became the basis for some of
Le Corbusier's more promising housing projects, and it is a pity
that none of them was realized. The designs for a pilgrim's
hostel at Sainte-Baume and for a vacation development at
Roquebrune (the famous "Roq et Rob" project of 1949) (fig. 86)
are easily identifiable as the sources for more recent developments, such as the Halen colony near Berne in Switzerland.
They represent a departure from the traditional concept of the
facade, for these developments unfold like carpets according to
the dictates of location, use, and time. They are cellular conglomerates displayed as a kind of dense web with "the accent
placed on their flexible, changeable fabric, thus precluding any
predetermination in terms of a particular form."[95] The analogy
with traditional vernacular settlement patterns that survive on

Mediterranean and Aegean islands is, of course, anything but coincidental.

The Roof as an Umbrella

Southern climates played a decisive role in dramatizing Le Corbusier's architectural palette. His first assignments for Algeria and his later visit to Brazil that resulted in the first uses of the sunbreaker are proof of this. In March 1951, when Le Corbusier visited India for the first time, he was once again confronted with the problem of regulating light and temperature. After his arrival in the Taj Mahal Hotel in Bombay, he carefully recorded how the architects of the colonial period had solved the problem by means of balconies, passages, and recesses of all kinds.[96]

These problems were, as we have seen, by no means new to him. In his first draft of the villa in Carthage (North Africa, 1928), he placed a free-standing roof-umbrella on top of the box (fig. 88).[97] This motif now reappeared in the same form on the Villa Shodan in Ahmedabad (1952–1956), while the "corps du logis" underneath was redefined in terms of a violent sculptural articulation of cubic volumes and hollows dramatized by heavy sunbreakers (fig. 87).[98]

In the chapel at Ronchamp—the first sketches were completed a month before Le Corbusier's departure for India—the roof, which sags into the dim interior like a heavy tent, is visually independent of the walls; a thin strip of daylight is revealed between the chapel walls and the roof. "A crab shell picked up on Long Island, near New York, in 1946, lay on the drafting table. It became the roof of the chapel," reports Le Corbusier (figs. 202, 204).[99]

Exposition pavilions

The separation between the living section and the roof is most clearly defined in the posthumously opened pavilion in Zurich (fig. 89). This "demonstration house," the only project by Le Corbusier to be realized with (however modest) official support in Switzerland, is a collage of earlier ideas.[100] Its most outstanding feature, the roof, consists basically of two steel umbrellas placed next to each other.

This idea dates back to 1939 when at the "Saison de l'Eau" exposition in Liège, two similar umbrellas were articulated in

terms of light steel skeletons (fig. 89); as in Zurich later on, the
load was not taken up at the corners but at the center of each of
the four faces.[101] Still earlier, for the Nestlé company's portable
pavilion for the Commercial Fairs of 1928, Le Corbusier used tin
and plywood for a roof that bears an obvious similarity to the
Zurich type (fig. 90).[102] Later, around 1950, there was the "Porte
Maillot 50" project for a center dedicated to the idea of the "synthesis of arts,"[103] and the same roof type cropped up again in
connection with Corbusier's museum projects for Tokyo, Er-
lenbach (near Frankfurt), and Stockholm.

What is the function of this dramatization of the roof as an
autonomous form? In Ronchamp, the thin slit of light filtering
between the walls and the shell roof creates a strong tension
between indoors and outdoors. On the roof of the Zurich
pavilion, allowing one's eye to be guided by the sweeping
contours of the steel umbrellas, one experiences a comparable
tension of spaces. In Le Corbusier's later buildings, the indoors
and outdoors do not flow together harmoniously; light and
space are not just admitted; they are either rejected or else virtually sucked into the interiors.

The Manipulation of Sunlight

On his return from Constantinople and Athens in October
1911, young Le Corbusier visited Hadrian's Villa near Tivoli.
He made careful notes about the manner in which the apse of
the Serapeum, cut into the rock, was lit through a chimney-like
clerestory. Decades later, when designing the underground
shrine of Sainte-Beaume (1948), he returned to these sketches
(figs. 92, 93).[104] But it was for the chapel at Ronchamp that he
first formulated the idea architecturally in the form of periscopic
light shafts capturing the sunlight and spilling it over the
cavern-like apses and the altars of the three side chapels. The
indirect lighting of Ronchamp, re-elaborated in the side chapels
of La Tourette and the "forum" of the Parliament at Chandigarh, is the dramatic finale of a development that also originated in the twenties. "I use light abundantly, as you may have
suspected; light for me is the fundamental basis of architecture.
I compose with light."[105]

Le Corbusier, himself a painter, knew that clerestories and

skylights have advantages over mere picture-windows, especially in studio-spaces, thus the brightly lit Ozenfant studio at
Montmartre (1922) (fig. 68). In a house designed for a painter,
but never built (1922),[106] he cut a large studio window into the
flattened barrel roof of the main room; ten years later, this form
was (at least partly) realized in Le Corbusier's private studio
(1932).[107] In 1929, he designed what he called "my house,"[108]
i.e., an ideal artist's studio with an elaborate system of
skylights and paraboloid-shaped concrete roof-shells directly
inspired by the contemporary work of the engineer Eugène
Freyssinet, who had used similar shells in the same year for his
well-known locomotive sheds in Bagneux near Paris (figs. 96,
97). "My house" was never built, but many years later (in 1952)
it served as a model for the Art School and the College of Architecture in Chandigarh (fig. 95). The form of the Freyssinet-
sheds was simplified here, but the principle remained the
same: a rhythmical sequence of sheds tilting northward in order
to avoid direct sun glaring off the large studio windows.[109]

Studios, workshops, and factories require vertical and/or
indirect lighting, and the same applies to museums. In Le Corbusier's museum projects we can follow the development from
an elementary crudeness to an almost baroque refinement: the
lighting of the museum at Ahmedabad (about 1954 to 1956) is as
poor as the illumination of the Tokyo museum is ingenious and
dramatic.[110] Other architects would have relied on electric
power, not so Le Corbusier: to him even a cavern only exists,
architecturally speaking, as a result of the sun.

The Venice Hospital
An extreme case of confidence in the virtues of indirect lighting is the rather unusual project for a hospital in Venice.[111] Le
Corbusier did all he could in order to extol its advantages, recalling that intense daylight streaming in through a window
had annoyed him during an illness. The experts may debate the
therapeutic virtues or drawbacks of the proposed Venetian
system: it was, after all, an urbanistic proposition, aiming at architectural and urban conglomerates of high density and flexibility at the cost of a view of the surroundings. During a press
conference in Venice, Le Corbusier put it in simple terms: "I
planned a hospital complex that can stretch like an open hand: a
building without facade, into which one enters from below, in

other words from the inside."[112] Once again the idea is not
new; it had been developed in a project for student quarters in
1925,[113] and it has an immediate antecedent in the "musée à
croissance illimitée" (museum of unlimited growth).

Spiral and Bowl

The Museum of Unlimited Growth

In a letter to Christian Zervos dated December 8, 1930, Le Corbusier formulated his idea of a museum of unlimited growth: a
cube standing on supports with an entrance from below into
the midpoint of the structure, from which the rooms spin out in
an endless spiral (fig. 102). "The museum rises in some suburb
of Paris, set in the middle of a field of potatoes or beetroot. If the
site is magnificent, so much the better. If it is ugly and sad-
dened by sprocket-wheel developments or factory chimneys,
it doesn't matter. . . ."[114]

In his later years, Le Corbusier designed a large number
of museums. Three of them were actually built (in Tokyo,
Ahmedabad, and Chandigarh), but in none of them was unlimited growth actually provided for; the only indication of the
non-structural and flexible character of the partitions is provided by the nature of the brick joints on the exterior walls.
Practical considerations were originally brought forward to justify the choice of the spiral, but more fundamental concerns
seem to have been involved. The spiral fascinated Le Corbusier
because it follows "natural laws of growth, laws which underlie
all manifestations of organic life"[115]—and this brings us back
to his studies of plants and animals made in the early years at La
Chaux-de-Fonds.

But in Corbusier's work the spiral remained an abstract
concept; it never became a powerful architectural image (as
it did in Borromini's lantern in the St. Ivo Church in Rome, or
Tatlin's grandiose project for the Third International, 1920) (fig.
100). It was Frank Lloyd Wright who gave the spiral evocative
power as an architectural form, although in doing so he compromised the function it was intended to serve. Compared with
Wright's Guggenheim Museum in New York, Le Corbusier's
museums may be of modest architectural caliber, but they fulfill
their purpose better.

The Stadium

It is obvious that this theme would interest Le Corbusier since for him sport was synonymous with mental and social hygiene. From his elegant apartment at the Porte Molitor, he used to look down on the Sunday crowds watching soccer games in the Jean-Bouin Stadium, and it is not surprising that he was impressed by the "gigantic and clean-cut concrete bowls" which he saw in 1936 in the United States: "Sixty thousand, even a hundred thousand spectators participate in these famous games, where everything has self-control, style, enthusiasm."[116] In Berlin and Rome, 1936 and 1937 were years of spectacular mass rallies; Paris could not be allowed to lag behind and so Le Corbusier worked out a grandiose design for a national sports and entertainment center approachable by wide ramps and large enough to seat a hundred thousand spectators (fig. 99).[117]

When he took up the idea again twenty years later, the result was more curious than colossal. In Firminy, a small town in the mountains of central France, Le Corbusier came up with a building shaped like a grandstand but intended to serve as a youth center (fig. 98) (design: 1956). For obvious reasons, the youth center was originally designed to be incorporated into the stadium. Later the administration decided to build the stadium elsewhere; but the plans had been made, and the architect held to his original idea. The final building is frankly paradoxical;[118] a monument to the fact that architecture never grows directly out of function, but results from a confrontation between needs on one side, and formal concepts on the other.

Typology and Design Method

How, then, is it possible to categorize Le Corbusier's work as an architect? Is it appropriate to break it up according to functional programs: social housing, villas, office buildings, assembly halls, churches, etc.? Is there a consistent formal development within these themes?

I do not think so. It is one of the characteristic paradoxes of this work that its forms develop with relative independence of the specific purposes they serve. Barely more than three or four

themes (or functions) led to definite architectural types: the
dwelling module (box), the museum (spiral), the stadium
(bowl), and to a certain degree the assembly hall (triangle). Out
of the functional requirements of these programs a few families
of forms and patterns were established. And these forms and
patterns were later developed, varied, and modified in the
context of a multitude of different tasks. Of course, the evolution of forms is not entirely independent of traditional architectural themes, but the connection between purpose (physical and conventional) on the one hand and form on the other
becomes loose, and at times even accidental.

A few examples taken from three clearly different functional categories may illustrate this apparent paradox. Le Corbusier was repeatedly involved with the design of schools: at
the age of twenty-three, he produced a project for the Ateliers
d'Art Réunis in La Chaux-de-Fonds (1910); almost half a century later he designed the Art School and the College of Architecture in Chandigarh (between 1958 and 1962) and the Carpenter Center for the Visual Arts at Harvard (1961–1964). In each
instance he was confronted with a somewhat similar program—
a program, incidentally, that was of great significance to him
—in each case he gave it an entirely different form. The Ateliers
d'Art Réunis are a secularized monastery, directly related to
the Florentine convent that he had visited shortly before. The
Chandigarh school is a variation of the Freyssinet-type rail-
way-shed (and of his own studio project of 1929), while the
Carpenter Center is an amalgam of the La Roche exhibition
wing and the Millowner's ramp, reformulated in terms of the
Chandigarh—and the La Tourette—idiom.

And the villas: in Ahmedabad two luxurious private residences were built at the same time on the basis of very similar
programs—the Villa Shodan and the Villa Sarabhaï. Yet they are
totally different in almost all respects: whereas the first belongs
to the Citrohan family, the second is a variation of the Monol
type.

But the point is best illustrated by Le Corbusier's churches.
In principle, they serve an analogous purpose: to gather a
crowd around an altar. Yet their form is radically different in
each case. Ronchamp is a system of curved and partly tilted
convex and concave walls covered by a shell that rises from the

center of the interior space. Its irregular shape recalls the African sketches from Ghardaïa and the M'zab (1931).[119] La Tourette is a strictly prismatic box of Cistercian austerity. Firminy is a cut-off cone that is slapped on the interior like a hat. The form resembles neither that of Ronchamp nor that of La Tourette; it is directly borrowed from the Parliament in Chandigarh or perhaps even from the industrial cooling towers—the Assembly Hall's ultimate point of reference (figs. 104–106).[120]

Le Corbusier's attitude toward function and symbolism in architecture is best illustrated by this category of buildings where function had traditionally been determined by practical needs as well as, and perhaps even more so, by tradition. The term "church" does not signify any preestablished code of forms in his work; and no doubt this constitutes a break with the conditions under which institutional buildings were conceived in the past. Le Corbusier refused to work with the notion of "the sacred" as it is conceived by modern theology, namely as the "political appearance of the religious,"[121] embodied in a firmly established building tradition. He had his own definition: "some things are sacred and others are not, whether they are religious or not."[122] Thus Ronchamp belongs, typologically, to the same building category as the small Assembly Hall of the Millowner's Association in Ahmedabad; it is not a chapel by virtue of its form, but by its intensive sculptural articulation— and the strong medieval overtones of the twilight interior.

The idea that similar functions create similar forms is continually questioned in Le Corbusier's works, and it is no longer necessary to emphasize that the concept of functionalism is of little help with regard to the interpretation of his architectural typology. More precisely, it is helpful only in a very limited sense: for it was only at the inception of a form that the data of the program and the materials played a determining role in the sense in which Sullivan postulated that "form follows function." Once this basic vocabulary was established, it became not totally but relatively autonomous with respect to specific social functions (and also with respect to physical execution). It could now be used, that is, it could be associated with the precise and individual data of a particular program. The results of such a procedure, which have been described by A. Colquhoun as a "displacement of concepts,"[123] may be quite efficient as far as the functional performance of the resulting buildings is concerned—if only because the vocabulary is, as we have seen, remarkably flexible. But—and this is the point—these results are not primarily determined by function or structure, nor indeed by the building's forming a part of an institutionalized tradition.

There is, in short, no longer a language of forms that coincides with established social functions and cultural meanings. In other words, form and function are no longer defined within traditional social conventions.

La fenêtre fut toujours l'obstacle. Son évolution à travers les âges, marque le perfectionnement de l'outillage.

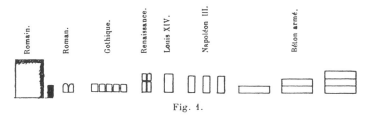

Fig. 1.

La fenêtre est l'un des buts essentiels de la maison. Le progrès apporte une libération. Le ciment armé fait révolution dans l'histoire de la fenêtre.

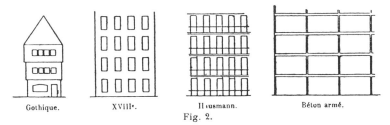

Gothique.   XVIII⁰.   Hausmann.   Béton armé.

Fig. 2.

La couverture étanche fixe la forme de la toiture La pénurie des moyens portait entrave au rêve *constant de monter sur la maison.*

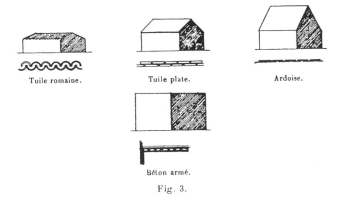

Tuile romaine.   Tuile plate.   Ardoise.

Béton armé.

Fig. 3.

Le béton armé apporte le toit plat et révolutionne l'usage de la maison.

42. Le Corbusier, the revolution of the window in relation to structure (from "Architecture d'Epoque Machiniste," *Journal de Psychologie* (1926):332)

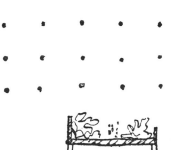

43. Le Corbusier and Pierre
Jeanneret, Pavillon Suisse
at the Cité Universitaire,
Paris, 1933: the Pilotis (from
Creation is a Patient Search)

44. "The Pilotis"; explanatory drawings of "the five
points of a new architec-
ture" (from *Oeuvre com-
plète*)

45. "The roof garden" (from
Oeuvre complète)

46. Le Corbusier and Pierre
Jeanneret, Villa Savoye in
Poissy, 1929–1931 (from
Creation is a Patient Search)

47. "The elongated win-
dow" (from *Oeuvre com-
plète*)

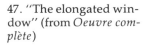

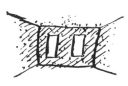
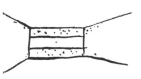

48. (a) Studio flat in the
Boulevard Rochechouart,
Paris; (b) saddler's shop
near the Place du Tertre
(from R. Banham, *Theory
and Design in the First
Machine Age*)

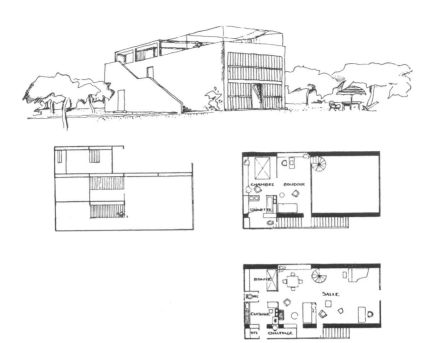

49. Le Corbusier, first proposal for the "Maison Citrohan," 1922 (after *Oeuvre
complète*)

50. André Lurçat, artist's
studios in the Villa Seurat,
Paris, ca. 1925 (photo: author)

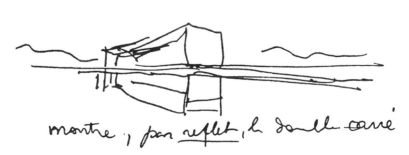

51. The system of dwelling units inserted into the structural "grid" of the Unité d'habitation. Model–photograph (archives: Willy Boesiger, Zurich)

52. The "box" of the Supreme Court Building, Chandigarh (from *Oeuvre complète*)

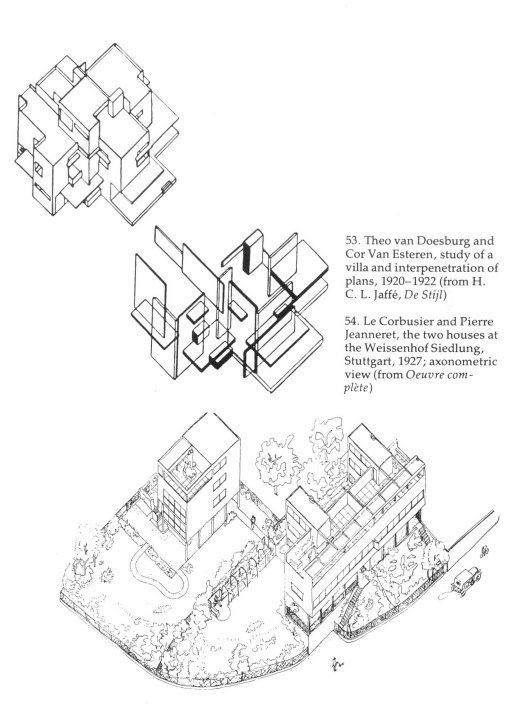

53. Theo van Doesburg and Cor Van Esteren, study of a villa and interpenetration of plans, 1920–1922 (from H. C. L. Jaffé, *De Stijl*)

54. Le Corbusier and Pierre Jeanneret, the two houses at the Weissenhof Siedlung, Stuttgart, 1927; axonometric view (from *Oeuvre complète*)

55. The "Petit Trianon" in
Versailles with "regulating
lines" (from *Vers une architecture*, 1923)

56. Le Corbusier, Villa in
Vaucresson, 1922; view of
the garden facade (from
Oeuvre complète)

57. Le Corbusier and Pierre
Jeanneret, residence and
studio for Mr. Planex, Paris,
1927; street facade (from
Oeuvre complète)

58. Adolf Loos, Moller
house, Vienna, 1928 (from
Müntz/Künstler, *Adolf Loos*)

59. Le Corbusier and Pierre
Jeanneret, Villa Stein-De
Monzie in Garches, 1927;
street facade (archives:
Willy Boesiger, Zurich)

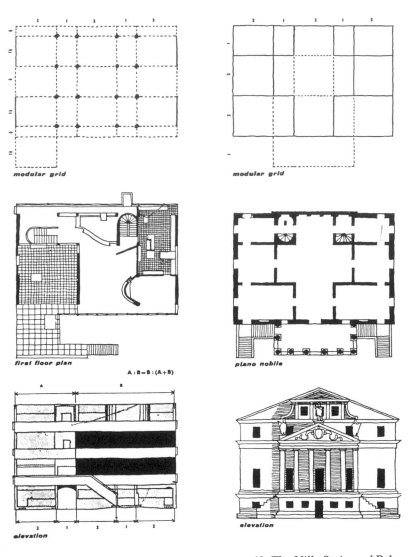

60. The Villa Stein and Palladio's Villa "La Malcontenta" compared (from Colin Rowe, *The Mathematics of the Ideal Villa*)

61. Villa Stein-De Monzie,
view of the balcony on the
garden facade (archives: Architectural Association,
London)

62. Le Corbusier, sketches
of the Villa in Vaucresson,
1922 (from *Oeuvre complète*)

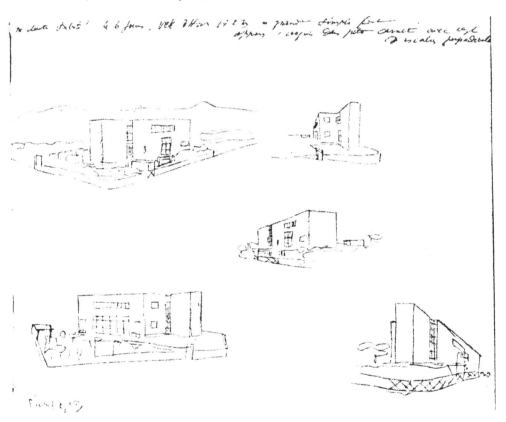

63. Le Corbusier and Pierre   64. Andrea Palladio,
Jeanneret, Villa Church in   Palazzo Chiericati in Vic-
Ville d'Avray near Paris,   enza, ca. 1552; stairwell
1928 (destroyed) (from   tower (photo: author)
Oeuvre complète)

65. Le Corbusier and Pierre Jeanneret, Pavillon Suisse at the Cité Universitaire in Paris, 1933 (archives: Willy Boesiger, Zurich)

66. Le Corbusier and his Voisin-automobile (from *Le Corbusier lui-même*)

67. Le Corbusier, "Pavillon
Suisse," preparatory
sketch, ca. 1931 (Fondation
Le Corbusier, Paris)

68. Le Corbusier and
Amédée Ozenfant, studio
house for Ozenfant, Paris
1922 (photo: Roger Viol-
let)

69. Le Corbusier and Pierre Jeanneret, open staircase in the garden of the Villa Planex, Paris, 1927 (from *Oeuvre complète*)

70. Le Corbusier, fire escape at the Unité d' Habitation, Marseilles, 1952 (archives: Willy Boesiger, Zurich)

71. Le Corbusier and Pierre Jeanneret, Maison La Roche-Jeanneret, Auteuil, 1923/24; hall (from *Oeuvre complète*)

72. Arthur Little, "Shingleside," house in Swampscott, Mass., 1881; hall with gallery (from *Building News*, 1882)

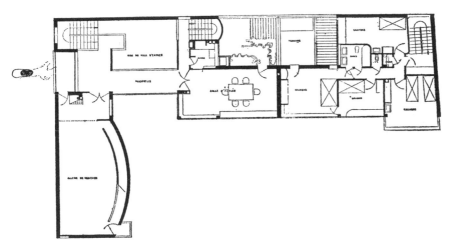

73. Maison La Roche-
Jeanneret, ground plan second floor (from *Oeuvre
complète*)

74. Le Corbusier and Pierre Jeanneret, Villa Savoye in Poissy, 1929–1931; ramp leading to the solarium (from *Oeuvre complète*)

75. Le Corbusier, Carpenter Center for the Visual Arts, Harvard University, Cambridge, Mass., 1960–1963; view of studio wing and access ramp (photo: Carpenter Center for the Visual Arts)

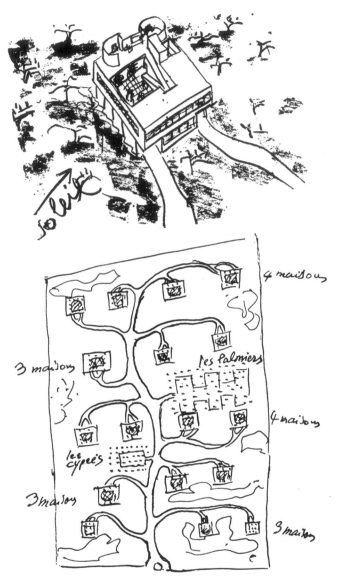

76. Le Corbusier, sketch of
Villa Savoye and proposed
suburban multiplication of
the type (from *Précisions*,
1929)

77. Pierre Chareau, maison
de verre, Paris, 1930–1932;
garden facade (photo: au-
thor)

78. Le Corbusier and Pierre
Jeanneret, Clarté flats,
Geneva, 1930–1933 (from
Oeuvre complète)

79. Le Corbusier and Pierre
Jeanneret, Centrosoyuz office building, Moscow,
1928–1934; axonometric
view with details showing
"Neutralizing wall" (Fon-
dation Le Corbusier, Paris)

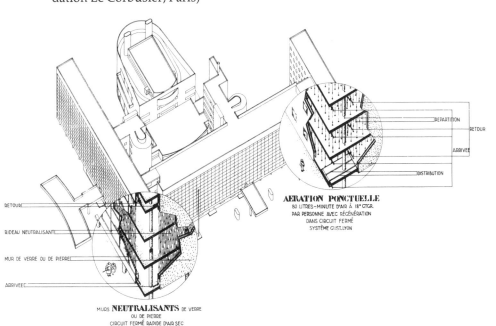

80. Le Corbusier and Pierre
Jeanneret, Villa Bézeult at
Carthage, Tunisia, 1929 (ar-
chive: Willy Boesiger,
Zurich)

81. Le Corbusier, the sunbreaker; explanatory
sketches (from *Oeuvre
complète*)

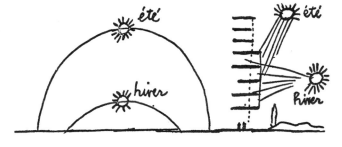

82. Le Corbusier, Villa Jaoul
in Neuilly, 1954–1956
(photo: Lucien Hervé)

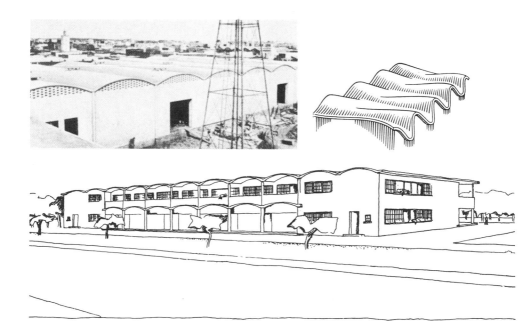

83. Auguste Perret, docks at
Casablanca with egg-shell
vault, 1915 (from Giedion,
Bauen in Frankreich)

84. Antonio Gaudí, roof of
the parochial school of the
Sagrada Familia, Barcelona
(from Sweeny-Sert, *A.
Gaudí*)

85. Ch.-E. Jeanneret, Monol
workers' houses, 1919 (from
Oeuvre complète)

86. Le Corbusier, preparatory sketches for the "Roq
et Rob" vacation settlement
for Roquebrune, Cap Mar-
tin, 1949 (from *Oeuvre complète*)

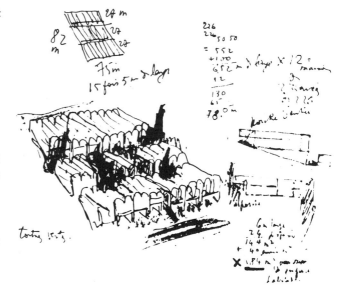

87. Le Corbusier, Villa Shodan in Ahmedabad, 1956
(archives: Willy Boesiger,
Zurich)

88. Le Corbusier, first project for the villa at Carthage,
Tunisia, 1928 (*from Oeuvre
complète*)

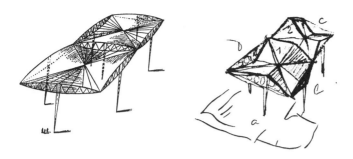

89. Le Corbusier, exhibition pavilions: commercial fair at Liège, 1938 (left); pavillon Le Corbusier at Zurich, opened in 1967 (right) (from *Oeuvre complète*)

90. Le Corbusier and Pierre Jeanneret, Nestlé pavilion, commercial fairs in Paris, 1928 (from *Oeuvre complète*)

91. Le Corbusier, Tavès and
Rebutato, architects, Centre
Le Corbusier, Zurich, inau-
gurated 1967 (photo: Jürg
Gasser, Zurich)

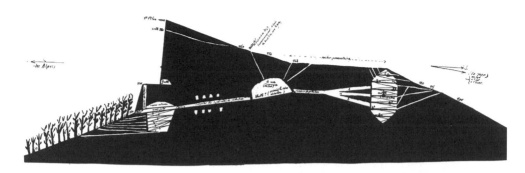

92. Le Corbusier, project for
an underground sanctuary
in Sainte-Baume, Southern
France, 1941 (archives: Willy
Boesiger, Zurich)

93. Le Corbusier, sketch
showing the interior of the
Serapeum at Hadrian's Villa
in Tivoli (from *Oeuvre complète*)

94. Giovanni Battista Piranesi (1720–1778), view of the Serapeum at Hadrian's Villa in Tivoli; engraving

95. Le Corbusier, Art School
in Chandigarh, India, with
studio windows oriented
toward north (photo: author)

96. Eugène Freysinnet,
locomotive sheds in Ba-
gneux, France, 1929 (from
Giedion, *Bauen in Frank-
reich*)

97. Le Corbusier, sketches
for an artist's studio, *My
House*, 1929 (from *Oeuvre
complète*)

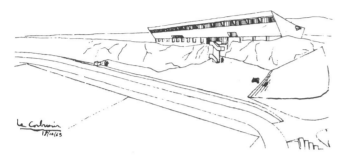

98. Le Corbusier, house of
culture at Firminy, France,
opened 1965; perspective
view (from *Oeuvre complète*)

99. Le Corbusier and Pierre
Jeanneret, project for a national center for popular
celebrations, 1936–1937
(from *Creation is a Patient
Search*)

100. Wladimir Tatlin, project of a monument for III. Communist International, Moscow, 1920

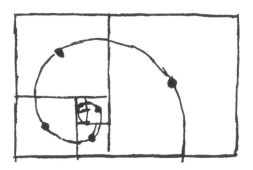

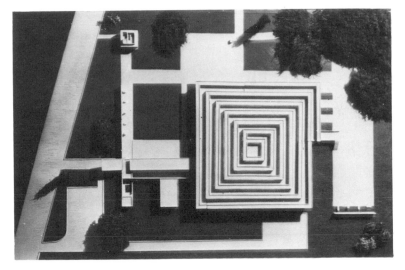

101. Le Corbusier, sketches illustrating the origins of the spiral motif (from *Oeuvre complète*)

102. Le Corbusier, project for a museum of unlimited growth, model, seen from above, ca. 1931 (archives: Willy Boesiger, Zurich)

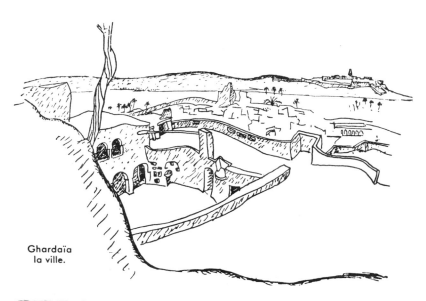

Ghardaïa
la ville.

103. Le Corbusier, view of
Ghardaia, M'zab, North Africa, 1931 (from *Plans*)

104. Le Corbusier, church at
Firminy, France, 1961 (from
Oeuvre complète)

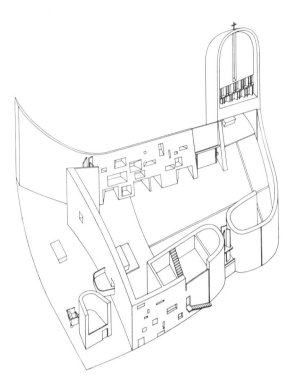

105. Le Corbusier, chapel Notre Dame du Haut at Ronchamp, 1951–1955; axonometric view of the interior (from *Oeuvre complète*)

106. Le Corbusier, Assembly building in Chandigarh, India; roof of the Upper Chamber (photo: Pierre Jeanneret; archives: Willy Boesiger, Zurich)

4 Variations on a Utopian Theme

Context: The Twenties

The redefinition of housing in terms of a new polarization of private and collective life was an accepted dogma in progressive architectural thought throughout the twenties. For political and economic reasons, the climate at the time was favorable to large scale experiments, especially in Russia and Germany where the provision of working class housing was largely a public matter that was placed under government control and often handled by radically modern architects.

In 1926, the City Soviet of Moscow organized a competition for a "communal house." A year later the leading Russian magazine *SA* (*Sovremennaya Arkhitektura*) dedicated an issue to the same topic, and from then on the idea of "collective living," which had played a considerable role in pragmatic approaches to the housing shortage ever since the revolution, became a central issue in discussions among progressive Soviet architects. Numerous competitions were organized, in particular by the OSA ("Society of Contemporary Architects"). Their results were often far-reaching; for example, A. Ol's project of a communal house with two-story split-level dwelling units and "interior streets" (fig. 108). Important, too, was Moses Ginsburg, who worked with a team of architects on proposals for new, minimal dwelling types. The studies carried out in the Strojkom (the State Commission of Housing) produced the well-known "type F" project of a dwelling unit with exterior gallery which was the basis of the "Narkomfin" apartments built shortly afterwards (1928) (fig. 107).

Perhaps the most straightforward and clear-cut interpretation of the idea of collective living was provided by the famous project of a communal house by Barshch and Vladimorov, with its juxtaposition of minimal dwelling units and spacious collective halls where food was to be served by an assembly line (1929) (fig. 109).[1] The OSA coined the expression "social condensers" for projects of this kind, that is, buildings that did not merely passively reflect the changes undergone by society since the revolution but that played an active part in the transformations by anticipating, under laboratory conditions, more developed forms of future social life. Their purpose was thus to help break away from the traditional small-scale household,

to free the woman from domestic slavery, to place education
more and more under the supervision of the community, etc.
As W. Kuzmin, one of the "supercollectivist" propagandists, put
it in 1928: "The proletariat must begin immediately with the
abolishment of the family as an organ of repression and exploi-
tation."[2]

Not that Ginsburg or, later, the Vesnin brothers would
have gone that far in their own propaganda rhetorics. They too,
however, would no doubt have considered the tendency toward the abolishment of the small household and the small
family as a characteristic quality of a new society. Moreover,
their Western colleagues, architects such as Walter Gropius and
Bruno Taut, would have agreed entirely, for they too were confronted with the dramatic housing shortage in the industrial
centers; and they too were convinced that the only way to re-
solve the problem was through the establishment of minimal
standards and the relegation of a number of domestic functions
to the communal or collective sphere. In European avant-garde
circles it was taken for granted that the small family was about
to become obsolete, not only as a unit of production but also as
a unit of consumption. The difference between Kuzmin's and
Gropius's position was based mainly on the fact that the former
talked about the abolition of the family as an urgent socialist
postulate, whereas the latter referred to it as to an established
and well-proven sociological trend of modern industrial society.[3] Thus the communal house idea as such was by no means a
revolutionary proposition. In fact, some of its most radical
propounders were well aware that the principle of the "technical collectivation of the domestic apparatus" had already been
realized in earlier, bourgeois forms of apartment houses, service houses, and luxury hotels built for the capitalist elite.[4]

The architecture chosen by the Russian constructivists as
an appropriate framework for the new way of life was clearly of
industrial extraction. Barshch and Vladimorov seem to have
chosen the fully Taylorized assembly line production system as
the correct model for a new, proletarian togetherness. The ideas
of the Germans (Ernst May, Bruno Taut, and others) were almost romantic in comparison. Although the formal vocabulary
of their numerous radically modern housing complexes was
anonymous and "functionalist," the syntax was frequently

romantic. The qualities of rural life in a quasi-medieval community continued to serve as an implicit guideline for most proposals of new housing complexes. It was the economic crisis of 1928 that set things straight in Germany and generated the form of the apartment block that has since become the controversial icon of modern working-class housing: the high-rise slab in the form propounded by architects like Hilberseimer and Gropius after 1928.

"Light, air, openness" were the qualities emphasized by this new building type—the qualities of lung sanatoriums. It is no coincidence that Giedion in 1929 referred to sanatoriums as prototypes of the new way of life: "The most recent studies in the field of medicine concerning hospitals coincide with the intention inherent in the whole field of architecture; the doctor, too, requires a maximum dissolution of the walls in glass, the freest possible access of light."[5]

It is thus not surprising that buildings such as Aalto's sanatorium in Paimio, Finland (1928), high and slender slabs exposing their convalescent inhabitants to sun and fresh air, become paradigms of the new architecture and its social ethos. One liked to believe—even if one didn't always say it explicitly—that the architect had a moral responsibility comparable to that of the doctor, that architecture must assume a therapeutic role in the cure of urban diseases, and that the city might ultimately become a huge hospital of social regeneration. Concepts like these were inseparable from the reform ideology of urbanists like those who, after 1928, used to gather in the International Congresses of Modern Architecture (CIAM). This biological model of urban reform was not of purely declamatory significance, for tuberculosis and other diseases directly related to urban over-congestion and lack of hygiene were (and often still are) urgent problems of big cities.

The strong symbolism of this form, revealing as it does the subrational motivations of architectural idealism, does not, of course, explain the triumph of the apartment slab as a solution to housing in many parts of the world, especially since 1945. This is largely due to the fact that the erection of a high-rise slab appeared (and still appears) faster and more economically under the conditions of centralized mass production and industrialization than any other building type. To reduce human needs to "light, air, openness," that is, to a parameter of criteria considered essential to biological survival (rather than for social well-being) was a way of fitting in with the partially assumed realities of industrial production at a given moment in time.

Le Corbusier: The monastic ideal

The "social condenser," the "garden city," and the apartment slab: how do Le Corbusier's ideas relate to these themes of urban renewal that became so important between 1920 and 1930? In fact, his work both contributed to and derived from this international development. But only an examination of the architect's own attitudes to the issues involved—together with these international trends—can help to reconstruct the context in which his projects grew.

It was the visit to a charterhouse in Galluzzo (fig. 114), near Florence (in 1907) that seems to have introduced young Le Corbusier to the virtues of "collective life"; he once mentioned to the Dominican Père Couturier (1948) that his visit to this Tuscan monastery set the course of his whole career.[6] Unlike Fourier and the French tradition of socialist utopianism, whose ideas reached Le Corbusier only much later in his life, this was a first-hand experience; and it is tempting to regard even the physical form of the Certosa as a point of reference for later Corbusian projects. Three sides of this cloister crowning a hilltop are composed of small houses for the monks, each equipped with a garden from where the Tuscan hills appear as a framed view. It is here that the daily life of the monks unfolds—study, meditation, and gardening—in perfect isolation (and solitude was to become a loaded word for Le Corbusier, a fundamental requirement for any creative mind). The "collective spaces"— the church, the refectory, and the meeting halls—are situated to the west of the cloister, and their splendor reflects the status of Niccolo Acciaiuli, the founder of the Certosa.[7]

A few years after his first visit to Florence, Jeanneret joined forces with his friends from the Cours Supérieur in order to found the Ateliers d'Art Réunis in La Chaux-de-Fonds. The form of the Tuscan charterhouse provided the model for an ideal building that was to house the newly founded community of artists (fig. 115): a sequence of studios alternating with gardens and clustered around a central lecture hall covered by a pyramidal roof. A cloister of young artists—the idea was in the

air around 1910. Heinrich Tessenow was about to realize it in
the "Bildungsanstalt Jacques Dalcroze" in Hellerau near Dresden, in many ways a model settlement for a colony of students.
As Jeanneret, who visited it late in that same year, 1910, put it:
"Hellerau is a truly collectivist manifestation."[8]

Immeuble-villas (villa-superblocks)

The systematic organization of daily life into two basic types of
activities: those that take place in the isolation of the individual
cell and those that are performed collectively, remained a point
of reference for Le Corbusier's social outlook. He regarded it
first and foremost as an economic principle that allowed him to
do away with the waste of space and labor characteristic of the
traditional bourgeois household. The idea formed part of the
"immeuble-villa" concept that developed from the early studies
of the Maison Citrohan. As early as 1922, Le Corbusier and
Pierre Jeanneret studied ways of inserting the Citrohan box into
large, multistoried apartment blocks—by sketching on the back
of a menu, as Le Corbusier later recalls.[9] The idea that these
agglomerations of dwelling units would be connected to a centralized system of services "like a hotel, like a commune" was a
crucial issue in Le Corbusier's comments in *Urbanisme* and
other books.[10] For example, an early version of immeuble-villas
shows these apartment houses organized around large rectangular courtyards; the apartment blocks are connected via a system of bridges across the streets containing children's day-care
facilities, meeting halls, clubs, and facilities for an around-the-
clock crew of servants (fig. 110).

Technically, in terms of program, and even in terms of architectural form, such projects clearly anticipate some aspects of
later Russian proposals like those referred to previously. But
despite his enthusiasm for monastic life Le Corbusier never really aimed at the abolishment of the small, single-family household. The new way of life was not intended to make the bourgeois family obsolete; on the contrary, it aspired to provide
a model of service that would enable it to survive. To Le Corbusier, housing reform meant the provision of a cell that would
allow even the petit bourgeois and the worker to have his
middle-class foyer fully equipped and open for the "essential
joys" of sun and air. He had no objection to the relation between master and servant in the modern household; although

he did propose to replace the *bonne de Bretagne* ("the maid from Britanny"), to whom he often referred as a charming requisite of domestic peace and cooperation between the classes, by an anonymous but efficient crew of uniformed stewards and stewardesses.

The Pavillon de l'Esprit Nouveau at the Exposition Internationale des Arts Décoratifs in Paris (1925) was designed as a 1:1 model of a villa that ideally was intended to be inserted into large, well-serviced multistory immeubles (fig. 39). The combination of split-level living room (à la Citrohan-box) and garden terrace owed much to the Tuscan monastery: it was a monastic cell adjusted to family scale. The "collectivation" consisted of decentralized services, not in socialist cooperation in the areas of management and other responsibilities. What these projects emphasize is the ideal of an urban middle class that prefers to live in the city, that might be interested in some collective services (given the increasing difficulties of maintaining large numbers of servants), and that would have no objection to more greenery and fresh air (given the increasing noise and other pollution brought about by automobile traffic). The life style suggested by this new urban form was that of the elegant apartment block or condominium where hardly anyone ever gets to know his neighbor: a nomadic way of life within the cosmopolitan anonymity of the metropolis.[11] This is what separates Le Corbusier's reform model from most of the contemporary Anglo-Saxon and German attempts at a "regeneration" of the city via a return to popular and pre-industrial forms of small town, or village, communities. In short, the "homme poli vivant en ce temps-ci" [well-educated man who lives in our times], this classless Mr. X, envisaged by Le Corbusier as the standard inhabitant of his immeuble-villa, was not identical with the "man on the street."

Pessac

It is interesting to note that the community idea and the socialist ethos that qualified the modernist housing proposals of the twenties—especially in Germany—had at this time, only a limited impact upon Le Corbusier's work, even in the context of a commission that would have lent itself to a more romantic approach. The Quartier Frugès in Pessac near Bordeaux (built in 1925) was primarily a demonstration of universally applicable dwelling types, a principle that had been worked out in a group of ten small worker's houses at Lège, near Arcachon (1923). A set of combinable space-boxes served as a base.[12] Compared with Gropius's earlier modular system for standardized housing (1921) this set of buildings is somewhat simple in character; for unlike Gropius's open and flexible compounds, Corbusier's house types are, once again, variations on the theme of the box. Naturally, these types underwent numerous changes during the design process. The final project of 135 dwelling units, which was never completed, offered a choice of house types ranging from the Z-shaped, two-storied compound of row houses interspersed by large, two storied bays, and three-storied blocks with roof gardens, which Le Corbusier called "skyscrapers" (fig. 118). He partly abandoned his original intention of building houses for absolute minimal requirements, and that which had been planned as a cheap working-class garden city ended up looking more like an elegant middle-class suburb.

Henri Frugès, an industrialist from Bordeaux, himself an amateur painter and musician, who had inherited a sugar-cube factory from his father, wrote to Le Corbusier, "Pessac should be a laboratory. I give you free hand to dispose of convention and to abandon traditional methods."[13] While Pessac is unthinkable without the English garden city tradition (with which Le Corbusier was extremely familiar, as early proposals for La Chaux-de-Fonds show),[14] in some ways the concept owes still more to Tony Garnier's *Cité industrielle*. This is particularly noticeable in the formal treatment of the concrete frame buildings in which we find quite as many elements from Garnier as from anonymous vernacular sources. The possibility of the endless repetition of identical units along a geometrical plan, and the fact that the perfect standard of the individual cell is more important than the clearly defined unity of the whole (in short, that no attempt was made to build a village), brings Pessac close to Garnier, and to the "Plan Voisin."

If it is true to say that Pessac was unsuccessful in the long run, then this was due to factors that have less to do with the project as such than with the circumstances of its realization, that is, financial, legal, technical, and administrative complications.[15] First, the shopping area, an important raison d'être of

the project, was never built; second, an incompetent contrac-
tor was employed on the site; third, due to some inconsistencies
of the project with local government standards, the commune
failed to connect the new estate to the public water supply
system until 1929; and fourth, as a consequence of these facts,
the buildings were finally inhabited by people other than
those for whom they were designed. After a few years of almost
total neglect, they were taken over by local residents who had to
finance and carry out the most elementary repairs. But even
without this unfortunate course of events, it can safely be assumed that the houses were of a kind that would have been
more readily accepted by an enlightened urban middle class
clientele than by a rural population of workers.

The two houses at the Weissenhof development in Stuttgart
(1927) would appear to be more eager to present universal solutions to universal needs of "modern man" than to offer precise suggestions of how to cope efficiently with the problem of
working-class housing. Architects like Mart Stam or J. J. P. Oud
(who both participated in the Weissenhof experiment with extremely interesting "minimal housing" proposals) had workers
in mind as the ideal inhabitants of their estates, but Le Corbusier once again designed for man *tout court*, that "well-
educated man who lives in our times." There is no doubt that
some among Le Corbusier's conservative critics defined the social affiliations of the supposedly universal modern man, for
whom the Weissenhof dwellings were built, far more clearly
than Le Corbusier himself was able to. To quote Edgar Wedepohl's critic in *Wasmuth's Monatshefte für Baukunst* (1927), "Certainly, the intellectual is one kind of present-day man, but is
he really *the* type whose claims and requirements should determine the forms of residential architecture?"[16]

Rue à redents ("Street with setbacks")
Between the two types of apartment blocks indicated in the Plan
Voisin—the blocks of the cellular principle and the blocks with
setbacks—it is the latter that will remain an established element
in the Corbusian urbanistic code. This type allows interesting
manipulation of urban spaces, contracting and expanding along
the street (figs. 116, 117). The principle is similar to that of the
Louvre embracing the Tuileries—an image that Victor Considérant had already chosen as appropriate for his Fourierist

Phalanstère. Le Corbusier, however, multiplies this modernized Louvre and spills it all over the city. It was the potentially endless sequence of the urbanistic form that counted rather than the isolation of the "Unité d'habitation," as in the case of the château. In this respect, the "maisons à redents" (as Corbusier calls his "setback" apartment blocks) are closer to Haussman than to Fourier. But both the form and the term ("à redents") are directly derived from Eugène Hénard (1849–1923), whose *Studies on the Transformation of Paris* were also an important point of reference for other urbanistic concepts by Le Corbusier.[17]

Apartment Houses after 1930

The upper class character of Le Corbusier's housing projects was not merely the result of his own social affiliations and sympathies. In a country like France, the promotion of progressive architecture was obliged to occur via the bourgeois elite, because the government, despite occasional lip service paid to progressive endeavors,[18] had no consistent planning and building policy that would have assigned an active role to modern architects. No commissions were available for working-class housing, and, significantly, only fragments of the "immeuble-villa" idea were ever realized in the years immediately following. The two apartment houses built by Le Corbusier and Pierre Jeanneret around 1930 in Geneva and at the Porte Molitor in Paris were too small to allow the introduction of collective services, although one of the two projects, the "Clarté" flats in Geneva, brought about some interesting typological clarifications concerning the spatial organization of the dwelling units.[19]

In the Pavillon de l'Esprit Nouveau, the two-storied living unit was L-shaped in plan and opened onto the terrace. The living room, and the dressing rooms and bedrooms in the recessed upper story, opened onto the front, toward the two-story picture window. At right angles to this portion was the lateral wing, which was situated at the rear of the terrace and contained the kitchen and the maid's room, while the bathroom and another bedroom were located upstairs. All the rooms led out onto the large covered terrace, the "hanging garden" of Le

Corbusier's ideal superblock. While working on the Geneva project Clarté, the architects took up the Esprit Nouveau box idea and modified the system of accesses and interior connections. Instead of galleries at the rear, they created an interior corridor on every other—and in later projects on every third—floor of the block. With this adjustment, the typical section of the later Unité d'habitation with its interlocking dwelling units had been established. At first, the architects called these connections "couloirs généraux" but soon the notion of the "interior street" was coined.[20] The idea had already been formulated clearly in 1928–1929, and it is probable that slightly earlier Russian projects like A. Ol's 1927 competition entry referred to above (fig. 108) were helpful in providing a workable solution.

Impact of the Russian avant-garde: The Pavillon Suisse
First, a few words about Le Corbusier and Soviet Russia as background to subsequent events. The Russian avant-garde was well aware of what was going on in the West; via Le Corbusier's books as well as Russian magazines, they knew about this architect's major projects and buildings, and indeed, it is hard to imagine that a project like G. Vegman's "communal house" (fig. 111) (1927) could have been conceived without Le Corbusier's earlier immeuble-villa idea. Nor is it likely that Ginsburg's "type F" dwelling unit, which was realized in the Narkomfim block with its exterior galleries (fig. 107) (1928), could have been conceived without the Pavillon de l'Esprit Nouveau (1925). Now, from 1928 onward—the year of Corbusier's first visit to Moscow—the feedback of information flowed in the other direction and all the major Corbusian projects of the following years refer in some (often polemical) way to what was being done in Russia.[21]

Much of what was being built in Moscow around 1928–1930 seems to have struck Le Corbusier as lacking in fantasy and scale. In 1930, he wrote in an unpublished manuscript:

In Moscow I had the chance of visiting a communal house. The structure was solid and well executed and the management impeccable, but the interior arrangement and architectural concept were entirely cold. . . . The subtle artistic intention that should have animated the building was totally lacking, and I was moved by the sadness of the thought . . . that several hundred individuals have thus been deprived of the joys of architecture.[22]

It is not clear to what building this criticism refers, but a look at J. Nikolaev's student hostel in Moscow (1928–1929) at least suggests what kind of architecture he may have had in mind, since only a few "social condensers" of the kind envisaged by Barshch and Vladimorov were actually built (figs. 119, 120, 122). Thus, in Moscow or elsewhere, the collectivist ideal was more enthusiastically received in situations where no particular sentimental barriers had to be overcome, as with the student hostel, a traditional paradigm of collective living. Nikolaev interprets the program in terms of a simple juxtaposition of the communal spaces (in a low adjacent wing) to innumerable individual cells (in a high slab).

This building may well have influenced Le Corbusier's own solution of a similar, somewhat more modest task. His "Pavillon Suisse," a dormitory for Swiss students in Paris, located in the Cité Universitaire and built in 1930–1932, looks almost like a cabinet version of Nikolaev's colossal slab (figs. 65, 67, 121).[23] But the comparatively small, "humanized" scale of the pavilion endowed the building with additional visual power: the slab became a cube, and the communal spaces on the ground and the curved stairwell were not merely attached to the building, but functioned as a violent contrast to the elevated box, as part of a sculptural whole. The image is charged with symbolic implications that refer to the student as a noble savage, placed in a habitat that metaphorically displays the healthy virtues of the new, ideal, radiant city.

This was the first Corbusian slab, "liberated from the soil" by massive pilotis, the glazed facade of which faced south over—yes!—a sport's field, and directly into the sun. It is not surprising that such a declamatory cult of sun and salubrity created more thermic problems than it resolved. In fact, it was necessary to equip the wall of glass of the main facade with complicated jalousies in order to keep out the glare on sunny days.[24]

Other proposals, more directly oriented toward the working class (and perhaps never realized for this reason) clearly refer to the Russian communal house projects. Le Corbusier's workers' housing complex designed to be built in Zurich (1933) was directly inspired by a project for a communal house in Kusnetsk by the Vesnin brothers (1930). A more elegant apartment house project, once again designed for Zurich and never built (1932), owes something to Ginsburg's Narkomfin.[25] Thus in the area of housing as well as in urban planning the Russian avant-garde became an important influence. So it was after all through Ginsburg and the Vesnin brothers that Le Corbusier came in contact with the reality of a Fourierist tradition of utopian socialism; a tradition that at this time was an important aspect of the Russian scene, but that seems to have played a minimal role in the French avant-garde.

Salvation Army: Cité du Refuge

It is symptomatic of Corbusier's career that his social reformism, despite its desperate attempts to appear confidence-inspiring and bourgeois, in France between the wars was destined to remain Platonic. Government programs comparable in verve to those in the Weimar Republic or in Soviet Russia simply did not exist. This frustrating situation explains to a certain degree the long and curious connection between Le Corbusier and the Salvation Army.

Around 1928—at the time of the impending Wall Street crisis—Le Corbusier claimed that what France needed most urgently was a moral leadership capable of channeling the nation's financial resources, made available by the recently passed housing act ("Loi Loucheur") into the right direction: a leadership that would coordinate and direct generous, centralized planning strategies. The point he made was that in foreign countries, and he must have had Russia in mind, this "apostleship" was assumed both by state institutions and by the press, "but France has not yet tried out such methods." However, he then added that in France there existed an institution that was not only familiar with the real needs of the people, but that also possessed the status of a "moral personality of high value": the Salvation Army.[26] In 1929 he went to see Loucheur, the minister of housing, to suggest that the government should appoint the Salvation Army as a sort of "people's commissariat of housing." "It was a paradox," he later felt compelled to concede, "but one thing is indisputable: the country's reconstruction in terms of housing is a business that involves the heart and that requires new techniques, cleanliness and elevated views."[27]

Le Corbusier's collaboration with the Salvation Army began in 1926/1927, when the studio at the rue Sèvres built a new wing of the Salvation Army's "Palais du Peuple."[28] In 1928, in a letter to Albin Peyron, who was then commander of the Salvation Army in France, Le Corbusier suggested further initiatives by which the institution might try to improve the housing situation. Interestingly enough, he seems to have been thinking of suburban garden cities. Commander Peyron, however, replied that garden cities were hardly a solution for the Salvation Army's clientele: "It seems to me that for the time being we should concentrate our efforts on bachelors without family and friends, often without a roof over their heads, with no resources and often entirely without hope."[29] Commander Peyron, in short, envisaged a large hospice, well-equipped with numerous collective services: a "service-house" or hostel that would offer competent medical care and legal assistance in addition to the first aid or long-term care needed by its visitors. The idea was actually realized only a few years later with Le Corbusier as its architect in the "Cité du Refuge."

It is interesting to look at some of the advertisements and pamphlets by which the Salvation Army tried to promote the idea and to obtain funds (fig. 125). Here Le Corbusier's reformism is placed in a perhaps unexpected, but not inappropriate context: housing was presented as a social rescue operation in the name of Christian benevolence. Justin Godard, another high official of the Salvation Army, a member of parliament and former minister, described the function of the Cité du Refuge in these terms: "Here . . . all those whom life has wounded and who have been caught in the web of misfortune or vice will find consolation and kindly treatment: work and contemplative life."[30]

An illustration in the Salvation Army magazine *En Avant* describes (in a style both expressionist and Art Deco) the function of the new establishment within the system of the existing charitable institutions in Paris: it was to be a harbor of refuge, from where those in need were to be redistributed among the other organizations of the Salvation Army and the public social services (fig. 125).

Were it not for the fact that Le Corbusier's liaison with the Salvation Army reveals a surprising and profound concordance between the philosophies of the client and the architect, it would probably be no more than a mere anecdote in his life's work. Idealism and Christian charity, organized with military determination in order to secure access to "work and internal life" for everyone (thereby avoiding social unrest and political change): this was a reform program that closely approached Corbusier's own convictions. The idea that the architect must be a benefactor of society—mitigating pain, healing wounds, and even sacrificing himself for the sake of the suffering—had been a central theme in Le Corbusier's concept of the architect's role in society since his student years. Thus the Cité du Refuge was something that appealed to him directly; to such a degree, in fact, that he wanted to have one of the dormitories named after his pious aunt, Pauline Jeanneret.

The imagery and intrinsic symbolism of Corbusier's Salvation Army projects are also important in the context of their charitable purpose. The boat that Le Corbusier built for the Salvation Army as a small hospice moored on the Seine embankment next to the Louvre (fig. 131) is an almost archetypal metaphor of the ethos that inspired both client and architect. It is a Noah's ark for those shipwrecked by life, designed to provide moral elevation by means of an improved physical environment at a low social level: essentially a paradigm of what urbanistic reformism is really about. There is even an echo of this naval image in the prow-like western corner of the Cité du Refuge; and in fact, to quote Peter Serenyi, the building is in a way a vehicle intent on transporting people quickly and safely from one stage of life to another.[31]

The construction of the Cité du Refuge began in 1929 and was completed in 1933. The spatial arrangement was designed to make a clear distinction between the areas assigned for permanent residence and those intended for a short sojourn.[32] The ground floor, two stories below the level of the rue Cantagruel where the visitor arrives, took the form of a kind of "digestive apparatus," the curved access street of which served both the "social services" wing and the grand, glazed slab of the "hôtellerie" itself (figs. 126–128). The social services are accommodated in an autonomous, compact volume outside the whole complex.

This way of exposing the "stomach" on the outside of the body itself lends the building the character of an almost didactic model of the functions that it serves.

The access from rue Cantagruel does not lack splendor in its grand gesture; its function is to receive the visitor and deliver him to the assembly line of Christian charity. The porter's lodge, an enlarged box-shaped *baldachin*, is the bridgehead from where the needy client is despatched over a footbridge into the circular lobby, where he is duly assigned to the appropriate "social officer." In this vestibule there are small cabins "for troubling confessions"[33] and medical consulting rooms. The first floor, below, contains a lecture hall (fig. 127).

The program is a first aid operation for social emergencies. The management is military, and the imagery is that of a factory; and it is no coincidence that Le Corbusier spoke of the building as of a *usine du bien* ("factory of goodwill"). Both in its functional setup and in its imagery, the *Cité du Refuge* recalls Russian communal houses of the later twenties and their "Taylorization" of everyday life. In fact, this building might be described as a Christian-humanitarian version of a social condenser, comparable to the Russian pendants in the edifying impetus of the idea, and in its definition of the dwelling as a transit camp preparing its inmates for a better, higher form of social life.

Unité d'Habitation à Grandeur Conforme

Le Corbusier's best known contribution to a modern typology of social housing, the "unité d'habitation," would be unthinkable without these realizations around 1930. Nor would it be conceivable without the projects of the Soviet avant-garde and their particular interpretation of the Fourierist legacy. In fact, the "unité" combines all these themes and uses them to serve a reform of the modern city as a whole.

The idea of large scale urban reform had itself become a key issue of architectural debate around 1930. The third CIAM Congress in Brussels (1930) almost managed to propose the high-rise, slab-shaped apartment house as a standard solution to the European housing crisis. The projects by Gropius, Breuer, and others did not fail to impress Le Corbusier, whose term *ville radieuse* ("radiant city"), coined shortly after the Brussels meeting, poetically dramatizes the idea of the freestanding slab in a wide open space. Among the few apartment slabs built in the thirties, W. Van Tijen's work in Rotterdam is particularly worthy of mention.[34] France, however, did not engage in any large scale experiments in this direction.

In fact, it was World War II that finally resulted in the realization of projects of this kind. In 1945, Raoul Dautry, then Minister of Housing,[35] commissioned a "Unité d'habitation à grandeur conforme" for Marseilles, and in 1947 the cornerstone was laid on the boulevard Michelet. It took five years for the work to be completed (figs. 135, 136).[36] Between 1945 and 1952 the client, that is, the French government, changed ten times, but the project had the support of each successive minister of reconstruction, of which there were at least seven.

Opposition to this project was violent. Among the various pressure groups, architects, especially those organized in the SADG (Société des Architectes Diplômés par le Gouvernement), proved to be especially eloquent. They objected to the Government's decision to allow the Unité to be realized outside the framework of the building codes then in force, while the "Conseil supérieur de l'hygiène" went as far as to prophesy that the building would produce mental illness among its occupants. In its turn, the "Société pour l'Esthétique de France" took legal action in order to have the site cleared.[37] All this, however, did little to influence the determination of the subsequent ministers of reconstruction to realize the building. Claudius Petit, a former cabinetmaker, was in office when the Unité was completed, and he presented the architect with the "Ribbon of Commander of the *Légion d'Honneur*"[38] at the opening ceremony in October 1952.

The idea underlying the Unité was the creation of a model solution to serve as a prototype for France's coming reconstruction campaigns. The structural principle is simple and consists of a huge reinforced concrete cage, with 337 structurally independent (and thus acoustically isolated) dwelling units inserted like bottles in a bottle rack (fig. 51). The typical dwelling unit is split-level with a two-story living room opening onto both the front and the rear of the slab: it is a variation on the Citrohan theme. The dwelling unit, however, comes in twenty-three different sizes and shapes, from the single hotel room to the large unit for families with up to eight children, in order to secure a reasonably mixed sociological situation. Every third floor has an "interior street" with access to the individual cells.

The organizing idea behind this building type can perhaps best be summarized in Le Corbusier's own term of *logement prolongé* ("extended dwelling"), proposed in 1953 at the CIAM meeting in Aix-en-Provence. By extensions of the dwelling, the architect meant the collective services that were to form a constituent part of the individual unit. There are twenty-six of these services; the most important is placed along a shopping street located halfway up the slab—both revealed by and hidden behind a screen of concrete lamellas. As an image, this "street in the air" suggests an ideal "ville radieuse" in the shape of a continuing screen serviced by an elevated highway (à la Plan Obus for Algiers; see fig. 149); a screen from which the Unité stands out as a fragment or sample.

The roof provides additional services such as playgrounds for children, a kindergarten, a stage for improvised spectacles of all sorts, and naturally (in such a machine for health and regeneration), a gymnasium. Altogether, these elements constitute a sculptural landscape that is not only one of Le Corbusier's most successful architectural compositions, but also, in many ways, a symbolic key to the ethos that underlies the concept of the Unité.

Thus the building as a whole crystallizes the idea of an extended dwelling. This crystallization, however, occurs via a set of concepts and images that represent, in Le Corbusier's mind, progress towards a new social harmony. Conceptually, the monastery is the ultimate source of inspiration, and the communal house of the twenties was its organizational model; thus Christian and Socialist tradition are both invoked.

Fourierist sources
In France, and in the context of architectural theory, socialist tradition means Fourierism. The fact that Charles Fourier (1772–1837) was one of the sources for modern theories of urbanistic reform is an accepted premise that does not need to be discussed here.[39] The form of the phalansteries, elaborated by Victor Considérant (1840) according to Fourier's theory, is a point of reference in any history of architecture; and in fact, this

and the project of the Unité d'habitation show surprising analogies: both are "miniature towns but without open streets" (Fourier), both are designed for approximately 1600 inhabitants;
both are based on the principle of radical separation between
private and collective spheres; and both envisage large, multistory "rues galeries" as meeting places for their inhabitants.

Fourier's "Phalanstère," as elaborated by Considérant, was
not successfully realized in France until Jean-Baptiste Godin
(1817–1889) constructed a slightly smaller version in Guise
(begun in 1859). Godin succeeded in setting up a cooperative
and in handing the management of both the housing units and
the factory of this productive unit over to his workers, thus
putting the experiment on an economic basis consistent with
the socialist philosophy. The dwellings of the "Familistère," as
the experiment was called, were concentrated in three places
built around large courtyards. A visitor's account of 1886 con-
fronts us with a situation that seems to anticipate all the essential qualities of the Unitè d'habitation:

The economic use of land enabled the "Familistère" to be surrounded by a large park of almost 20 acres. Each apartment has
windows looking out onto it, both in front, behind, and to the
sides. . . . Since there is no building facing the "Familistère,"
it is not possible for curious neighbors to peer through the windows, whether open or closed. On fine summer evenings, each
inhabitant has only to close the door opening onto the great
hall, to be able to sit at the open window and smoke his pipe or
read his book in complete privacy, for all the world as if he were
the owner of a separate villa standing on its own grounds.[40]

It is not certain whether Le Corbusier was familiar with these
prototypes; Fourier's name is mentioned only incidentally in
his books—at least once in the context of a discussion of the
Unité.[41] But while his direct familiarity with Fourier seems to
have been limited to a few basic lexicon-notions, his immediate
sources, including of course Soviet communal houses, were all
part of the Fourierist tradition, so that he could not help being a
Fourierist himself.

The nautical metaphor
Whereas Considérant used the French château at Versailles as a
model for his "societal palace dedicated to humanity," this
image was not, of course, acceptable to a modern architect a

hundred years later. Le Corbusier chose the ocean liner that he had praised so extensively in his rhapsodies on "eyes that do not see." Later, in the context of social housing, he discovered that—beyond its qualities on the level of pure form—the liner represents an interesting model for a rational distribution of private and collective spaces. Furthermore, he was well aware of the biblical connotations of the ship as an ark. Finally, the liner had the unquestionable aura of upper-class good life which enabled it to play a symbolic role similar to that of Considérant's château, thus indicating popular appropriation of the signs of elite affluence.

In *La ville radieuse* (1933), Le Corbusier describes the pleasures of traveling on a luxury liner as a realized urbanistic utopia. Next to an illustration taken from a travel agent's brochure on the famous Italian liner *Augustus* (figs. 133, 124), he evokes this paradise on earth (or rather on the sea) as: "All this in the middle of the ocean, on a ship: tennis, a swimming pool, sunbathing, conversation and entertainment: the ships are 22 to 27 meters wide, and so are the buildings of the 'ville radieuse.' "[42] The liner as a Grand Hotel: this is the mundane alternative to the proletarian communal house of Soviet extraction—and Le Corbusier's ecstatic prose at times comes close to that of the travel agent. The relaxed pleasures of an ocean liner are possible only if a small army of servants guarantees perfect happiness on board; and indeed the luxury of a cruise means being served like a king by an omnipresent crew of servants.

The liner is the paradigm of a closed system that can only work with a clear division of labor and a strict hierarchy. At the top of the hierarchy stands the captain, a gentleman-officer who guarantees both the flawless course of the trip and perfect service on board. It is thus not surprising that captains—men firmly in command of delicate and important tasks—are a frequent motif in Le Corbusier's early books (figs. 129, 130). Both ship and captain are established accessories of the Corbusian mythology, reminiscent of primeval nautical archetypes of shipwreck and salvation from distress at sea.[43]

Béton brut

Behind the image of the ocean liner, however, the formulas of Le Corbusier's typology emerge: the slab, the split-level dwell-

ing unit, the sunbreaker, the pilotis, and the roof garden. The
liner furnished a unifying visual and symbolic metaphor of the
building as a whole—but when it came to organizing the physical bulk of the Unité, it proved useless. The light, naked, clean
perfection of the international style was entirely rejected in
favor of a violent orchestration of the concrete mass treated as a
gigantic sculpture. The roof terrace has rightly been praised as a
climax of Corbusian space conception. It shares with the roof
decks and solariums of the twenties—Poissy, Garches, etc.—a
solemnity that transcends the ordinary purpose: the roof is a
stage set for the rituals of a secularized sun cult. In this context,
Adolphe Appia and his early stage designs come to mind once
again. But while the roof decks of the twenties are smooth and
mundane, the deck of the Unité is rough, austere, and primitive
in character. The ensemble is cramped: a solid cluster of free,
organic shells (exhaust shafts, gymnasium, etc.) contrasting
with the elemental stereometry of the freestanding walls and
prismatic boxes (elevator tower and day nursery). The surfaces
are left rough and partially painted in subtle nuances of white
and grey since Le Corbusier refused to clean up the (unin-
tended!) effects of the primitive wooden form-work.[44]

Success or failure?

The "Unité" has been judged as "perhaps the most important
hypothesis in present-day town-planning thought"[45]—and yet
so many visitors to Marseilles speak of failure. In fact, neither of
the two judgements is really plausible.

As an organizational model and a formal prototype of
urban renewal, the Unité is of questionable relevance today,
but as an individual building the "Marseilles Block" is no doubt
a remarkable success. The definition of the urban habitat
in terms of a series of closed, self-sufficient neighborhood-
communities (the architect himself spoke of "vertical villages")
is romantic; it may suit the needs of certain social groups, but it
certainly conflicts with the life-styles of most others. In no way
is it universally applicable. The form, however, heroically
dramatizes the idea of the Unité, and thus it became (especially
in countries like England and Switzerland) a sort of an ar-
chetype of social housing in the welfare state. But, due to its
sculptural bulk and generous social equipment, it proved too

expensive for a widespread application in postwar reconstruction in France.

As an individual building the Marseilles Block has its faults: the forest of the pilotis on the ground floor is simply lugubrious, the individual cells are too narrow, and the spacious shopping street on the eleventh floor is too large compared with the size of the building.[46] Designed for a working-class clientele, the Unité d'habitation is now inhabited by a mixed middle-class community that seems to appreciate and use the generous social equipment. The inhabitants have formed an association that cooperatively controls the collective facilities and sponsors social events. [47] Thus the architecture has actually succeeded in generating the kind of community that it glorifies through its forms.

As for the architecture per se, the Unité is among the most carefully designed and supervised building campaigns ever undertaken by this architect. The bulk of the béton brut would be overwhelming were it not controlled by a subtle sense of scale, semantic complexity, formal wit, and ironic juxtaposition of surfaces, volumes, and spaces.[48] The roof summarizes it all: its forms, framed by a high wall and thus cut off from the immediate surroundings, seek a dialogue with the horizon. In a way, this giant architectural still life incorporates the Homeric austerity of the landscape that it overlooks.

None of the subsequent Unités d'habitation built by Le Corbusier achieves this degree of controlled architectural power. Nantes-Rézé (1953–1955) illustrates how many cuts (both in form and social equipment) were needed in order to make the Unité an economically reasonable proposition for working-class housing. The French sociologist Paul Chombart-de-Lauwe, however, has shown that Le Corbusier's block still remains an interesting alternative to the then current low-cost housing practices in France.[49] And the Unité in Briey-en-Forêt (near Metz), located in the middle of a forest, is a grandiloquent symbol of its underlying ethos, but a poor and dramatically neglected place in which to live—no better, in fact, than any French immigrant's ghetto.[50] If proof was needed that meaningful architecture need not be synonymous with successful building and vice versa, this latter day Unité would provide it in full force.

La Tourette

There is a certain logic in the fact that Le Corbusier concluded his career as an architect of houses with a convent and a student hostel. Both programs represent traditional forms of collective life in Western society, and both played, as we have seen, a considerable role in defining Le Corbusier's stand on the issue of housing.

Only the monastery of La Tourette will be discussed, as it is undoubtedly one of the most important late works (fig. 137).[51] The convent was consecrated in 1960, but the commission dates from 1952. It was partly the result of the intervention of Alain Couturier, a Dominican priest and an exponent of progressive forces within the Church, who suggested Le Corbusier's name to the Dominican order's Lyons chapter. He also encouraged Le Corbusier to visit the abbey of Le Thoronet in southern France, a Romanesque complex built in the late twelfth century, which made a strong impression upon the architect.[52]

Le Corbusier would not have considered the medieval typology of monastic building as a valid model for his own project. In fact, both the program and the site favored a departure from traditional approaches. La Tourette was *not* to be a monastery in the strict sense, but was planned as an educational and research center of the Dominican order. This explains its location in the country, unusual for preaching orders' monasteries, which are usually situated in a city.[53] The site demanded a fresh approach, for to define the buildings in terms of monastic tradition would have meant building colossal foundations upon which the cloister, church, refectory, and dwellings could be grouped.

The final solution is based, not surprisingly, upon an idea for an urban megastructure proposed as early as 1929. For the wholesale urban renewal of Montevideo, Le Corbusier had then suggested a system of highways that would connect the high point of the hilly site with the residential facilities, offices, etc. inserted underneath. A city built from the top down, not from the bottom up, with the traffic network on the city's top level serving as a base (fig. 138). La Tourette, with its difficult sloping site, provided the opportunity for the realization of the idea.

The main entrance of the U-shaped residential and study unit is, paradoxically, situated at the highest level. A crown of cells with deep loggias marks the residential area. Classrooms, service areas, the library, and the dining room are located below, so that the building, suspended upon its pillars, meets the ground at certain points. The public areas are again, as in the Unité d'habitation, indicated by a screen of lamellas whose delicate rhythms accompany and contradict the massive bulk of the concrete pillars and sunbreakers.[54]

Apart from this "linguistic" analogy with the Unité, the way of putting the forms together is different. There are less curves and sensuous volumes (like those of the Unité's pilotis or exhaust shafts), and more right angles and sharp corners; less unity through smooth transitions from angular to organic forms, and an increased effect of a montage of heterogenous parts. From the corridors on the upper floors, only thin, horizontal slits open onto the courtyard (exactly at eye level): the pyramid which crowns the prayer chapel, the staircases, and the stepped connecting corridors form a kind of sculptural machine framed on three sides by the elevations of the monastery wings, themselves a background charged with sculptural drama. One is tempted to think of superimposed beams, the aesthetics of the lumber yard blown up and cast in concrete.

Not only does the building look cheap, it was cheaply built and was financed largely by benevolent gifts. A sense of austerity prevails: only a few of the walls are whitewashed, and pipes and ducts, painted in flashy colors, are exposed throughout. Thus La Tourette, too, ended up as a machine, but beneath the tough mechanical symbolism of its overall form, the building displays images both of escape and of retreat from modern civilization, from the city and from the international, clean, plastic slickness of prosperity that had started to penetrate even France at the time.

Whereas the U-shaped residential wing is a "radiant city" open toward the woods, the box-shaped church that closes the courtyard is entirely introverted: a *boîte à miracles* (a "miracle-box," to quote a term Le Corbusier used for one of his theater-projects). Inside, the sharp sequence of sculptural and spatial "give and take" continues. The church itself is a grand, simple and silent box. Attached to it is the crypt on the lower floor, which bulges out into the sloping landscape: a rough cave, flooded with light pouring in and over the colored walls through giant "light canons."

In terms of pure form, the exterior of La Tourette conveys a turbulent sense of drama, as if the architect wished to speak in ever more desperately forceful images about his vision of social harmony, once it had become clear that society had definitely refused to adopt it.

107. M. Y. Ginsburg and J. Milinis, Narkomfin housing project, Moscow, 1928–1929 (from A. Kopp, *Town and Revolution*)

108. A. Ol, project of a
split-level dwelling unit
of a communal house with
"interior street," 1927 (from
A. Kopp, *Town and Revolution*)

109. M. Barshch and V. A.
Vladimorov, project of a
communal house, 1929;
dining hall (from A.
Gradow, *Gorod i byt*)

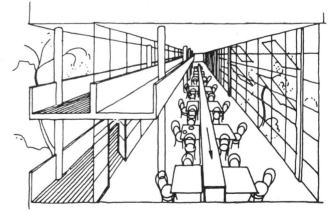

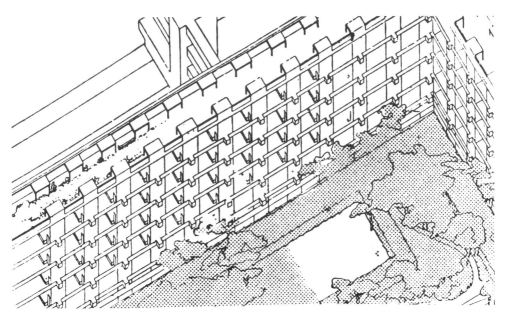

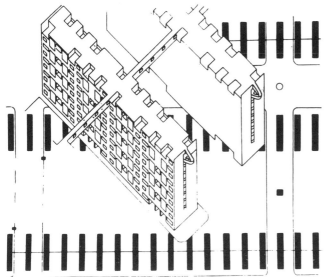

110. Le Corbusier and Pierre Jeanneret, "immeuble-villas" with connecting bridges containing collective services; 1922 (from *Oeuvre complète*)

111. Vegman, project of a communal house, 1927 (from A. Gradow, *Gorod i byt*)

112. Ch.-E. Jeanneret,
Athos; 1911 (from *Le Corbusier lui-même*)

113. A. Pfleghard, M.
Haefeli and R. Maillart,
Queen Alexandra lung
sanatorium in Davos, Swit-
zerland; 1907 (from S.
Giedion, *Space, Time and
Architecture*)

114. Carthusian monastery
at Galluzzo near Florence;
fourteenth century (photo:
author)

115. Ch.-E. Jeanneret,
project for the Ateliers
d'Art Réunis, La Chaux-de-
Fonds; 1910 (from *Oeuvre
complète*)

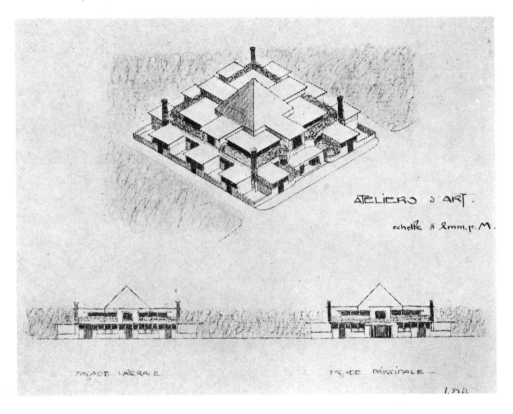

116. Victor Considerant, a phalanstery after Charles Fourier's theory

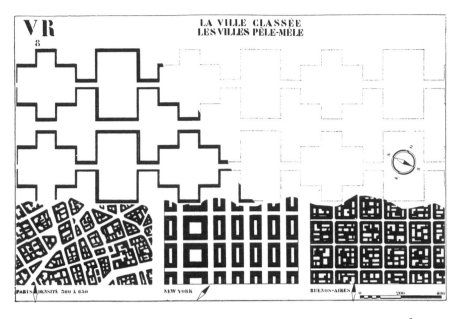

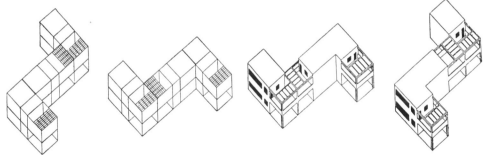

117. Le Corbusier and
Pierre Jeanneret, apartment
blocks "à redents," op-
posed to traditional urban
patterns; ca. 1925 (from
Oeuvre complète)

118. Le Corbusier and
Pierre Jeanneret, Pessac
workers' housing, 1925;
type of two-story dwelling
unit (from Oeuvre complète)

119. J. Nikolaev, student
hostel in Moscow; ca. 1928,
main facade (from A. Kopp,
Town and Revolution)

120. Student hostel, with
communal spaces to the
right (from A. Kopp, *Town
and Revolution*)

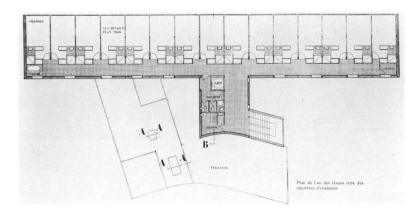

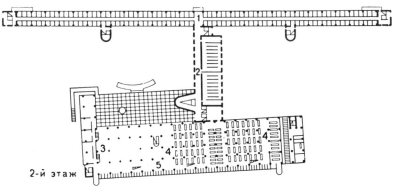

121. Le Corbusier and
Pierre Jeanneret, Fondation
Suisse; hostel for Swiss students in Paris, 1930–1932
(from *Oeuvre complète*)

122. J. Nikolaev, student
hostel in Moscow, plan
(from A. Gradow, *Town and
Revolution*)

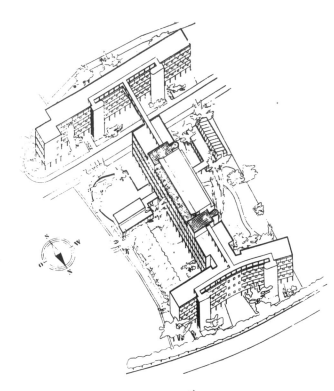

123. Le Corbusier and
Pierre Jeanneret, Hardturm-
strasse, workers' housing
project for Zurich, 1933
(from *Oeuvre complète*)

124. A. and V. Vesnin,
communal house, project
for Kusnetsk; 1930 (from A.
Kopp, *Gorod i byt*)

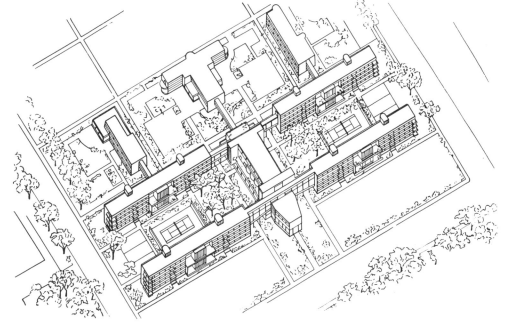

125. Special issue of *En Avant*, the magazine of the French Salvation Army—section, published in order to get funds for the Cité de Refuge, 1929 (Fondation Le Corbusier, Paris)

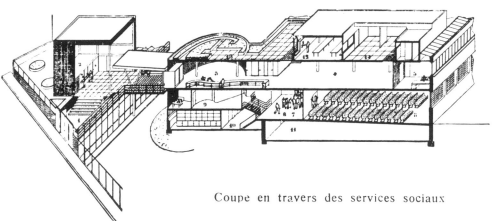

Coupe en travers des services sociaux

126. Le Corbusier and
Pierre Jeanneret, "La Cité
de Refuge," Paris, 1932–
1933, main facade (archives:
Willy Boesiger, Zurich)

127. Cité de Refuge; collective equipments, entrance
(left), reception, lecture,
and meeting halls (right)
(from *Oeuvre complète*)

128. Cité de Refuge; side
view (photo: Roger Viollet,
Paris)

129. The captain as a hero of
the twenties. Poster for the
Anchor Line (collection
Kunstgewerbemuseum,
Zurich)

130. Page from Le Cor-
busier's book, *L'art dé-
coratif d'aujourd'hui*, 1925

131. Le Corbusier and
Pierre Jeanneret, "Asile
flottant," Salvation Army
boat in the Seine, opposite
the Louvre, Paris, 1929
(photo: Roger Viollet, Paris)

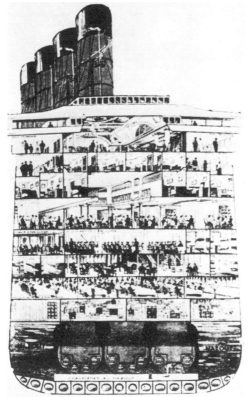

132. Le Corbusier: the size of an ocean liner and that of a Paris avenue compared; ca. 1925 (Fondation Le Corbusier, Paris)

133. Section of an ocean liner; from a poster of the Cunard Line (from Le Corbusier, *La ville radieuse*)

Ceci en plein océan,
sur un bateau : ten-
nis, piscine, bain de
soleil, conversation et
   divertissement ;
les bateaux ont une
largeur de 22 à 27 m.
Les immeubles de la
Ville Radieuse aussi.
Sur toute l'étendue
de la ville au-dessus
de la mer des arbres,
un nouveau sol serait
      ainsi gagné.

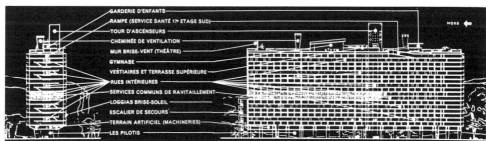

134. View of the deck of the
Italian liner Augustus; from
a travel agent's folder (from
La ville radieuse)

135. Le Corbusier, Unité
d'habitation in Marseilles,
1947–1952; section and elevation (from *Oeuvre com-
plète*)

136. Unité d'habitation in
Marseilles; general view
(photo: Lucien Hervé; ar-
chives: Willy Boesiger,
Zurich)

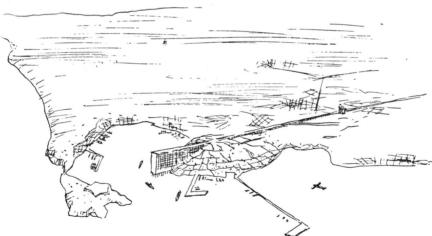

137. Le Corbusier, La
Tourette; School of the
Dominican order at Evreux
sur L'Arbresle near Lyons;
1958 (photo: C. Mossbrug-
ger, Zurich)

138. Le Corbusier, sketch
for the urban redevelop-
ment of Montevideo; 1929
(from *Précisions*)

5   Urbanism

Any discussion of Le Corbusier's ideas on urbanism must inevitably be colored by mixed feelings of fascination and disillusionment, for to have gained recognition as a pioneer and a precursor of modern town planning is not a safe guarantee of glory. Both critic and historian must face the fact that contemporary urbanism has caught up with, and partly compromised, the dreams of the 1920s. However, to lay the shortcomings and failures of recent urban renewal and other large-scale developments at Le Corbusier's doorstep would be both presumptuous and naive.[1] Planning policies are not determined by the influence of one single architect "great" as he may be, but by socioeconomic forces and interests, institutional patterns and ideology. Although Le Corbusier created an imagery for such forces at an early date, he obviously did not bring them to life.

However, he will—and with good reason—continue to be blamed or admired, according to the critic's own philosophy, for having accepted modern technology and centralized bureaucracy as guidelines of action and for having elevated these realities to the level of universal and natural laws, as indeed he did in his early projects. These qualify him as a protagonist of the ideology of the modern welfare state, and part of his personal fate was that his first large-scale renewal projects were developed some twenty-five years before their underlying ideology became universally accepted in the industrialized world.

From the City for Three Million Inhabitants to the Plan Voisin

The mechanics of urban life had been one of Charles-Edouard Jeanneret's major concerns since 1910.[2] But as in the area of architecture, the leap from occasional study and speculation to systematic invention occurred only after 1920. In 1922 Le Corbusier was invited to submit an urbanistic project to the Salon d'Automne of that same year. Asked by the architect what he meant by "urbanism," Marcel Temporal, the organizer of the exhibit, explained that he was interested in benches, kiosks, street lamps, signposts, and billboards. "Look, why don't you design a fountain for me?" Le Corbusier accepted, "All right, I will make a fountain, but behind it, I will place a city for three million inhabitants."[3]

The project was entitled "Ville Contemporaine," and was
not intended to be understood as a utopian project for a distant
future (fig. 144), but as its title suggests as a model of contemporary city: "It is this that confers boldness to our dreams: the
fact that they can be realized."[4] Nevertheless, the Ville Contemporaine was visionary in its outlook and permeated with
the idea that in order to change present conditions there must
be a clear goal. And even if it were not possible to attain this
goal in a day, Le Corbusier insisted that, at least from a technical point of view, the project must be immediately workable.

He started from scratch, as he had done earlier in the case
of the Citrohan house, creating a model situation which was to
be universally adaptable. "The goal is not to overcome the
preexisting state of things but to arrive, through a rigorous
theoretical structure, at the formation of fundamental principles
of modern urbanism."[5] The plans were exhibited at the 1922
Salon d'Automne without commentary, and they generated as
much indignation as enthusiasm. Much of the discussion that
took place during and after the exhibition is summarized in the
book *Urbanisme* published in 1925.

Unlike *Vers une Architecture*, which is a journalistic collage
of rhetorical assertions, *Urbanisme* offers a thorough documentation and discussion of the facts upon which Le Corbusier's
theory is based.[6] He opens his line of reasoning with general
aesthetic and moral postulates borrowed from history; but from
the very first pages, his remarks reflect the explosive mixture of
love and animosity, of enthusiasm and revolt, that characterized
his relationship with Paris, its history, and its current architectural situation. In order to give his theses the strength of
imperative postulates, he cites statistics of the demographic
explosion and of the problems of transportation in the Parisian
region. In addition, he includes newspaper excerpts testifying
to the state of human and social misery in the capital at a time
when postwar parades were marching through the great avenues.[7] It was, in short, the Paris of dust and of air pollution,
the Paris of tuberculosis and of slums, and also the Paris of petit
bourgeois conventions that provided the background for his
categoric proposals.

Thus the Ville Contemporaine of 1922, although conceived
as an abstract model of urban reform and not as a remedy for

specific problems of the French capital, is as directly dependent upon the situation of Paris as Tony Garnier's "Cité Industrielle" (1903) was on Lyon, or as Sant' Elia's "Città Nuova" (1914) was on Milan and its railroad station. The functional program of the Ville responds to the immediate needs of postwar Paris for large-scale housing, office buildings, and a new traffic pattern. Although these needs were more urgent than they had ever been, they were not new, for early in the century they had already generated a number of projects that were never realized.

The most important of these were Eugène Hénard's proposals entitled *Études sur les transformations de Paris*, published in eight parts between 1903 and 1906.[8] Since 1882, Hénard (1849–1923), a professor at the Ecole des Beaux-Arts in Paris, had worked for the Travaux de Paris, the office in charge of municipal architecture. Due to his experience as a municipal architect and his involvement in the planning of the Paris World Fairs of 1889 and 1900, he was an outstanding technical expert in the field of town planning. As the Ville Contemporaine and the Plan Voisin of 1925 demonstrate, Le Corbusier was very much aware of Hénard's work, although of course he was far removed from his taste and stylistic outlook. While Hénard anticipated the need for large open spaces and efficient transportation, he embedded these postulates in the eclectic and decorative imagery of Parisian fin-de-siècle architecture (figs. 145, 147). Le Corbusier, on the other hand, did not merely state the problem in terms of new social requirements and new transportation techniques, he also aimed at an urban form consistent with the "spirit of the age."

In 1922, next to the grandiose scheme of the Ville Contemporaine Le Corbusier exhibited a smaller plan proposing an adaptation of the plan to the specific situation of Paris.[9] In 1925, the reorganization of Paris became the great issue. In a sidewing of the Pavillon de l'Esprit Nouveau at the Art Deco exhibition, Le Corbusier displayed a large diorama of the Ville Contemporaine facing another, similar diorama of what he called the "Plan Voisin" of Paris (figs. 39, 144). This Plan Voisin relegated the Ville to where it originated: to the city of Paris, the "eye of Europe."

The name "Voisin" points to one of the essential features of the project: it was based upon a new traffic pattern. Convinced that the crisis of the French capital, as well as its need for future transformation, was a direct consequence of motorized traffic, Le Corbusier sought financial support for the Pavillon de l'Esprit Nouveau and the town planning project displayed there from various automobile firms: Peugeot, Citroën, and Voisin. It was Gabriel Voisin who promptly granted him patronage for the project and lent his name to it.

To render Paris habitable, Le Corbusier recommends massive surgery and makes the total razing of the area between the Seine and Montmartre a preliminary condition of any renewal. Only a few isolated buildings—the Louvre, the Palais Royal, and the Place des Vosges (of which he was particularly fond; fig. 168), the Place de la Concorde, the Arc de Triomphe, plus a few selected churches and town houses—are to be spared. The architect declares "the historical past, a universal patrimony, will be respected. More than that, it will be saved."[10] But he adds, more modestly, "The Plan Voisin does not claim to provide a complete solution to the problems relating to the center of Paris."[11] The plan's primary concern was to move the urbanistic discussion from the level of small and uncoordinated renovations to a level more in keeping with the times,[12] in which housing, business accommodation, and traffic are but single aspects of one great problem: urbanism.

Although nobody regrets that this Promethean project was never executed, decades later it exerted a lasting influence upon large-scale planning throughout the world, and thus a brief survey of its dominant characteristics is appropriate.

The towers

Le Corbusier had already published his first ideas of a tower city in *L'Esprit Nouveau* as early as 1921.[13] Laid out along a cross-shaped plan, the towers were to reach a height of sixty stories (about 825 feet), and to be placed at a distance of 800 feet from each other. He comments that the idea had been suggested to him by Auguste Perret, but when Perret's first drawings were published in August 1922, the difference between the two concepts was striking (fig. 142).[14] While the urbanistic setting proposed by Perret corresponds to Le Corbusier's later concept, the style of the towers is relatively traditional. In fact, Le Corbusier condemned Perret's project altogether, including the curiously futuristic aspect of the proposal: the elevated bridges connecting the towers.[15]

It is clear that in Le Corbusier's view, Perret's solution was not "pure." In order to be pure, the skyscraper needed a cruciform plan, straightforward cubic elevations, and fully glazed surfaces. To provide good lighting of the interiors, these surfaces were to be à *redents*, that is, organized in terms of bays and recesses that enabled maximum sight and lighting. Neither the cruciform shape nor the bays were Corbusier's invention, and he may well have been aware of Sullivan's cruciform skyscraper projects and the frequent use of bays in Chicago around 1890.[16] But the rigid elementary geometry of this type *was* new, and it was closer to the aesthetics of machines or grain silos than to anything that had been proposed in the field of architecture before 1920.

Thus the cruciform skyscraper (for offices) and high-density apartment blocks (for dwellings) appeared to be the only possible rational solution to the overwhelming evidence of facts. These facts were in themselves not new. Overcrowding, social chaos, and traffic congestion had been the characteristic diseases of large cities since the beginning of industrialization. But while the traditional remedy of planners ever since Ebenezer Howard had been decentralization and spread,[17] Le Corbusier proposes concentration and increased densities. He shares with the Garden City Movement a profound belief in the salutary effects of natural surroundings upon urban man, yet he also believes in urban density as the premise of cultural progress, and he thus rejects the reformist trends toward the limitless expansion and multiplication of individual homes. Le Corbusier argues that even if the highly concentrated metropolis no longer works, it should not simply be dissolved, as advocated with such success by the exponents of the Garden City Movement or, later, by Frank Lloyd Wright in his Broadacre City. If the modern metropolis no longer works, it should be brought back under architectural control, equipped with proper tools, and remain a cultural and architectural "whole" clearly distinct from its rural surroundings.

Hence he pursues two goals which would appear to be mutually exclusive: to increase the density of the urban fabric

and to reaffirm the supremacy of its business center, and at the
same time to bring greenery and nature back into urban life. In
his description of the Ville Contemporaine the two goals appear
as aspects of one and the same postulate.[18] On the one hand,
after a quick sociological analysis of urban populations, Le Corbusier advocates an increase of their density; on the other, he
aims at a multiplication of green spaces.

Nature and space

Most of the city's soil was to be transformed into a vast recreation zone: 95 percent of the soil in the business district and 85
percent in the dwelling area were to be turned into public
parks.[19] Why this obsession with parks and greenery? Once
again the answer lies partly in the context of Paris. In order to
give proposals credibility in the eyes of the bourgeois elite, it is
necessary to legitimize them in terms of its widely shared
ideals: thus Le Corbusier's insistence upon the necessity of
large public parks is a direct response to the traditional rhetoric
of reformist planners and politicians in Paris. Around 1920, to
conceive of the city as one vast recreation zone was not only a
proof of social-mindedness but also of an awareness of the city's
splendid past: it meant bringing the work of the French kings
and emperors to its grandiose fulfillment. The Tuileries, the
Jardins du Luxembourg, etc., time and again reproduced in Le
Corbusier's books, are constantly called upon as reference
points for his plans.[20]

He spices his argumentation with more personal touches.
Recalling his trip to the Orient he quotes a Turkish maxim:
"Where one builds, one plants trees"—and he adds sarcasti-
cally, "We root them up."[21] Plants and greenery appear to him
as the biological guarantee of sound urban living. Parks are the
"lungs" of the city, its respiratory system. But he pushes his
point even further: the city itself becomes one great "lung." To
Le Corbusier, respiration is not merely a physiological phenomenon, it is a process that involves all his sensitivity and
imagination. Even more than his lungs, his eyes want to
"breathe," as it were. Naturally, he bases his arguments on
biological grounds, but ultimately the overwhelming presence
of plants and trees in his ideal city is a matter of cultural idealism rather than physical well-being. It is an aspect of his al-

most mystical belief in nature, rooted in his sensibility ever
since his early years in La Chaux-de-Fonds.

But while his early studies are characterized by a sympathy
for the laws governing organic growth in plants, leaves, flowers, and trees, he now started to develop a hunger for grandiose
vistas and the sensation of limitless space. Previously, he may
have experienced this sensation on the Jura heights; now, in
Paris, it was the Eiffel tower that provided the inspiration:

When I ascend, I experience a feeling of serenity; the moment
becomes joyful—solemn too. Step-by-step, as the horizon rises
higher, it seems that the mind is projected into wider trajec-
tories, when everything becomes physically broader, when
one's lungs inhale more vehemently, when the eye takes in vast
horizons, the spirit is animated with nimble vigor; optimism
reigns. [22]

This love of panoramic views, this craving for vast horizons, became so compelling that Le Corbusier soon lost sight of
the starting point of his belief: the reestablishment of natural conditions in the modern city. Eight hundred feet above
ground one no longer perceives the rustling of the leaves at the
foot of the towers. Both the green vegetation and the grayish
urban carapace grow faint and become no more than a pleasant
decorative carpet. Nature appears in the grandiose (although by
no means vital) form of distant perspectives and infinite spaces.
In the residential areas, the large parks have a more plausible
function; here the height of the buildings reaches no more than
six stories of duplex apartments, and the contact with nature is
thus maintained. [23]

The axes and the myth of speed

With a grand sweeping gesture, Le Corbusier's city is inscribed
into the landscape. Its axes reach out toward the four corners of
the horizon, and Versailles and Baron Haussmann's grandiose
vision, partly realized in his reorganization of Paris at the time
of Napoleon III, are called to mind.

For Le Corbusier, the rigor of the axis constitutes an essential principle, both moral and aesthetic: "Man walks in a
straight line because he has a goal and knows where he is
going." [24] The straight line is the line of man, the curved line
that of the donkey. Le Corbusier rejects the romantic and pic-

turesque idea of basing urban design on the random forms resulting from the growth of medieval cities; in his opinion, this
was the principal error of Camillo Sitte, "an intelligent and sensitive Viennese who simply stated the problem badly."[25] In his
eyes, the chessboard or gridiron plan is the only correct way of
approaching the problem of city planning, and this point can be
substantiated by historic evidence. Thus in *Urbanisme* we find
the layouts of a large number of orthogonal cities, from the
thirteenth-century bastides in the south of France to the plans
of American colonial cities of the sixteenth, seventeenth, and
eighteenth centuries, including L'Enfant's plan of Washington,
D.C.[26] One gridiron plan, however, does not appear among the
documents published in *Urbanisme*, although it must have
played a major role in the determination of Le Corbusier's urbanistic preferences: the plan of his native town of La Chaux-
de-Fonds. This town had been heavily damaged by a fire in
1794, and it was then rebuilt according to a "plan américain"
with a grand axis in the middle, the avenue Léopold-Robert,
where, incidentally, young Charles-Edouard Jeanneret spent a
part of his youth.

   Thus ultimately this architect's obsession with monumental axes was not based upon an abstract theoretical postulate,
but upon an urban experience that had to be preserved. It
comes as no surprise that Baron Haussmann was the subject
of his admiration as well as of his constant criticism: in Le
Corbusier's eyes, the great axial thoroughfares with which
Haussmann pierced the Parisian maze from 1853 to 1868 were
the answer to an imperative necessity, even though he did not
sympathize with Napoleon III's utilization of the boulevards
and avenues for parades and military displays.[27]

   Time and time again, he uses Haussmann's approach to the
renewal of Paris as the background for his own argumentation.
In 1937, for instance, he points out that in Baron Haussmann's
city, "tradition . . . required that all straight avenues should
be climaxed by a set piece: the Opéra at the end of the avenue of
the same name, the church of Saint-Augustin at the end of the
boulevard Malesherbes."[28] Le Corbusier, on the other hand,
wants traffic arteries running through the entire city without
interruptions. He is against the idea of closed squares, à la Place

de la Concorde: "It is a square of glory like an honor hall. But
. . . it is not a street, even less an artery. Let us get it clear: this
was the era of the coach and of the pedestrian."[29] For Le Corbusier, the straight axis is not a mere formal principle; it is justified only by its function as a tool of modern traffic. It is thus
not surprising that in 1936 he admired the ten-mile long avenues of Manhattan, symbols of an efficient traffic pattern determining the entire physiognomy of a metropolis.

In order to articulate the system of the axes in the Ville
Contemporaine and in the Plan Voisin, the architect reverts to
the most classical means. The main axis of the Ville is a superhighway laid out between two triumphal arches. A closer
look at the obelisks, columns, and monumental domes along
the main traffic arteries as well as the general layout reveals a
composition worthy of any Beaux-Arts student.

Once again, the ideals of the classical tradition are inter-
mingled with those of the machine age. We are reminded of the
quasi-magical character that Le Corbusier ascribes to speed.
"The city that has speed has success," he claims.[30] This sounds
like a futurist slogan; and indeed Sant' Elia's projects of about a
decade earlier were based upon an analogous worship of veloc-
ity. I am not, however, sure of to what degree Sant' Elia's "Città
Nuova" was an actual source for the Ville Contemporaine. Le
Corbusier hardly ever refers to the Italians at this time (which
may perhaps be regarded as an indication that in fact he *was* influenced by them).

But he liked to refer to the rhetoric of French automobile
advertisements. In *Urbanisme*, he quotes an article by one of the
directors of the Peugeot plant, Philippe Girardet, who saw in
the automobile the vigorous and brilliant confirmation of an
age-old dream of humanity. Girardet describes man as one of
the slowest animals in creation: "a sort of caterpillar dragging
himself along with difficulty on the surface of the terrestrial
crust. Most creatures move more quickly than this biped so ill-
constructed for speed, and if we imagined a race among all the
creatures of the globe, man would certainly be among the 'also
rans' and would probably tie with the sheep."[31] It was, of
course, motorized traffic that ultimately enabled man to
triumph over this deplorable condition.

Differentiation of traffic lines: the death of the street
Again, the situation of Paris forms the background for Le Corbusier's redefinition of the urban street. The traditional complexity of its functions seems obsolete to him in the age of automobile traffic. The increase of urban density and the sudden advent of motorization turned the street into a scene of paralyzing chaos and constant danger. So far, the argument is convincing. But for Le Corbusier, the question is not so much to analyze the crisis of the traditional urban streets as to justify its radical disappearance in the Ville Contemporaine. Thus the argumentation becomes resolutely polemic when, in an article published in *l'Intransigeant* in May, 1929, he fires off against that secular element of the city, the *rue corridor*: "It is the street of the pedestrian of a thousand years ago, it is a relic of the centuries; it is a nonfunctioning, an obsolete organ. The street wears us out. It is altogether disgusting! Why, then, does it still exist?"[32] In 1924, he publicizes his redefinition of the street in terms of the modern superhighway. It is a "machine for circulation" he insists, "a circulatory apparatus . . . a kind of factory in length."[33] Hence his placement of the superhighway as the central axis of his urbanistic schemes, and hence, also, his constant urge to separate automobile traffic from pedestrian circulation and to layer the different levels of mechanical transportation according to function, range and speed.

This was, of course, not new. The idea of a city efficiently served by a vascular system of streets, canals, and tunnels is as old as scientific speculation about the city as an "organic" whole; it was one of Leonardo da Vinci's hobby-horses, as a number of famous sketches show.[34] In the nineteenth century, the differentiation of urban traffic lines became a frequent concern in progressive town planning proposals. Myriads of widely publicized urban utopias and renewal projects promoted around 1900 gave pride of place to the idea of the separation of traffic lines. Long before 1900, the great metropolises—Paris, Berlin, London, New York, and Chicago—had all built their subway systems and elevated railways (fig. 143).

In Paris, it was again Eugène Hénard who, as early as 1903, suggested a number of important urban changes in order to cope with the increasing dangers of traffic. His *carrefour à giration* (fig. 145), probably the first traffic roundabout in the mod-

ern sense, was designed for horse-drawn carriages; the concept
was published by Le Corbusier in *Urbanisme*, and it obviously
served as an inspiration for the great central station in the heart
of the Ville Contemporaine.[35] While Hénard proposed two
levels of circulation—vehicles on the surface and pedestrians
underneath—the author of the Ville Contemporaine suggested
no fewer than seven superimposed layers (fig. 146). At the lowest levels, the terminals for the main lines; above, the suburban
lines; then the subway; above that, all pedestrian circulation;
then the throughways for rapid motor traffic; and last, at the
top, the airport.

Chaos in the general layout; uniformity in detail
The aesthetic rules to which Le Corbusier's doctrine is committed were established by the great French academic tradition.
He quotes the axiom of Abbé Laugier, the eighteenth-century
theoretician, as a guideline of urbanistic strategy: "chaos, disorder, and wild variety in the general layout; uniformity in detail."[36] In Le Corbusier's Ville Contemporaine however, the
"uniformity in detail" seems to be the main point, while the
"chaos" of the general layout is a rather regularized elemental
variation of "disorder and wild variety." Be that as it may, in
Urbanisme Le Corbusier presents and discusses a large number
of historic examples for the kind of uniformity he has in mind.
The examples range from the Procurazie Vecchie in Venice
where, as he comments, "the pigeons of Saint Mark's themselves add their own uniform module, providing a varied and
effective note in the scheme,"[37] to Bramante's Belvedere Palace
at the Vatican; and the Place Stanislas in Nancy; the Place des
Vosges, the Place Vendôme, and the rue de Rivoli in Paris.[38]
Thus again we are left with the reassurance that the boldness of
the architect's proposal is actually nothing but the result of a
correct understanding of the great French tradition.

Social and economic aspects
As to the social and economic aspects of the scheme, Le Corbusier is well aware of which card to play. He leaves no stone
unturned in order to prove the great virtues of the Ville Contemporaine as a guarantor of business profits and social peace:
"Paris, the capital of France, must build up in this twentieth
century its position of command,"[39] he announces. The whole
urbanistic imagery of the Ville Contemporaine as well as of the

Plan Voisin—the huge, 800-foot-high steel and glass office towers lined up on the flat land between the superhighways like
figures on a chessboard—is indeed a glorification of big business and of centralized state control.

"But where is the money coming from?"[40] Le Corbusier
was enough of a businessman himself not to be embarrassed by
such a question; his closest friends from the Swiss colony in
Paris were, after all, bankers. "To urbanize means to increase
value," he proclaims. "To urbanize is not to spend money, but
to earn money, to make money."[41] How? The key word is density: the greater the density of land use, the greater the real estate value. And again the reassurance: the colossal towers are
not "revolutionary," they are a means of multiplying business
profits.

The Plan Voisin thus characterizes itself as the ideal city of
capitalism, and not of French big business alone; foreign capital
should have its share in it too. Le Corbusier argues that the
distribution of land among French, German, and American
trusts would minimize the danger of possible air attack.[42] A
downtown made of glittering office towers reflecting the power
of multinational corporations—it took a few decades for Europe
to catch up with this vision. Yet in economic terms, if not in
those of urban imagery and planning procedure, the Quartier
de la Défense north of Neuilly and other recent large-scale developments inside Paris are based on the very forces with
which Le Corbusier had hoped to put his Plan Voisin into
action.

This insistence upon the city as a machine to make money
throws a shadow upon the social and political ethos of these
projects—and part of this business-oriented rhetoric certainly
needs to be seen in the context of the promotional aims of the
book *Urbanisme* itself. There is also the socially questionable
impact of the Corbusian imagery in the context of urban renewal, especially in the United States. The cruciform busi-
ness-towers of the Plan Voisin literally anticipate the imagery
of more recent social housing schemes[43]—but we should not
forget that his building-type was not proposed for housing in
these early projects and that after 1930 it was altogether rejected
by its inventor.[44]

These early schemes, in short, incorporate a dream with

consequences that have often proved fatal. But the housing situation in Paris *was* difficult for the poor living in its center: services like plumbing, heating, and electricity were either scarce or lacking altogether. It is not surprising that Le Corbusier approached these problems from above, that he addressed himself not to the poor, but to those in command. His solution appeared to him not as a pretext for revolution, but as a means of avoiding it: "Architecture or revolution. Revolution can be avoided."[45]

With the keen insight of a La Bruyère, (a seventeenth-century satirist and moralist), Le Corbusier exposes in *Urbanisme* the petty distractions by which the average Parisian consoles himself on an evening in Montmartre or Montparnasse, away from the dirt and squalor of his small, badly ventilated and unheated apartment.[46] People, he argues, have a right to live in comfortable apartments; after working for hours on end in the factory or office, they should be granted the pleasure of sweet reveries in the midst of nature; they should know the "essential joys" of leisure. What he promises is a weekend paradise—a paradise where it would be easier to play a game of tennis in the parks surrounding the villa-superblocks than to find a café in which to drink a glass of wine with friends.[47]

Like the immeuble-villa concept, the Plan Voisin as a whole reflects not so much his own, personal life-style, as the values of that sector of French society to which Le Corbusier addressed his message. It explicitly proposes a way toward social and economic security for the working class. This did not prevent Le Corbusier from being placed among the bolsheviks by his conservative critics:[48] centralized bureaucracy and modern technology in building were considered communist propositions incompatible with freedom and liberalism by the French middle class.

The years since World War II have witnessed a certain shift in the political evaluation of these issues. What was then seen as a bolshevik threat is now, at least in the West, in general viewed as the expression of advanced capitalism and its system of technocracy. Behind the apparent contradiction lies a consistent tradition of attempts to improve the world from above, through expertise, humanitarian ideals, and massive technol-

ogy; and no doubt Le Corbusier has to be regarded as a spokesman of this tradition within the broader field of modernist
thought in architecture.

Foreign Contacts: South America, Africa, and the USSR

Paris provoked Le Corbusier's urban utopia, but at the end of
the twenties, new factors intervened. First of all, there was his
trip to South America and his involvement with Africa; second, his increasingly frequent contacts with Russia, the
promised land, with its rational architecture and large-scale
planning policy. While the sudden contact with the non-
industrialized world—South America and Africa—generated a
new awareness of the vernacular roots of building, Russia
seemed to place Le Corbusier's views into a context of technical
feasibility and of immediate social need.

In the summer of 1929, Le Corbusier made his first trip to
Latin America at the invitation of the magazine *Stil* and a group
called *Amigos del Arte*. He traveled in a Zeppelin and delivered
ten lectures in Buenos Aires, two in Montevideo, two in Rio de
Janeiro, and two in São Paulo. In December, on his way back on
board the ocean-liner *Lutetia*, he wrote a summary of these
talks. The steamship company put a luxury suite at his disposal
where he had enough space to display the sketches he had improvised during his lectures and which he had brought on
board in a large roll.

The outcome was a book, *Précisions sur un état présent de
l'architecture et de l'urbanisme*, which was published after his
return. Besides summarizing his architectural and urbanistic
vision in extremely animated prose, the author pays tribute to
the country and the people of South America. Unlike *Vers une
architecture*, the book is not didactic. Inspired by the scale and
splendor of the South American landscape, it is the epic of an
architecture and an urbanism that responds to the turbulent
skyline of the mountains, and to the great expanses of the
plains, rivers, and seas. The wide plains crossed by waterways
and rivers meandering majestically toward the sea—a view Le
Corbusier observed from the plane and described with Balza-
cian eloquence—added a new verve to his urbanistic ambitions.

In the light of South America's realities, the earlier schemes developed for Paris proved to be too rigid and lacking in vitality and flexibility. For instance, how could a business center be established on the steep coast of Montevideo? Ever since the Ville Contemporaine of 1922, Le Corbusier had regarded the central traffic artery as the backbone of an urban plan. Given a hilly coastal site, however, he is obliged to change his views: in order to have a straight main traffic artery, it is necessary to elevate it from the ground and place it at the crowning point of the city. Thus, from the top of the coastal hill, three viaducts reach out toward the horizon, forming three platforms that overhang the port by 250 feet (fig. 138). Here the offices of the business center are to be suspended underneath. What is needed is not a skyscraper, as Le Corbusier put it, but a "seascraper."[49]

His "solutions" to the problems of Rio de Janeiro are no less adventurous. He arrived there in October 1929, and at first he seems to have been speechless: "To urbanize here is like trying to fill the barrel of the Danaides."[50] In a landscape as imposing as that of the Pão de Açúar, the Corvocado, the Gàvea, and the Gigante Tendido, architecture even on an urbanistic scale no longer has a chance. A few weeks later, however, he had recovered from the shock, and the solution to the problem was ready. Just before returning to Europe in December, he explains his ideas in a lecture. "From far away, I saw in my mind the vast and magnificent belt of buildings, crowned horizontally by a superhighway flying from mount to mount and reaching out from one bay to another."[51] Thus Corbusier's response to the burning challenge of this landscape is an immense elevated viaduct winding between the hills like a gigantic folding screen of glass and metal (fig. 148). The idea received further elaboration in 1936, when Le Corbusier was back in Rio again, but in the meantime it had become the basis for no doubt one of his most extravagant proposals, the "Plan Obus" for Algiers.

Algiers: The Plan Obus

Between 1931 and 1942, Algiers was the focus of Le Corbusier's town-planning endeavors. It is difficult to assess to what degree this city, around 1930, really *was* expecting great things to

come. Far-reaching renewal projects were no doubt in the air.[52]
Yet, however real the prospects of making Algiers into a capital
of business may have been, the city's capacity to stimulate this
architect's enthusiasm cannot be described in terms of its economic future alone. Le Corbusier seems to have found in Algiers what he had looked for in his youth in Constantinople and
Athens: the white city under the sun, facing the sea. In his eyes
Algiers not only outdid all the cities of the French mainland as a
center of business and trade, it also preserved the remnants of
an authentic and centuries-old folk tradition. The Casbah, un-
spoiled by nineteenth-century industrialization and taste, was
a lively cluster of folk architecture and pre-industrial forms of
life. All these realities, around 1930, forcefully entered the orbit
of Le Corbusier's thinking.

Encouraged by France's recently renewed interest in North
Africa, through a number of lectures, articles, and pamphlets,
Le Corbusier tried to convince the local administration that the
moment had come to act. In a letter of December 1933 to M.
Brunnel, the Mayor of Algiers, he draws a magic square out-
lined by four letters:

P

B   R

A

The initials stand for Paris, Barcelona, Rome, and Algiers: "A
unity stretching from north to south along a meridian, encompassing the entire gamut of climates, from the Channel to
Equatorial Africa, containing within itself all the needs as well
as all the resources." And he adds, "Algiers is no longer a colonial city. It is now becoming the head of Africa. It is a capital
city. . . . The hour of urbanism has arrived in Algiers."[53]

The first contacts had taken place a few years earlier. In
1931, Le Corbusier had been invited to deliver two lectures on
modern architecture at the recently opened Casino of Algiers. In
1932, he returned in order to present his first projects to the
public, as part of an exhibition on town-planning. He called his
master plan "Plan Obus" (figs. 152, 199).[54]

The concept is reminiscent of the plan for Rio. Downtown, in the "quartier de la Marine" close to the harbor, an office skyscraper was to be built upon a site that had been due for demolition for some time. From its roof terrace, an immense road bridge leads to the elegant apartment blocks on the hills of Fort l'Empereur. Thus the seat of public administration would be safely linked to the quarters of the ruling class. Just below, parallel to the coast and at right angles to the bridge, the great traffic artery serving the entire region was to be built as a viaduct forming an enormous hairpin bend in the west. The underlying principle of the plan is simple. First of all, the highway department would build this system of viaducts crossing the coastal landscape at a height of 350 feet; later, the population of the overcrowded center would gradually move into the levels underneath the road. Thus the building of superhighways would not reduce but actually multiply the built-up surface of the city—and the Casbah could remain physically intact.

A well-known drawing by Le Corbusier demonstrates how he planned the utilization of the filled-in land gained through the plan. On each level, individual houses would be built side by side, each according to the desires of the occupants. For example, a Citrohan-type dwelling adjoining a small Moorish house halfway between the Algerian Casbah and the Californian bungalow in style. Instead of the rigorous visual hygiene of the Plan Voisin and its implicit dictatorial "freedom through order" we have a kind of open planning, founded on broad-based participation and initiative.

The "Plan Obus" contains two versions of "road-buildings." The long ribbon of apartments parallel to the coast has a superhighway on its top; the large, curved buildings crowning the Fort l'Empereur have their access road in the form of galleries halfway up. It may be easy to ridicule the idea, but it is hard to refute its underlying logic: in a capitalist economy, public funds for automobile highways are more easily available than funds for housing or urban renewal. Here, then, is a proposal that shows how to improve the housing situation in downtown areas with the help of an urban superhighway. In the light of recent urban history, where superhighways usually played the opposite role, it is hard to say which is more sur-

prising: the ingenuity of the physical plan itself or the paradox
of its supposed economic base.

Precedents and implications

On June 12, 1934, the Plan Obus was officially rejected by the
City Council of Algiers, a decision that must have encountered
little opposition since the plan had never really been asked for
by the city's officials. Since then, the Plan Obus has taken its
place as part of the history of urbanistic science fiction. Its explosive quality and its nerve consist of the combination of various, seemingly conflicting concepts forcefully controlled by a
new approach to form, and enthusiastically promoted with the
help of a political philosophy that accepts the existing class
hierarchy and colonialism as a positive cultural and economic
force.

There are historic precedents for Le Corbusier's combination of viaduct and habitat: the medieval "urbanized bridges"
of London, Paris, and Florence; Edgar Chambless's "Project for
Roadtown" of 1910; and some contemporary Russian schemes
(figs. 150, 151). Giacomo Mattè-Trucco's Fiat factory in Turin
(1920–1923) with its trial run installed on the roof may be considered as an immediate source[55] (fig. 153). Le Corbusier praised
the factory in *L'Esprit Nouveau* and in *Vers une architecture*. Finally, in 1934, he had an opportunity to visit the site and to use
it with the latest sports model. This was, for him, the ultimate
proof that the Plan Obus was feasible:

The Fiat factory has gained a lead over the urbanism of our
machine age. The superhighway on the roof, for instance, actually proves the possibilities of modern technology. It is no
longer a dream but a reality: certain cities like Genoa, Algiers,
Rio de Janeiro could thus be saved from the impending disas-
ter.[56]

Thus motorized traffic, speed and its infrastructure served once
again as a key to town planning. Then there was the overall
urban form, the sensuous curves of the highway winding along
the coast. This new imagery will have to be discussed in another context; it owes as much to the voluminous nudes that
had just replaced the earlier glasses, bottles, and pitchers on Le
Corbusier's canvases as it does to the airplane and the new
ways to "read" the landscape that it suggested.

Algerian Tribulations: Last Project

For twelve years, between 1931 and 1942, Le Corbusier put forward no less than seven projects for the transformation of Algiers. The majestic vision of a viaduct-city, the Plan Obus, was followed almost year by year by more realistic proposals until 1942, when the adventure finally found its conclusion in the well-known skyscraper project for the quartier de la Marine (fig. 155). None of his propositions had any immediate consequences: the skyscraper was rejected in 1942, and it took another decade until the city administration rediscovered Le Corbusier's plans and some of their intrinsic virtues. It was a story of constant frustration, interrupted by extravagant hopes.

No doubt the ambiguous nature of Le Corbusier's contacts with government agencies and planning boards did little to improve the chances of success.

In 1937, at Emery's suggestion, the Governor General Le Beau appointed him to the Algerian Regional Planning Committee. Le Corbusier believed that by his participation in the work of this committee he would be able to exert his influence on the transformation of the city. It was a vain hope. On the contrary (and the same was true later for the UN and for UNESCO) having Le Corbusier serve on a committee was the best way of neutralizing him, both as an architect and as a city planner. Later, he tried hard to gain the support of French government and thus exert pressure upon the local authorities from above. In 1941 and 1942, he arrived in Algiers in the high official capacity of delegate of the Vichy government, and General Weygand gave him an honorable welcome. But Le Corbusier was a poor diplomat: while he placed his liberal and anti-fascist friends of the CIAM of Algiers in such a position as to make it impossible for them to intervene in his favor, his own political opinions were independent enough to puzzle Pétain's Algerian friends. In such a situation, little more was needed to compromise Corbusier's Algerian mission, and it was a polemical article published in a local professional magazine that seems to have brought about the decisive shift.[57] The article pompously "provided proof" that modern architecture was the fruit of "international Jewry" and bolshevism. This was enough to eliminate Le Corbusier from the scene, and a few days after the publication of the article on June 12, 1942, the municipal council of Algiers decided to reject all his proposals, including the latest project for a 500-foot-high skyscraper at the Cap de la Marine.[58]

The mission in Algiers thus ended in a fiasco. But the actual influence of the Algerian projects could hardly have been more far-reaching if they had actually been realized. The last skyscraper project (fig. 157)[59] was almost as influential as the Plan Obus itself, which has inspired a number of significant schemes in Brazil and Italy. The drama of the sunbreakers was the harbinger of Chandigarh—especially the Secretariat (fig. 190)—while the rhomboidal plan, already used in a project for Zurich in 1932, had a clear impact on buildings like the Pirelli tower in Milan (Gio Ponti, 1958) and the Pan Am Building in New York (Gropius and TAC, 1958).

USSR and USA

Le Corbusier made at least three trips to Moscow between 1928 and 1930. Having won the competition for a large office building (Centrosoyuz; fig. 79), he was obliged to visit the city from time to time in order to supervise the development of the project.[60] Like most West-European architects in the twenties, he realized that Russia around 1930 was the "New World," where the concepts of modern town planning were most likely to be realized on a grand scale, and where the architect was in the long run most likely to be assigned a leading role in the transformations of society.

In fact, whereas the economic crisis in Western Europe had jeopardized the prospects of radical architects and planners, Russia with its first five-year plan (1928) had established a program of nationwide industrialization and urbanization that surpassed the most utopian projects of the West. A number of avant-garde architects from Germany, Holland, and Switzerland moved to Russia where they remained for a number of years and were put in charge of important planning projects. These architects included Ernst May, Erich Mendelsohn, Bruno Taut, Mart Stam, Hannes Meyer, Hans Schmidt, and others. During his visits, Le Corbusier met the leaders of the architectural avant-garde, including the Vesnin brothers and, in 1930,

Moses Ginsburg, who was then working on his project for the
de-urbanization of Moscow. Later, in 1931, he submitted a
master plan for Moscow that, although it was rejected by the
Russians, became the basis for his book *Ville Radieuse* (1933).[61]
  Whereas his project for Moscow as a kind of Soviet Plan
Voisin is based on his earlier Parisian proposals, the Plan Obus
(which he developed at the same time) seems to owe something
to contemporary Russian schemes, for example, the "linear
city" project by Ginsburg (fig. 150). No doubt the Plan Obus,
determined as it is in its function and form by traffic arteries,
owes much to the Russian ideas and rhetoric of around 1930. Le
Corbusier was aware of Russian concepts, as is clearly demonstrated by his later proposals for linear industrial developments
along railway lines, rivers, and canals (fig. 158).[62] The linear
industrial cities proposed after 1940 by the ASCORAL group
(*Assemblée de Constructeurs pour une Rénovation Architecturale*),
which was headed by Le Corbusier, not only anticipate the
sort of industrial sprawl along highways typical of the present
American landscape,[63] they are directly based on Miljutin's
proposals for industrial cities in Russia, particularly for Trac-
torstoj (1928) (fig. 157).

New York

Although the USSR had appeared to be the "promised land" for
the new architecture for some time, the Western avant-garde
quickly lost track of Soviet developments once the Stalinist
bureaucracy returned to the dogma of socialist realism (1934)
—particularly since the USA began to adopt at least some
of the ideals of "modern architecture" at about the same time.
In 1931, New York received its first "modern" skyscraper—the
McGraw-Hill building by Hood, Godley and Fouilhoux (1931).
In 1932, the Museum of Modern Art drew the attention of the
elite to what it called the "International Style";[64] the Rockefeller
Center was under construction at the time, and George Howe
and William Lescaze were supervising the completion of the
PSFS Tower in Philadelphia. The principles of rational design,
as demonstrated and advertised by these buildings, were suddenly regarded by many architects as the only possible approach to the vast social and economic issues of the Depression

years. American interest in European urban utopias grew in
intensity, and on January 3rd, 1932, the *New York Times* published a long, lavishly illustrated article on Le Corbusier's
"Ideal Metropolis," in which the architect pays a tribute to what
he calls the American "juvenility"; "The United States is the
adolescent of the contemporary world, and New York is her expression of enthusiasm, juvenility, boldness, enterprise, pride
and vanity. New York stands on the brink of the world like a
hero." [65]

It was not until some years later, however, in October 1935,
that Le Corbusier sailed on the famous French liner *Normandie*
to the United States whose skyscrapers and grain silos had
so often served to illustrate or clarify his arguments in his
articles and books. On the evening of his arrival in New York,
he surprised the local press somewhat by stating that "the
skyscrapers (of New York) are too small." [66] Later he added,
"It is a catastrophe, but a beautiful and worthwhile catastrophe. . . . America is not negligible! Compared with the
Old World, she has established, after twenty years, the Jacob's
ladder of modern times." [67] His prose reaches a climax of enthusiasm when he attempts to evoke the "violent silhouette" of
the city as it appeared to him at sunrise on a clear day: "like a
fever chart at the foot of a patient's bed." [68] In this he was not
alone, for architects such as Eliel Saarinen, Eric Mendelsohn,
and Richard Neutra had also stood petrified with awe before
the phenomenon of New York, struggling with the contradictions of an urban paradox with underlying principles which
they could not accept, but with a wild silhouette that forced
them into unwilling admiration.

His book entitled *When the Cathedrals Were White*, which
bears the subtitle *Journey to the Country of the Fearful Ones*,
summarizes Le Corbusier's violent and contradictory response
to the American reality and the American dream. [69]

I return from the United States. Good! On the example of the
USA, I want to show that although the times are new, the
houses are uninhabitable. The table has not yet been cleared
after the meal; the leftovers of the departed banquet guests
remain—congealed sauces, carcasses, wine stains, bread-
crumbs and dirty dishes. [70]

With a characteristic mixture of fresh insight and a patronizing
display of cultural superiority, this ambassador of the Old
World offers his advice on traffic congestion and sprawl, downtown development, and regional planning. Much of what
the book contains is in fact a repetition of what Le Corbusier
had said earlier in articles, lectures (of what he gave twenty-
three in twenty cities during his travels through the USA), and
interviews.

In fact, the coverage given by the press to his visit to New
York was extraordinary and may have disturbed some of his
American colleagues (fig. 156).[71] Despite this, the hoped-for
flood of important commissions never occurred; the New Deal
had no use for a Colbert from the Old World and ascribed more
importance to good technicians and managers. Le Corbusier's
New York proved to be yet another crusade that ended in dis-
aster, for it was based on a fundamental misconception of the
possible role of the architect in an advanced industralized society governed by liberalism and big money.

The Cartesian Skyscraper

The numerous proposals by which Le Corbusier tried after 1930
to induce the urban future into the reality of existing cities are
all based on an established catalog of building types. Apart
from his studies for Paris, Algiers, and New York, he had in fact
developed renewal projects for Barcelona, Stockholm, Antwerp,
Geneva, Buenos Aires, and various other cities, usually without
any sort of commission from those concerned. It is noteworthy
that he has eliminated, around 1930, the cruciform tower from
his vocabulary. It was replaced by the so-called "Cartesian
Skyscraper": Y-shaped in plan, "like a hen's foot."[72] The principle is obvious: like a reflector, the building is oriented toward
sun and light (whereas in the cruciform skyscraper fifty percent
of the facades remained in the shade during the whole year).
The new type shows up for the first time in the master plan for
Barcelona by José Luis Sert and the GATEPAC group, a study
made in collaboration with Le Corbusier and Pierre Jeanneret
(1932–1935).[73] Later, it appears in the Antwerp master plan as
well as in that of Hellocourt,[74] not to mention the "Plan de Paris"

of 1937 and finally, the project for Buenos Aires (1938) with its five glass skyscrapers lined up like soldiers standing at attention and facing the sea.

The Role of the CIAM

Le Corbusier's urbanistic imagery, as it was established in the twenties and thirties, was to a large degree an academic set of formal rules, rigorous and static as the Beaux-Arts tradition it tried to escape. There is of course more to Le Corbusier's town planning than mere aesthetic choice. Social progress through quantitative analysis, scientific management, and large-scale planning in all areas were the concerns discussed in and later championed by the CIAM (Congrès Internationaux d' Architecture Moderne), a sort of multinational lobby for the promotion of modern architecture, whose members were carefully selected from various European avant-garde circles and represented the "hard core" of the movement. Le Corbusier had been among the founders of the group.

Urbanism was not the CIAM's primary concern right from the beginning.[75] It was only among many concerns expressed in the manifesto of La Sarraz (1928). Later on, however, the problem became the center of the CIAM's discussions, and the two subsequent meetings in Frankfurt (1929) and Brussels (1930) were devoted to housing. It was in Brussels that Cornelius van Eesteren, the city planner of Amsterdam, was elected to the CIAM's presidency, succeeding the Swiss architect Karl Moser. Also at that time a special working committee, the CIRPAC (Comité International pour la Résolution des Problèmes Architecturaux Contemporains), was formed with the aim of establishing a method of comparative analysis in city planning, and of preparing a subsequent congress entirely devoted to urban planning. This congress was to be held around 1930 in Moscow, the Mecca of progressive architects and planners.

Despite the challenge of Russia, where at this time some 360 cities were to be built from scratch, the meeting in Moscow scheduled for 1933 never took place. The avant-garde's enthusiasm for Russia had been somewhat dampened by the result of the Soviet Palace competition of 1931 that indicated a shift of official taste in favor of traditional academism. The Rus-

sians also seemed to have lost their earlier interest in an international exchange of views. Whether they officially withdrew
the invitation is not clear, but in any case the CIAM leaders decided to cancel the meeting in Moscow. Marcel Breuer came up
with an almost equally attractive alternative: a congress in the
form of a cruise.

This idea appealed to Le Corbusier, and he immediately
telephoned the art critic Christian Zervos, whose brother was
the director of a Greek navigation company. The decision was
quickly made, and the fourth CIAM congress took place on
board the S.S. *Patris II* between Marseilles and Athens, in
Athens itself, and finally on the return voyage to Marseilles.
The theme of the congress was "The Functional City."

During the cruise, the members of the congress analyzed
thirty-three great cities on the basis of preparatory work by
the CIRPAC. The party was joined by a number of painters
including Fernand Léger and Moholy-Nagy (who made a
documentary film of the meeting) and some art critics (Jean
Badovici, Christian Zervos, and Carola Giedion-Welcker).
These intellectuals must have contributed to the creation of an
atmosphere rather different from that of a meeting of special-
ists. In addition, there was Greece itself with its landscape and
its architectural past both monumental and vernacular, which
emerged with unexpected force.

Sigfried Giedion, the general secretary of the CIAM, speaks
of Greece's impact upon the subconscious of the "new tradition":

These problems of the subconscious became fully clear only
after the congress was over. They were in fact a development of
the purely functional tendencies in architecture toward a more
comprehensive inclusion of other elements—aesthetic, social,
and biological. The full evaluation of this new, independent
platform had been helped immeasurably by the contact with the
past and our Hellenic heritage.[76]

The immediate results were summarized in a series of carefully
written "statements" published in Switzerland and Holland
after the conclusion of the congress.

It is interesting to note that the famous "Charte d'Athènes," which is usually regarded as the outcome of the congress, was in fact written and published in France only a de-

cade later, in 1943. Although based on the original "statements" of 1933, this solemn document is to a large degree a personal manifesto by Le Corbusier himself.[77] However, since no real debate seems to have taken place among the CIAM members as to whether the "Charte" is to be regarded as the official document of the 1933 meeting, it was thus universally accepted as such.

The moment for a publication of this kind was well chosen for it is unlikely that any progrssive town-planning manifesto published in 1943—a time of increasing worry with respect to postwar reconstruction—would have passed unnoticed. But the "Charte" had even more to recommend it to a wide circle: unlike the earlier CIAM documents that dealt with precise questions such as minimal housing or the industrialization of building, the "Charte d'Athènes" is, as its title suggests, an Olympian statement concerned less with specific information than with broad generalizations. Most of its eighty-four points call in some way or other for sound and detailed urban studies as the essential basis for any planning. The need for systematic coordination of the different interests and competences involved (traffic systems, housing, etc.) was equally important in the "Charte." But of all the statements contained in this document there is one that stands out as the key issue, and has done so ever since its publication: the definition of the "functional city." This states that the city has to accommodate four essential functions: "Dwelling, working, recreation, and circulation." There is nothing wrong with this list as long as it serves as the basis for topographical analysis and surveying. The implication, however, was that—in a new plan—these functions were to be articulated in terms of separate urban units, and it is here that the idea becomes controversial.

Careful research is required to determine the real importance of Le Corbusier's role within the CIAM. One thing, however, can be taken for granted: the visual fascination of Le Corbusier's own urbanistic projects was one of the most powerful propaganda vehicles for the CIAM ideals. Of all the concepts mentioned in the "Charte," it was the rigorous differentiation of urban functions that is most strongly emphasized by Le Corbusier's projects. The Plan Voisin, for example, was based on a clear division of functions, and in *Urbanisme* (1925), he had al-

ready proclaimed the strict separation of dwelling and traffic:
"In an orderly house, the back stairs do not go through the living room, however pretty the 'maid from Brittany' may be."[78]
The plan for Nemours (1937; fig. 154) may be regarded as a
crystallization of all the elements mentioned in the "Charte
d'Athènes." As in Algiers, the business center was to be
situated on the seashore, near the harbor. In the background, a
group of hills forming a vast amphitheater facing the shore was
to have been the site for eighteen housing units, and industry
and workshops were to have been located in a recessed position
by the river. Civic administration, churches and facilities for
leisure and tourism were planned as a kind of acropolis towering over the sea from the top of a cliff. This city was, however,
never built.[79]

War and Reconstruction

Although Nemours was never built, the project's underlying
concept of radiant high-rise grandeur on the grounds of a differentiation of the city's functions influenced many planners of
the postwar years in some way or other. As for Le Corbusier
himself, the war did not merely stimulate his dreams of Cartesian reconstruction, it inspired him to more immediate action.
The victims of Nazi devastation were not interested in urbanistic concepts: what they needed was a roof over their heads.
Shortly after the invasion of Belgium and Holland, Le Corbusier
came up with his concept of the "Murondin houses"—a proposal for direct self-help based on the rational use of clay,
quarry-stones, and branches: a strategy of instant reconstruction by the people for the people.[80]
    The war years were characterized by hopes and disap-
pointments. Le Corbusier tried hard to maintain good working
relations with the government, and these seemed to be well-
established around 1940, when he was commissioned by the
Ministry of Defence to build an ammunition factory. The factory never progressed beyond its foundations, however, for the
entry of the Germans into Paris on June 14, 1940, brought the
project to an untimely end. Le Corbusier, who happened to be
in Aubusson at the time, fled with his wife and his cousin
Pierre to Ozon, a small village in the Pyrenées where he was

subsequently commissioned to build a chemical plant. Whereas
Pierre later joined the Résistance in Grenoble, Le Corbusier remained in Ozon for an extended period, spending his time
painting and writing and hoping that he would be called upon
sooner or later by the pro-German regime of the demilitarized
zone of France.

Instead, a new law issued by the government made it
impossible for him to carry on working as an architect, although this did nothing to weaken his belief in Maréchal Pétain
and his circle as the guarantee of an imminent French "renaissance." This belief was strong enough to govern most of his ac-
tions, and he made several pilgrimages to Vichy, the puppet-
government's headquarters, in the hope of being allotted a
share in the responsibility for France's postwar resurrection.
Here he lived for some time in the Carlton Hotel where he wrote
a series of recommendations for the reconstruction of France (*La
maison des hommes*) in collaboration with François de Pierrefeu.
His prime concern during the whole of 1941 and 1942 was the
establishment of a theoretical basis for a large-scale French
reconstruction: three books appeared in 1941 (*Destin de Paris*,
Sur les quatre routes, and *Les constructions Murondins*); three
more in 1943 (*La maison des hommes*, *Charte d'Athènes*—which
was unsigned and contained a solemn introduction by Jean
Giraudoux, and *Entretien avec les étudiants des écoles d'architecture*); and another two one year later (*Les trois établisse-
ments humains* and *Propos d'urbanisme*). The amount of work he
got through in these years is almost unbelievable for, in addition to his frenetic writing and editing, he also chaired the
twenty-two subsections of the ASCORAL Group in Paris, drew
up proposals for regional planning in the Pyrenean district (together with Marcel Lods), and established the layout of a new
town there, Saint-Gaudens.

In 1941, Le Corbusier was appointed head of a government
commission for the study of housing, but circumstances made it
impossible to accomplish anything.[81] Thus, in effect, all these
years were taken up with more or less unsuccessful attempts—
at all levels—to establish the premises for large-scale recon-
structions.

At last, however, after the liberation he received two size-
able commissions from Raoul Dautry, who had been appointed

Minister of Reconstruction in the provisional government: he
was asked to draw the master plans of La Rochelle-Pallice in
Northwest France, and Saint-Dié in the Vosges which had been
totally destroyed toward the end of the war. But, once again,
these projects required a political setup very different to that of
France just after the war. In the end, it was a poor country with
a firmly established and basically feudal power structure that
was able to realize Le Corbusier's vision—at least in its essential parts: India.

Chandigarh

Thanks to Le Corbusier's own books on the subject, Norma
Evenson's important monograph, and numerous studies published since, Chandigarh is probably the best-documented
urban venture of recent history.[82] To some the word Chandigarh signifies progressive, socialist planning and outstanding
architectural achievement; to others it is a symbol of arrogant
Western planning ideology ruthlessly inflicted upon the Third
World.

   Today it is obvious that Chandigarh's problem lies in the
fact that it was built on the basis of a prospective utopia that
we find increasingly difficult to regard as realistic. However,
whereas its master plan must be interpreted within the context
of Le Corbusier's work as a whole, its realization can only be
comprehended as a response to the political situation of India at
a particular moment in her history: her newly-gained independence from British rule and her struggle with Pakistan.

   The state that made Chandigarh possible was not the
pan-Indian community based on agriculture and cloth-making
which Gandhi had anticipated.[83] It was a new nation, eager to
become an adult member of the family of industrial powers
to which it had been attached for so long as a mere servant or
slave, a nation whose leaders were waiting for the occasion to
create a monument to the new national self-awareness. And
Chandigarh seems to have provided this occasion.

   As a result of the 1947 Independence Bill, the western part
of the Punjab—including the old state capital of Lahore—was
ceded to Pakistan in 1948, thus leaving the Indian part of the
Punjab without a capital and millions of Pakistani refugees

without a home. After some hesitation as to whether the state
government should be permanently accommodated in one of the
existing rural centers, the decision was taken to build a new
town. P. L. Varma, chief engineer of the state of Punjab, and
P. N. Thapar, a former member of the Civil Service, chose the
site and the name.[84]

From the very beginning, the central government in New
Dehli was involved. Nehru himself suggested that Albert
Mayer, an American architect whom he had known as a
lieutenant colonel of the American army in India, should be
commissioned to produce a master plan (fig. 159). The central
government also agreed to cover one-third of the estimated
building costs ($34 million) and agreed upon the appointment
of one of Le Corbusier's former collaborators, Matthew Nowicki, as the architect responsible for the design of the government buildings among other things.[85] Unlike Mayer's initial
plan, Nowicki's sketches show a marked interest in a monumental orchestration of the capitol complex; the Assembly was
to be placed like a mastaba in the midst of a ceremonial plaza,
and the Secretariat was to be covered by a huge shell-like
structure (fig. 189). Both Mayer's master plan and Nowicki's
sketches for the capitol area illustrate that the general concept
and layout of the city was established to a large extent around
1950—well before Le Corbusier took over the command.

This occurred in late 1950. Nowicki's sudden death in a
plane crash over Egypt in the spring of 1950 and the difficulties
incurred in coming to a financial agreement with Albert Mayer
had interrupted the planning of Chandigarh, and two Punjab
officials traveled to Europe in search of a new team of planners
and architects. Their first contacts were Maxwell Fry and Jane
Drew, and it was they who suggested that the Indians should
get in touch with Le Corbusier. Although his first reaction was
anything but enthusiastic, he finally agreed to become the
"Planning Advisor of the Punjab Government for the Creation
of its New Capital" at a monthly salary of $420 and with the in-
junction to spend four weeks twice a year in Chandigarh during
its construction. In addition, he was appointed architect of the
capitol complex. In February 1951, he flew to India together
with Pierre Jeanneret where he met Maxwell Fry and Jane Drew.

In a small hotel on the road to Simla, the new plan for Chandigarh was drawn up within four days (fig. 161).[86]

In fact, this was not a new layout but a revised version of the existing—and accepted—master plan by Albert Mayer. All the distinctive features of Mayer's plan were adopted: the location of the government center outside the city, so to speak as its "head" (an idea which happened to coincide with one of Le Corbusier's own earlier planning concepts), the creation of a business center within the city, and the division of the territory into sectors. The changes to the plan were mainly concerned with the size of the neighborhood units, which now received roughly rectangular outlines and measured about 1200 by 800 meters—Le Corbusier's "module" of a "sector." The most obvious modification, however, was to the roads. Mayer had envisaged them as large curves; Le Corbusier established a system of rectilinear axes, and only the lateral streets crossing the Jan Marg, the grand avenue of the city, were slightly curved for better protection from the sun.

The monumental axis had been a central aspect of Le Corbusier's urbanistic proposals ever since the Project of a Contemporary City for Three Million Inhabitants (1922), and it was loaded with moral, aesthetic, and functional symbolism (fig. 144). To Le Corbusier, speed and motorization were elements of the "lyricism of modern times," a lyricism too Olympian to be judged on purely utilitarian grounds. In fact, one of the sketches of the Contemporary City shows an urban superhighway connecting the two triumphal gates; outside the city, where an access highway would be justified, the urban axis reverts into a simple cross-country road (fig. 162). Chandigarh corresponds to the utopia of 1922, for after six hours of bumpy country roads, the traveler by bus from New Delhi suddenly finds himself on a smooth highway, and while he thinks he is now finally approaching Chandigarh, he is actually being driven through the city's main street (fig. 163).

Le Corbusier's plan of changing Mayer's original layout seems to have been readily accepted by the Indian officials. Whereas Mayer's plan was reminiscent of the organic patterns of English garden cities and their American descendants (Mayer had played a considerable role in introducing Ebenezer Howard's ideas to America), Le Corbusier's modifications reestablished the plan in the tradition of Western pre-Howardian town planning. His project evoked the grandiose urban geometry of L'Enfant's Washington or Haussmann's Paris. Furthermore, it must have appealed to the Indian officials through its implicit analogy with the plan of New Delhi with its "King's Way"—India's showpiece of enlightened (though colonial) planning (fig. 188).[87]

It was analogies of this kind that made Chandigarh into a symbol of national pride and self-awareness. Not that the gridiron plan had been introduced to India by the British Empire; the city of Jaipur, for instance, dates from the early eighteenth century and is as Indian an ancestor for Le Corbusier's master plan as could be wished (fig. 164); its avenues, however, are not traffic arteries alone and serve as multifunctional public spaces. The declamatory gesture of Chandigarh's axis is, on the other hand, a definite legacy of New Delhi.

Many other monumental aspects of Chandigarh can be understood in terms of their often concealed analogy with the Indian capital (a fact which has been noted by Norma Evenson). Le Corbusier's only realization of an enclosed city space is the vast pedestrian plaza of the city center in Sector 17, which appears to stretch out its arms toward the surrounding (empty) traffic arteries (fig. 167).[88] This area's mono-functional character of a mere business district dervives from the "Charte d'Athènes," and its form—a vast open space surrounded by long arcaded office buildings—reflects Le Corbusier's delight in French squares and Roman fora, leitmotivs in his sketchbooks and early publications. The plaza is, in short, a colonial variation on the theme of the Venetian Piazza San Marco. Functionally dessicated and dramatically overscaled, however (the plaza is 550 meters long from street to street while the Piazza San Marco is "only" 200 meters deep), it also lacks the densely packed cluster of the surrounding city that gives the Venetian piazza its meaning as a public amenity.

The core of Chandigarh is just the opposite of what the Western tourist expects to find in an Indian urban center, the complete contradiction of the bazaar, shaded and noisy, crowding a maximum of people and goods into a minimum of space. Nevertheless, these vast plazas, which become ovens

under the glaring sun, are the pride of the administration, and
many Indian visitors from Calcutta and Bombay seem to experience the spaciousness and openness of this plaza as a promise
of relief from age-old poverty and overcrowding. And indeed,
"wide-open spaces," "space, air, and light," and the condem-
nation of the "horror of slums" were recurring themes in Nehru's speeches.[89] The city center also has its counterpart in
New Delhi, and its scale and neoclassical serenity (though
somewhat stiffened by the narrow-minded repetition of an elevation code which Le Corbusier had intended to be used in a
varied and flexible fashion[90]) recalls Sir Herbert Baker's Palladian arcades in Connaught Place (fig. 166).

Convergence of ideologies

It was, of course, no mere coincidence that Le Corbusier "happened" to be the right man at the right moment and that his
urban imagery and architecture—especially that of the Capitol
Palaces which will be discussed later—seemed capable of in-
corporating the very ideas and values that the new Indian elite
wanted to celebrate far more dramatically than Mayer's or
Nowicki's would have done. Since the very beginning of his
career, these values had been a central aspect of Le Corbusier's
own political philosophy. His enthusiasm for "authority,"
strong leadership, and great men at the head of important
tasks is proverbial, and the call for strong political authority
is a recurring motto in his publications. It was his opinion
that the realization of the new architecture of collective happiness required a strong, well-informed government with *Pleins
Pouvoirs*, to quote the title of a book by Jean Giradoux (1939)
of which Le Corbusier was highly appreciative. Thus his book
La ville radieuse (1933) was dedicated to "The Authority."
He entertained a paternalistic and even patriarchal concept of
state rule, which he compared to the authority of the "père de
famille" who knows what is best for his children.[91] At the end
of *Urbanisme* (1925), he reproduced a print of Louis XIV ordering the construction of the Hôtel des Invalides with the caption:
"Homage to a great urbanist" (fig. 169). Later, he confessed, "I
have been haunted for years by the shades of Colbert."[92]

In the context of Chandigarh, it is interesting—though
perhaps somewhat distressing—to note that Le Corbusier had
always naively admired Western colonization as a spectacle of

"force morale."[93] His book *Précisions*, written after his first trip to South America in 1929, abounds in enthusiastic statements about the great efforts of investors and industrialists to "build up America": "In many offices, I have seen that the Germans and the English have sent technicians in order to equip the country; in particular, I have felt the enormous financial and industrial power of the USA. People are coming to Argentina from all corners of the world, and all efforts are useful."[94]

Most of these earlier statements on the salutary nature of modern technology and industrial development for the well-being of mankind would probably have met with the approval of Prime Minister Nehru. In India, Le Corbusier was frequently blamed for not having been interested enough in local customs. When an Indian visitor asked him why he hadn't stayed longer at Chandigarh, he replied, "I was frightened of being bitten by a snake," and then added: "What is the significance of Indian style in the world of today if you accept machines, trousers, and democracy?"[95]

With this in mind, it is easy to understand what Nehru must have meant to Le Corbusier: after the latter's frustrated attempts to become a Colbert of the League of Nations, of Stalin, of Pétain, and of the UN, he had finally met a political leader whose outlook was in tune with his own architectural philosophy and whose authority was strong enough to enable it to be realized.

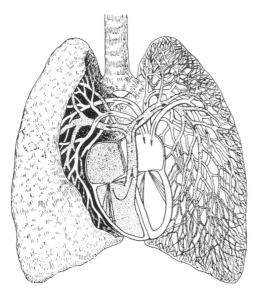

139. Illustration in Le Corbusier's book *Urbanisme* (1925), underlying the claim that the city is essentially a system of circulation

140. Le Corbusier, mural illustrating the principles of the "radiant city" at the Pavillon des Temps Nouveaux, World Fair, Paris, 1937 (from *Oeuvre complète*)

141. Diorama representing a
blimp in a natural setting;
shown at Salon d'automne,
Paris, 1922 (from catalogue
*Exposition de demonstration
de l'aeronautique Francaise*)

142. Auguste Perret, pro-
posal for a "tower-city" of
the future (from *Illustration*,
1922; photo: Werner
Oechslin)

143. Separation of traffic levels in New York, (6th Avenue and 33rd Street), around 1910 (from Le Corbusier, *Urbanisme*; copied from Hegemann, *Amerikanische Architektur und Stadtbankunst*)

144. Le Corbusier and Pierre Jeanneret, Diorama of the "Contemporary City for Three Million Inhabitants," shown in the Pavillon de L'Esprit Nouveau at the International Arts and Crafts Exhibition, Paris, 1925 (archives: Willy Boesiger, Zurich)

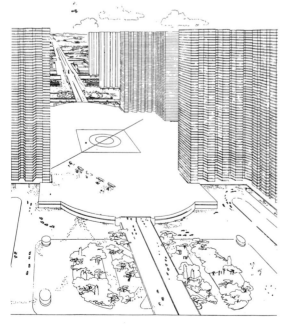

145. Eugène Hénard, "Carrefour à gitation" (traffic roundabout) for Paris (from *Etudes sur les transformations de Paris*, 1903–1906)

146. Le Corbusier and Pierre Jeanneret, Central station and airport of the City for Three Million Inhabitants, ca. 1922 (from *Oeuvre complète*)

147. "Rues à Redents": (a) after Eugène Hénard, ca. 1903 (from Hénard, *Etudes sur les transformations de Paris*; (b) after Le Corbusier, 1922 (from *Vers une architecture*)

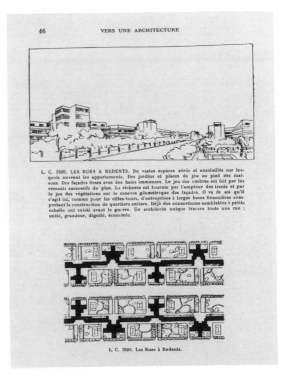

148. Le Corbusier; sketch of
the bay of Rio as seen from
the airplane, with proposed
megastructure for the new
city; 1929 (from *Aircraft*)

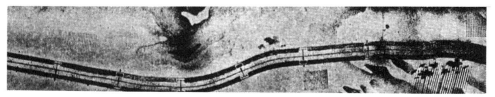

149. Le Corbusier, sketch
illustrating the Plan Obus
for Algiers, 1931 (Fondation
Le Corbusier, Paris)

150. M. Barshch and Moses
Ginsburg, "Green City";
project for Moscow, 1930
(from A. Kopp, *Town and
Revolution*)

151. Edgar Chambless, project for Roadtown (with railway track under ground), 1910

152. Le Corbusier and Pierre Jeanneret, Plan Obus for Algiers, 1931; view of model (from *Oeuvre complète*)

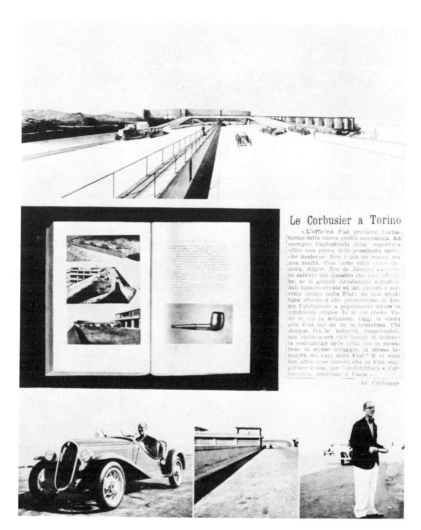

153. Page from *Oeuvre complète 1929–1934*, juxtaposing the Plan Obus (top) to Le Corbusier's visit to the Fiat plant in Turin, 1934

154. Le Corbusier and
Pierre Jeanneret, plan for
Nemours, North Africa,
1937 (from *Oeuvre com-
plète*)

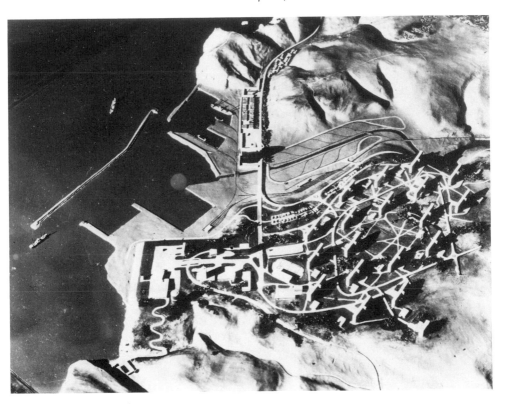

155. Le Corbusier and
Pierre Jeanneret, office
tower for Algiers, Quartier
de la Marine (project)
1939–1942 (from *Oeuvre
complète*)

10　　　THE NEW YORK TIMES MAGAZINE, NOVEMBER 3, 1935

LE CORBUSIER SCANS GOTHAM'S TOWERS

The French Architect, on a Tour, Finds the City Violently Alive, a Wilderness of Experiment Toward a New Order

The City of the Future as Le Corbusier Envisions It.

By H I BROCK

THE citizen of the French Republic who is known as Le Corbusier—he was born Jeanneret and his given name is Charles-Édouard—is just now paying his first visit to America and has had his first eyeful of the man-made miracle which is New York. In circles where disputing about art is a major sport, Le Corbusier is identified as the founder and public exponent of the mood in architecture which has been labeled the International Style and which certain stiff conservatives insist does not look like architecture at all.

The basic principle of this style is to regard the architect's function as primarily one of household efficiency engineering. His job is to furnish human creatures with a convenient "machine for living in." As stated, the principle applies specifically to the family dwelling. But it applies also to the composite arrangement of buildings which takes care of the complex employments and the complex human activities of a city where great numbers of people must live and most of them attend to business. Since the modern dwelling and the modern city have each new demands to meet, since each has at command a service of machinery and materials which no dwelling and no city has ever had before, Le Corbusier and his school begin by discarding traditions and dismissing prejudices which would perpetuate formulas of building evolved from conditions of life that have ceased to exist

THE rough idea is that the machine age, with its vast concentrations of population and its prodigious accumulation of mechanical devices for quantity production and for mass movement of goods and men, has created problems which the older architecture is incompetent to solve. The new architecture must face these problems squarely and find a solution on a sound mechanical basis, let the chips of academic aestheticism fall where they may.

New York City, for example, is planted thick with skyscrapers—filing cases of millions of human beings at work or stowed away for the night. The streets of New York are jammed with automotive vehicles engaged in distributing the quantity-production output or moving these millions of people about, back and forth between home and business, and generally where they want to go, creating in the process no end of traffic tangles and even seriously endangering in life and limb those who still have to get about on their own feet.

Le Corbusier has built in France and other European countries machines for living in—machines also for doing business in. Whether these machines are, in fact, more efficient than the houses other architects build is a question which will not be argued here. But it is true that, at three years short of 50, he is more famous than the articulate

Too Small?—Yes, Says Le Corbusier; Too Narrow for Free, Efficient Circulation.

New York Times Studios

MODERN architecture—that is, machine-made architecture—was born, as even its most ardent European advocates admit, in this country. The Europeans who have taken it up have made it much more "modern" than we have dared or cared to make it. Nevertheless, New York—the part of it, at least, which enjoys high visibility—is the creation on the greatest scale that the world voice of the new architecture than as the executant of its projects. He represents a vision of the future rather than a proved practice of the present.

knows of the new architecture which is our own. That architecture pierces the sky with pinnacles that lift the level of our rocky little island (which in a state of nature could not boast a really respectable hill) into rivalry with the lesser mountains.

Le Corbusier, from the deck of the giant liner Normandie, looked up the harbor and saw (as he says) afar off a dream city hanging in the blue sky above the horizon of the water—a vision of enchantment. He went below for déjeuner and came up again with the solid substance of the vision right on top of him. He was appalled by the brutality of the great masses—the "sauvagerie"—the wild barbarity of the stupendous, disorderly accumulation of towers, tramping the living city under their heavy feet, like a herd of mastodons.

As the ship moved up the river and he got the city broadside on, as the clutter of bunched towers of the stronghold of finance thinned out and other towers began to stand out separate, gleaming in the sunlight in the open space above their lowlier neighbors, his dispondency abated. Hope revived for the future which the first bright vision had seemed to embody. That vision might not, after all, be a mirage.

LATER, while touring the city in the company of the writer, he stood at the base of the steep sheer cliff of Raymond Hood's slab in Rockefeller Center and said that it was good, then began ruefully to rub the crick out of the back of his neck that was the result of trying to look up to the very top of anything so tall and uncompromisingly perpendicular.

He found the smaller buildings on the Fifth Avenue front—dedicated to France and the British Empire—out of scale, both with the upreared mass and the human beings walking about the central plaza. That plaza itself, all bare (as it is apt to be when the tourist season is on the wane), struck him as decidedly dull—in spite of Prometheus and his fountain.

Then he was shot in an elevator (at the rate of 1,200 feet a minute) to the very top of the big slat—the deck under which lurks the Rainbow Room—and looked out upon the map of the city, by that time half veiled in a soft gray mist, which cut off the horizons far short of the two extremes of our narrow island but revealed the bounding ribbons of water on either side North, south, east and west, the skyscrapers nevertheless stood out boldly. Now and again the sun thrust through the thin clouds and bathed their faces in a brief glory of high light or gilded the fancy tops which some of them have borrowed from all the styles—unimportant to M. Le Corbusier—that came before the steel skeleton revolutionized large-scale building. It was excellent theatre—spectacular drama.

BUT the modern architect was not particularly impressed. He was looking for architecture, not theatre, and shy, besides, of succumbing to drama so melodramatic. Moreover, he was looking for architecture in his own sense of the word—in this case, the city that is a machine for living in—not merely frightfully expensive scenery built to knock the beholder's eye out.

"They are too small," he said, looking straight at the Empire State Building, tallest in all the world of rising cases for men and standing on one of the biggest pieces of ground devoted to that purpose in the city.

Somebody pointed out a building with "modern" horizontal lines, belting continuous windows about it, down by the Hudson, and " building with "modern" vertical lines, stacking up windows in parallel slits, over toward the East River.

"I am not interested," said Le Corbusier, "in that sort of thing—both sets of lines are all right as expressing the idea of horizontal and vertical circulation respectively. But what counts is the actual existence in the building of the two kinds of circulation. That is the combination which creates adequate machines for business for swarms of people—human beehives—if it is joined, of course, with free circulation among the buildings."

The skyscrapers that thrust up

(Continued on Page 23)

Le Corbusier Looks—Critically

© André Steiner

156. "Le Corbusier Scans Gotham's Towers," report on Le Corbusier's first visit to New York in *The New York Times Magazine*, November 3, 1935

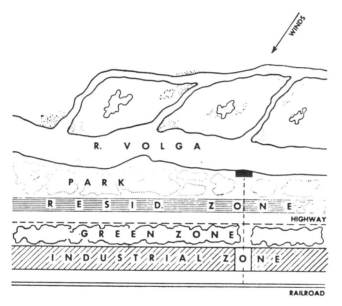

WINDS

R. VOLGA

PARK

RESID. ZONE

HIGHWAY

GREEN ZONE

INDUSTRIAL ZONE

RAILROAD

0 1 2 KM

0 5 10 KM

157. N. Miljutin, Trac-
torstoy. Schematic plan of a
settlement at the Stalingrad
Tractor Plant

158. Le Corbusier, "linear
city" (from *On the Four
Routes*)

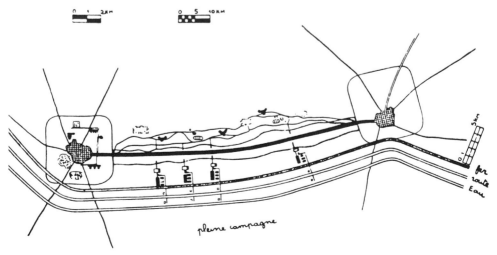

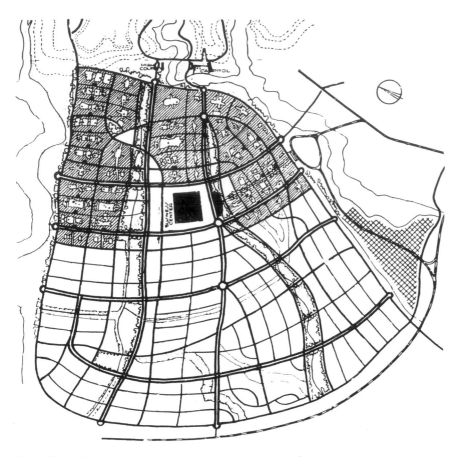

159. Albert Mayer, pro-
posed master plan for
Chandigarh, 1950 (from N.
Everson, *Chandigarh*)

160. Matthew Nowicki, the
"leaf plan" for Chandigarh;
ca. 1950 (from N. Everson,
Chandigarh)

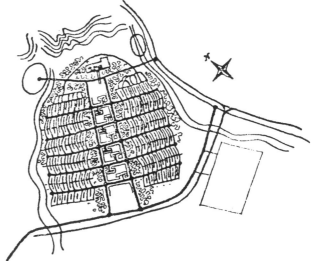

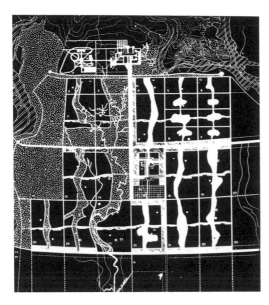

161. Le Corbusier and collaborators, master plan for Chandigarh, 1951 (from *Oeuvre complète*)

162. Le Corbusier and Pierre Jeanneret, Contemporary City for Three Million Inhabitants, 1922 (from *Oeuvre complète*)

163. Chandigarh, view of Jan Marg, the city's main axis. Right: Museum and Art Gallery (photo: author)

164. Main street in Jaipur,
India (photo: author)

165. Jan Marg with wall
"protecting" residential
sector (photo: author)

166. New Delhi; Connaught
Place (photo: author)

167. Chandigarh, city center
(photo: author)

168. The Place des Vosges in Paris, as reproduced in *Urbanisme*, 1925

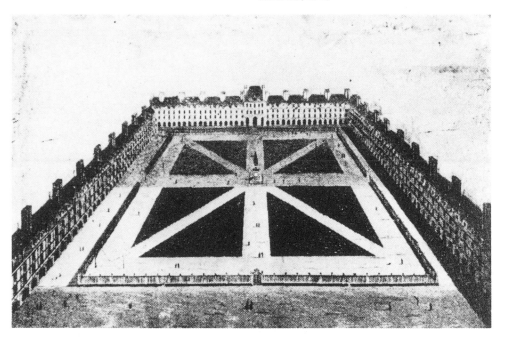

169. Louis XIV ordering the building of the Hôtel des Invalides from his architect; print, seventeenth century, as reproduced in *Urbanisme*, 1925

170. Prime Minister Nehru and Le Corbusier studying plans for Chandigarh; ca. 1954 (from *Oeuvre complète*)

Public Buildings

Town halls, castles, and churches have always taken their place among the most important architectural undertakings and those most likely to bring the architect public esteem and glory. Public buildings demand expertise in the handling of conventional programs as well as a feeling for the representation of the institution involved—the state or the church, whose authority is to a large degree determined by its age. It is therefore not surprising that in the early decades of modern architecture the large-scale public commissions were usually assigned to traditionalist architects, particularly since most protagonists of Modern Architecture regarded the idea of "representation" as obsolete in the context of architectural design.

In his *Ville Contemporaine* (1922), Le Corbusier did not even make provision for public buildings and considered anonymous office towers suitable accommodation for state and local authorities. Only a few years later however, he participated in an international competition for the public building of the twenties *par excellence*: the Palace of the League of Nations. Not only that: he used this competition and its ensuing controversies as a pretext for a massive attack on the academic taste and the established decision-making processes of the government authorities, and he experienced the eventual debacle of his project both as a proof of the jury's moral corruption and lack of understanding for the real needs of the era, as well as a confirmation of his own tragic role as a martyr to the cause.

The League of Nations Competition

Le Corbusier shared the widespread enthusiasm for the League's political purpose; for the first time in history, the building of a world parliament was under consideration. He must also have been extremely intrigued by the possible promotional effect that could be expected from the adoption of modern architecture for such an official and international purpose. For its headquarters, the League of Nations (founded in 1919 immediately after World War I) had chosen a picturesque lakeside site near Geneva. According to the competition program, the new palace was to include an office building, accommodation for the various temporary committees, and a general assembly hall. Three hundred and sixty-seven projects—a

total of eight miles of plans—were submitted to the jury before
the deadline at the end of January 1927. There was reasonable
hope for even the most modern competitors since the jury included people closely allied to the modern movement, such as
H. P. Berlage (Netherlands), Victor Horta (Belgium), Joseph
Hoffmann (Austria), and Karl Moser (Switzerland). France,
Great Britain, and a number of other countries were represented by established Beaux-Arts architects.

Right at the start the jury seems to have acknowledged ex-
ceptional qualities in the project by Le Corbusier and Pierre
Jeanneret, and in fact it was the only project of a modern character to be seriously considered (fig. 171).[1] But the members
of the jury were unable to come to a clear decision and, contrary to the previously agreed rules, they eventually awarded
nine tied prizes. Among the winners were Le Corbusier
and Pierre Jeanneret and had it not been for the fact that the
French delegate, M. Lemaresquier, claimed that Le Corbusier's plans were not original drawings but only copies and
thus failed to meet the requirements of the competition, their
project might have won first prize. With this award of nine tied
prizes, the jury passed the choice of project over to the politicians, who subsequently added to the confusion by requesting
four of the winning teams to develop a final project in close
collaboration with one another. The resulting neoclassical pastiche was realized several years later (Secretariat 1936, Assembly Hall 1938) in the (by then) International Style of government
buildings (fig. 178).[2]

Although there was no chance of the project ever being
realized, in 1927 and the years immediately following, Swiss
experts estimated the cost of Le Corbusier's proposal to be 12.5
million Swiss francs. The cost of the Palace that was actually built
amounted to 50 million Swiss francs. The building was moved
to higher terrain than had originally been planned, and when
the architects were obliged to adapt their project to the new location, their final scheme turned out to have a great deal in
common with Corbusier's second project, elaborated in 1929
(fig. 177). All Le Corbusier's and Jeanneret's efforts to save the
commission proved to be of no avail,[3] and finally in 1931, they
filed a thirty-six page lawsuit, written by a well-known lawyer

in Paris; the reply, however, was laconic: the League of Nations cannot comply with the claims of private persons.[4]

The Humanist versus the Utilitarian Ideal

Le Corbusier and Pierre Jeanneret were not the only protagonists of the modern movement in this competition, for Richard Neutra, the Polish group Praesens, Hans Wittwer, Hannes Meyer from Basel (fig. 172), and others[5] also made interesting contributions. Compared to these projects, Le Corbusier's proposal is less extravagant than it must have appeared to its critics. In fact, it does not really offer a radical alternative to a conventional neoclassical composition, but is more of an attempt to bring traditional monumentality up to date by the grand-scale incorporation of the "five points": pilotis, roof garden, free plan, free facade, and elongated windows. Kenneth Frampton has argued that the organization of space in Le Corbusier's scheme is hierarchical and that his Palais des Nations with its axes and gardens has characteristics of a Renaissance palace.[6] One of the sources of the project may have been the Grand Palais in Paris (built in 1900).[7]

Be that as it may, there can be no doubt that Le Corbusier's project was intended as an efficient tool designed to serve its purpose as an office building and not merely as a monument. Le Corbusier insisted that, contrary to all the academic projects presenting combinations of closed courts, it affords free views of the parks and mountains to all the members of the administrative staff. The critical reactions at the time suggest that the project's classicizing layout was far less obvious than its radically modern architectural forms; yet without this underlying classicism, the project would not have been a serious candidate for the first prize, nor would the architects eventually entrusted with the construction have been able to use—and despoil—the characteristics of its plan (fig. 177).[8]

Whereas the syntax of forms is classical and humanistic, the vocabulary of this architecture is of machine-age extraction. While the accesses to the Palace reveal grandiose symmetries, the details refer to the aesthetics of engineering. The grand entrance porch to the Assembly Building which looks onto the

"Cour d'honneur" is placed within the composition like a colonnade, and looks something like the canopy of a gas station (although it is impossible that a gas station of such streamlined design could have served as a model at the time); thus the visitor would have entered the building via something very similar to a railway platform.

The Assembly Hall itself (fig. 173) is a secularized, machine-age version of a theater; intended for an audience of 2600 delegates, the auditorium is designed in accordance with acoustic requirements, and Gustave Lyon himself[9] participated in working out the specifications for the form. Thus the auditorium is not a mere box within which communication would have been dependent upon earphones (which were not available at the time), but a kind of a resounding board. The external shape of the auditorium is a trapezoid with the roof slanted toward the lowest base like a piece of cake with the front part of the wedge cut off. This form, the "pie slice," became the prototype of all assembly halls planned by Le Corbusier up to his project for the United Nations (1947); moreover, it remained *the* standard solution to the problem of auditoriums in rationalist architecture for the next twenty-five years.

The composition as a whole is characterized by a mixture of classical severity and picturesque improvisation—a witty give-and-take between nature and geometry. In the "cour d'honneur" the baroque unity is somewhat blurred by the odd arrangement of the plants and trees—an English garden superimposed upon a French park (fig. 171). Not only are the buildings and gardens constantly juxtaposed as elements of a sharp and often contradictory dialogue, the building itself is treated like a three-dimensional collage of heterogeneous parts. Sculptural elements are placed in front of the Assembly Hall's symmetrical facade facing the lake (fig. 173): the curved, concave "box" of the presidential pavilion towering into space on high pilotis and, behind it, the staircase tower, comparable to a thick oval pipe, supporting a monumental equestrian group. The sculptures, exposed in front of a white wall, determine the focal point of the architectural whole. Le Corbusier liked to place grand modern sculptures in situations like this: "These sites control space. . . . It is the sculptor who, from the lofty heights

of his work resembling a blazing star or a beacon, must control
and hold at a fitting distance these large, pure and silent prisms
of crystal or stone."[10]

The Mundaneum

The debacle of his League of Nations project did not end Le
Corbusier's desire to build a palace that would serve no less a
cause than the well-being of humanity as a whole. Paul Otlet, a
member of the Union of International Associations in Brussels,
informed Le Corbusier about his aim of giving the League of
Nations a broader cultural mission; it was not politics alone, he
argued, that should be placed on an international level, but
culture as well. His idea was that the League should form a
world center of cultural cooperation, an institute where all
forms of civilization would be documented, compared, and
studied: "The idea is to create one point on the globe where the
image and meaning of the world may be perceived and understood; a point that may become a sacred shrine, inspiring and
coordinating great ideas and noble deeds."[11] The idea was not
entirely new, for as early as 1913, H. C. Anderson and E. Héb-
rard had published a project of a *Centre Mondial de Communications* ("World Center of Communications"). This proposal can
hardly have escaped Le Corbusier's attention.

The program of the Mundaneum foresaw a university, administrative offices, sports fields, conference rooms for international associations, and a "World Museum" situated in the
midst of open spaces reserved for temporary gatherings of the
continents, countries, and cities involved in the institute's
celebrations. This entire "Capitol" of humanity was to be located on a site not too far from the League of Nations Palace,
overlooking Lake Geneva. While it is not quite clear whether
this ambitious project was ever much more than the personal
dream of an idealist, it certainly met with Le Corbusier's enthusiastic response.

From the Temple of Wisdom to the Museum of Knowledge

Whereas the League of Nations project is in a way an updated,
secularized version of the Grand Palais in Paris, the design of
the Mundaneum evokes the imagery of a Mesopotamian ziggurat within its sacred precincts. This acropolis of cosmo-

politism and international collaboration (located just outside
of Calvin's Geneva, one of the birthplaces of modern capitalism) is dominated by a "World Museum" in the shape of
a step pyramid placed upon a platform from which two ramps
lead down to a large, rectangular court. Parallel to this "sacred"
core two additional, symmetrically designed systems of buildings and gardens are arranged, one of which (or so it appeared
in the final version of the project) has an axis leading down to
the shores of the lake (fig. 176).

It is tempting to speculate about the possible sources for
this extravagant project. Curiously, the most likely source of inspiration has never been taken into consideration. In 1925, the
architectural firm of Helmle & Corbett, New York, published its
reconstruction of Solomon's Temple, and the fame of this reconstruction, with the support of the spectacular renderings by
Hugh Ferriss, soon made its way to not only an American but
also a European public (fig. 174).[12] In fact, Le Corbusier could
not have found a more appropriate typological model for his
"World Center of Cultural Documentation" than Solomon's
"Temple of Wisdom" which had suddenly become available as
a clear-cut image through Helmle & Corbett's work.[13]

Le Corbusier's idealist roots and aspirations were so evi-
dent in the Capitoline aura of this building complex that the architectural left wing violently criticized the project as being
academic and reactionary.[14] Museums were of crucial importance in Le Corbusier's education, and this World Museum can
be regarded as the crystallization of his student years as an assiduous visitor to the Musée de l'Homme and the Musée
Guimet in Paris. He designed the project in the form of a promenade starting from the highest point of the ziggurat and descending toward its base. This promenade was divided into
three parallel naves, each devoted to a specific field of scientific
information, in such a way that it was possible to juxtapose the
artistic creations of man to historical facts and geographical
context at any point.

The library's main purpose was to promote contact between different peoples and cultures, and in addition to books
and documents, it also housed what Le Corbusier later called
"round books"—films, microfilm, and magnetic tapes. When,
in 1946–1947, he elaborated his proposals for the United

Nations headquarters in the United States, the recollection of the
Mundaneum served as a guide. It was the Mundaneum, too,
that started his fascination with electronics as a means of communication. When, toward 1960, he proposed the inclusion of a
"Museum of Knowledge" in the capitol area of Chandigarh, his
idea was to create a reservoir of knowledge in the form of films
and tapes that would give the deputies of the Punjab all the
necessary information about the country's problems such as
hunger, overpopulation, and industrialization. This way they
might, in his words, avoid the red tape, verbosity, and empty
phrases that paralyze institutions like the UN.[15] Needless to
say, the Punjab was no more in the position to build this "Temple of Wisdom" of the electronic age than the League of Nations
had been thirty years before.

Centrosoyuz and the Palace of the Soviets

Some ideas from the League of Nations project were eventually
carried out in Moscow where, in 1928, Le Corbusier won a
competition for the headquarters of the Union of Cooperatives
in the USSR (the "Centrosoyuz"; fig. 79).[16] The assembly hall of
this project is a reduced version of the Geneva auditorium prototype, and the facades of the office wings are the first large-
scale adoption of the "neutralizing wall" idea. Most surprising,
perhaps, is the lobby with its complex system of ramps; Le
Corbusier was adamant that the communication between the
ground floor and the first floor should take place by means of
ramps alone.[17]

The shape of the auditorium and the insistence on ramps
as the means of circulation within the buildings are the two
themes that Le Corbusier chose to develop further in his proposal for a Soviet palace. The result was a project that seems to
break away from his entire previous work, and especially its
elements of classical severity which had been particularly man-
ifest in the Centrosoyuz's main facade facing the Miasnitskaya.
One of the factors that facilitated this fresh approach was no
doubt that the new palace was planned to contain not offices,
but a huge cluster of meeting halls and auditoriums.

The USSR government had decided to celebrate the
achievements of the first five-year plan (1928–1933) through the

construction of a center for political meetings and congresses. Facing the Kremlin on the opposite bank of the Moskva, a new palace was to be built as a monument to young socialist Russia. Together with the Perret brothers, Walter Gropius, and Erich Mendelsohn, Le Corbusier was among the few Western architects to be invited to participate in the Soviet Palace competition.[18]

The program called for an exceptionally large building. Le Corbusier's project consists of six assembly halls, the design of which once again raises problems of acoustics and visibility (and here, too, Gustave Lyon contributed his calculations), but this time they are on a new scale. The large auditorium is planned to accommodate 15,000 spectators and no less than 1500 persons on the platform. The second assembly hall provides accommodation for 6500 persons; two further halls were for 500 each, and still another two for 200 persons each. On the outside, there are ramps and platforms to accommodate up to 50,000 participants during demonstrations and marches. Le Corbusier's sketches show the step-by-step development of the project, from a casual summation of the compound's individual requirements to the final, overall composition organized in terms of straight axial symmetry.[19]

The two large halls face each other like two gigantic, three-dimensional fans. Seen in plan (fig. 181), the project resembles an hourglass: the halls are connected by a kind of enclosed bridge which also serves as the central axis of the whole, and the smaller halls are arranged like leaves on a branch. A high wall, concave like a radar screen, is the focal point of the whole composition, and it is at this point that sculpture enters the scene. The immense, curved front wall of the large hall serves as the backdrop for mass demonstrations descending and ascending the huge ramps. The model of the project (now in the Museum of Modern Art in New York), reveals an affinity with the forms of crabs and oysters. To their inventor, these forms bore a resemblance to organic structures only inasmuch as they differed from traditional schemes,[20] but the zoomorphic character of this colossal skeleton brings to mind the surrealist animal and plant forms in Alberto Giacometti's sculptures of around 1930.

For the roofing of the large auditorium, Le Corbusier proposes an adventurous system of huge girders from which the acoustic shell is suspended as from the rays of a fan. The structural elements of this system are themselves hung by means of metal rods fixed to a huge parabolic arch that dominates the composition. This idea is directly based on Freyssinet's realizations such as, for example, the bridge at Saint-Pierre-du-Vauvray (1922) or the airplane hangars at Chartres (fig. 179).[21]

Viewed in the light of the Palace of the Soviets, Le Corbusier's earlier proposals for public buildings seem classical by comparison. In the Soviet Palace, in place of the earlier straight, symmetrical facades organized through regulating lines, we find shells and vast, concave glass surfaces, colossal girders stretched like the fingers of a hand from which the auditoriums and assembly halls are suspended.

What were the reasons for such a change? After 1928, when Le Corbusier traveled to Moscow to present his various Centrosoyuz projects, he was certainly impressed by the evolution of constructivist architecture. On the other hand, a number of his Marxist colleagues from the CIAM had labeled some of his earlier work—especially the Mundaneum project—as reactionary and formalistic. Through his project for Moscow, Le Corbusier set out to prove that the time had not yet come to rank him among the academicians. There is no doubt that he avidly studied the great constructivist projects that circulated in the magazines, for example the projects for the new theaters for Svedlorsk by G. and M. Barkhin (1930) or for Charkow by V. Gerasimov and S. Kravets (fig. 180) (1931).[22] The result of this study, however, is something rather different from Russian constructivism, precisely because of its organic and humanistic aspects.

But although his Soviet Palace project may have surprised and convinced his Russian friends, it failed to persuade the jury. Le Corbusier himself states the reasons for the official choice of Jofan's colossal neoclassical palace (fig. 182). Although he was by no means a friend of majority decisions in architectural matters, this time he regarded the jury's verdict as

reasonable in the context of the times. . . . A palace that, through its form and technique, expresses the modern spirit is clearly a product of a civilization in the process of conquering and not of a civilization in its beginnings. A beginning civilization like Russia requires for its people the substantial elements of flowering and seductive beauty: statues, columns and pediments are easier to understand than chaste, flawless lines that result from the solutions to problems of a technical gravity and difficulty previously unknown. Thus, at Moscow, it was a verdict of sagacious psychology. I repeat: I bow to the decision, I admit it. All the same, I am sorry.[23]

Diplomatic considerations may have influenced this realistic, and perhaps in part sarcastic, assessment of the relationship between avant-garde culture and official art in Russian society, since at the time it was written the project of the great CIAM meeting in Moscow was still up in the air, and there was nothing to be gained by sacrificing the remaining Russian "goodwill" to the ideals of Modern Architecture. Be that as it may, Le Corbusier's lucid conclusions are valid not only in the context of the Soviet Palace competition, for they also throw light on the mechanics of the painful and eventually frustrated struggle for a modern League of Nations palace in Geneva.

The UN Headquarters

It was World War I that brought about the League of Nations, and World War II was the reason for the establishment of the United Nations. Once again, Le Corbusier was determined to play a key role, and once again, the grand coup appeared to be just round the corner. In the meantime, however, the situation had changed: Beaux-Arts classicism was compromised, at least in Europe, through its association with fascism. Modern architecture was no longer the cause of a small intellectual elite, for in countries such as Holland, Sweden, and the United States, a large public had become familiar with its imagery. After 1945, an international organization committed to republican and cosmopolitan ideas could hardly have visualized its headquarters in terms of a neoclassical palace.

In May 1946, Le Corbusier returned to New York (where he had been some months previously) having been nominated by the French government as the delegate to a five-member commission in charge of finding an ideal site for the UN offices: it had been decided that the headquarters of the organization (which was founded on June 16, 1946, by the San Francisco Charter) would be situated in the United States. In a booklet entitled *UN*

Headquarters, Le Corbusier describes the situation; as he puts it
in a speech at the closing session of the "Permanent Headquarters Committee of the UN" on December 13, the search was "an
incredible journey into illusion and reality."[24] Vast sites on the
outskirts of New York, San Francisco, Philadelphia, and Boston
were under consideration. The idea was to build a "world
capital"—a universal center that would include, in addition to
the UN Secretariat and its Assembly Hall, an entire city for the
functionaries and employees of the organization, including a
world legislation center, an international library, headquarters
for international associations, and a "world museum." It really
seemed as if something akin to the Geneva Mundaneum was at
last becoming real, this time on a grand scale. The capital was to
be built on virgin soil for, to quote Le Corbusier, "to implant
the headquarters in the very shadow of the skyscrapers of Manhattan would be inadmissible."[25]

After several months spent examining all the possibilities,
a practical decision became imperative. A film showing a syn-
opsis of the commission's work was made to furnish "scientific proof" that the UN Headquarters must occupy an area
of 20 to 40 square miles, but the problem of where to find a site
for this "radiant city" of international bureaucracy remained
unsolved. According to Le Corbusier's calculations, the site
must be twice as large as Manhattan (which covers an area of 17
square miles, 11 of which are occupied by parks, parkways,
streets, docks, and factories). In December 1946, however,
when John D. Rockefeller, Jr., offered $8.5 million as a down
payment for the area between 42nd and 48th Streets on the
banks of the East River, Le Corbusier—in spite of his previous
megalomania—suddenly became convinced that this was the
right spot for the UN Headquarters. Now that the realization
seemed close at hand, the shadows of the Manhattan skyscrapers were no longer an insuperable impediment to the organization's flawless functioning. On the contrary, Le Corbusier
proclaims that with a building conforming to the concepts of
the "radiant city," the United Nations would usher in the urban
regeneration of Manhattan.[26] He took a quick look at the suggested site, and the very same evening he showed his first
sketches to his friend Tino Nivola, who lived on 8th Street, with
the words: "Here you are, it is all done."

His first sketches combine the Ville Radieuse imagery with the American reality of the downtown office building in the form of a slab (fig. 185). It is interesting to note that, as in Moscow (and later in Chandigarh), it was the sudden acknowledgement of the genius loci that gave his proposal its definite shape and that made it acceptable—or almost so—to its public. Le Corbusier's earlier vision of a Manhattan replaced by functionally integrated Cartesian skyscrapers[27] was virtually forgotten, and in its place was a realistic assessment of recent American work. He admired the PSFS building,[28] and it was no coincidence that Le Corbusier now pointed at the Rockefeller Center as a demonstration of the advantages of his proposal, and especially as an illustration of the futility of large open spaces beneath office towers! (fig. 156).

For a while, he seems to have taken it for granted that the UN would assign him the job, and late in January 1947, he was back in New York in order to work out his proposals. Two months later, he was joined by the other members of the ten-man team of experts: Oscar Niemeyer (Brazil), Sven Markelius (Sweden), and a group of lesser-known architects from the USSR, Belgium, Canada, China, Great Britain, Australia, and Uruguay.[29] Project "23A," which Le Corbusier had developed by the end of March 1947, easily became the working basis for this team (fig. 185).

The execution of the project, however, was assigned to a local architect, Wallace K. Harrison,[30] who had collaborated with Le Corbusier on project "23A" and also played an important part in the realization of the Rockefeller Center. Harrison's building (fig. 186) respects the outlines of the project "23A," but it lost much of the concept's original verve in the course of its technically elegant realization (fig. 186). Parts of Le Corbusier's idea seem to have been completely misunderstood, particularly with regard to the auditorium: to Le Corbusier, the "pie slice" form had a precise functional meaning, for the audience sits in the wide, raised part looking toward the pointed end of the hall. In Harrison's realization, however, the enormous, slightly streamlined back of the triangle merely contains an exaggeratedly large lounge, into which the assembly hall is painfully jammed. The project proved to be about "as easy as getting a mermaid into a pair of pants" and as successful.[31]

Seen within the context of Le Corbusier's biography, the UN building was just another episode in a long sequence of frustrated grasps for positions of command, an episode experienced and suffered by the architect as part of a Nietzschean tragedy: Harrison's takeover of the realization of the project seems to have hurt him like the betrayal of a friend.[32] There seemed to be no way of restoring his confidence—not only in Harrison, but in the United States at large. Le Corbusier's extravagant financial demands became notorious and when, in the fifties, Arthur Drexler, director of the Department of Architecture in the Museum of Modern Art in New York, wanted to organize a Le Corbusier exhibition, he was forced to abandon the idea because of the master's excessive claims.

The UNESCO Headquarters

The tragicomedy of the UN headquarters found its epilogue in the UNESCO headquarters, when the United Nations decided to locate the headquarters of their organization for education, science, and culture in Paris. For forty years, official Paris had ignored Le Corbusier, and he now hoped that an international organization would finally do justice to his genius. During the opening session of talks on the new palace the Brazilian delegate formally suggested Le Corbusier as architect. The rejoinder of the US State Department representative was: "Impossible." And since the United States played an important role in the financing of the project, this rejection was final.[33]

Some time later, Le Corbusier was elected with several of his friends from the CIAM (Walter Gropius, Sven Markelius, Lucio Costa, and Ernesto M. Rogers) to serve on the committee of five members entrusted with setting up the program for the project. His four partners readily admitted Le Corbusier's primacy, and Gropius did all he could to convince the UNESCO and the French authorities that Le Corbusier should be entrusted with the assignment. This, however, proved to be impossible since he had accepted membership in the committee of five; thus once again, his election on a commission proved to be the impediment to his realizing the project.

After this defeat, it was no easy task for Gropius to convince his friend to participate actively in the work of the committee. He achieved it, however, on May 13, 1952, and the day after Le Corbusier sent him a letter, at the bottom of which he added: "This is what Baudelaire wrote: 'Sois sage, ô ma douleur, et tiens-toi plus tranquille. . . .' Let us date this: UNESCO, Paris, May 13th, 1952."[34]

Ronchamp

Le Corbusier failed to become an official architect in Europe, and it is highly significant that the only institutional buildings he was able to complete in France were churches. This was made possible by a complex convergence of interests: a part of the French clergy interested in a spiritual reform of the church and a relative autonomy from Rome had established contacts with modern artists (including Léger, Chagall, and Bazaine) in order to bring about a long desired rejuvenescence of religious art in France.[35] Early in 1950, one of the protagonists of this cultural reform movement within the church, Pere Alain Couturier, suggested Le Corbusier as the architect of a new pilgrimage chapel to be built near Ronchamp, a few miles northwest of Belfort.

Le Corbusier's response to the proposal was cold. Only a few years previously, in 1948, his plans for the reorganization of an old subterranean sanctuary in Southern France (the caves of Sainte-Beaume, where Mary Magdalene is said to have lived) had been vetoed by the French ecclesiastic authorities (fig. 92).[36] The persistence of Lucien Ledeur, secretary of the Fine Arts Commission of the Archbishopric of Besançon, however, finally made him change his mind.

Architecture for Le Corbusier not only implied an attitude toward form, but also toward people, and it was a part of his personal tragedy that the ideal community for whom he longed to build either did not exist or refused to accept him as its architectural spokesman. In a way, after the sequence of debacles from the League of Nations controversy to the UNESCO headquarters, the Ronchamp commission seemed like a return to the humble facts of life after a long journey into Cartesian illusions. The atmosphere of pious devotion seemed to have struck a chord in Le Corbusier's rational soul. The *Livre de Ronchamp*, published by Jean Petit, celebrates the faith and

hope of the pilgrims who approach the chapel in long pro-
cessions as if it were a primeval sanctuary.[37] Thus, when a cor-
respondent of the Chicago Tribune asked, a few days before the
chapel's consecration, whether it was necessary to be a Catholic
to build such a church, Le Corbusier's answer was: "Get away
from here!"[38] "Your Excellency, when I built this chapel, I
wanted to create a place of silence, of prayer, of peace and inner
joy," Le Corbusier declared when he handed over the key of the
chapel to the archbishop of Besançon, Monseigneur Dubois,
during the consecration ceremony. "The feeling of the sacred
inspired our efforts. Some things are sacred, and others are not,
regardless of whether or not they are religious."

He tackled the problem first of all as a matter of "pure"
space—responding to the distant horizons which seemed to call
for an echo in terms of constructed form (fig. 202). In this context, Le Corbusier himself spoke of "landscape acoustics."[39]
The forms he finally came up with did equal justice to the practical purpose of the sanctuary and the evocative challenge of the
land. For large-scale celebrations, the ceremonies are held outdoors with the congregation facing the altar, which serves as
the focus of an open-air stage set. The interior, covered by a
mushroom-shaped roof, is large enough to accommodate 200
people. Following the shape of the hill, the nave of the church
inclines toward the east, and provision is made for small groups
of pilgrims in the lateral chapels which, like periscopes, receive daylight from above (fig. 105).

Many critics claim that Ronchamp is in "violent opposition" to Le Corbusier's previous work and ideas, if not in contradiction to the ideals of modern architecture as such. To quote

Notre-Dame-du-Haut is situated on the southern foothills
of the Vosges; to the south, beyond the Jura, the peaks of the
Alps can be seen when the weather is fine, and vast horizons of
forests and pastures recall the nearby ranges of the Jura mountains. Here, as early as the twelfth century, a statue of the Virgin
Mary was worshipped. Due to its strategic position, the hill has
time and again been the scene of bloodshed, and in World War
II, the neo-Gothic chapel on its summit was completely destroyed. A reconstruction seems to have been out of the question, and Le Corbusier was given total freedom to interpret the
program in his own terms.

Nikolaus Pevsner, "Le Corbusier has . . . changed the style of
his own buildings completely, and the pilgrimage chapel of
Ronchamp . . . is the most discussed monument of a new irrationalism."[40]

Yet Ronchamp is not entirely without precedents in the architect's earlier work. The theatrical, stage-set quality of its
"volumes in space" recall the solariums of the earlier villas, and
the thick, curved, inclined whitewashed walls with their irregular openings seem to emerge directly from the architect's
North African sketches of 1931 (figs. 206–208).

At the same time, the chapel owes something to the space
dynamics of modern sculpture (Gabo, Pevsner). The concrete
shell that descends into the nave, leaving a narrow slit between
the dark shell and the whitewashed walls—the roof resting on
the walls "like a hovering bird" and turning toward the outside like "an eye that is opening"[41]—is both an experiment in
structural engineering and a joke with "objets à reaction poétique." According to Le Corbusier, a shell he once found on
a beach in Long Island served as his inspiration.

Ronchamp's "irrationalism" is ultimately not a matter of
style, but of cultural commitment. The client had given the architect a free hand to abandon the established typology of sacred architecture—and the architect responded in terms of an
atavistic mysticism of nature. In Ronchamp, Le Corbusier finally realized the dream of a "sanctuary dedicated to nature"
that half a century previously had inspired the students of the
La Chaux-de-Fonds Art School. To quote Karl Ledergerber:
"Ronchamp's religious character does not result from the sacred
or the cultish. Here nature achieves a degree of reality that was
never attained by the sanctuaries of earlier periods."[42] Thus
Ronchamp is both more and less than a church: it is a religious,
but not a sacred building—if we accept Ledergerber's definition
of sacred as the political manifestation of religion, as opposed to
Le Corbusier's purely emotional distinction between things
which are sacred and others which are not.

Chandigarh's Capitol Complex

The palaces of the three powers in Chandigarh's Capitol Complex mark what is probably the climax of Le Corbusier's career

as a designer, for they represent the fulfillment, in many respects, of ideas and concepts that he had developed, questioned, and redefined during a long and partly obscure process
covering the whole of his creative lifetime. Like Ronchamp,
these palaces have their prehistory in Le Corbusier's earlier
work, not in an established imagery of monumental building.
They are indeed unique in their typological context.[43]

For all their originality, however, these buildings are very
much a part of the great theme of Chandigarh: the appropriation and transformation of older architectural and urbanistic
metaphors of rule by the new political establishment. This appropriation was carried out in terms of architectural ideals
that corresponded with some of the essential cultural beliefs
upon which the new society was built. The Capitol houses the
judiciary, legislative, and executive powers of the Punjab—or at
least it was for this purpose that it was designed.[44] But its powerful imagery aims at more than the mere glorification of a provincial government: it celebrates the recently established, independent rule of the young Indian nation (figs. 187–198).

This theme was not new in Le Corbusier's work and some
of his most spectacular projects had grown out of similar programs. The capitol of Chandigarh must be considered against
the background of never-realized palaces for the state and for
international associations such as the League of Nations and the
UN. The Mundaneum (1928–1929) is architecturally a clear anticipation of Chandigarh's Capitol (fig. 176), and it is no coincidence that some of this project's key concepts, such as the
"Museum of Knowledge," finally found their way into the
Chandigarh Capitol-project; and had it ever been realized, the
Palace of the Soviets (1931) would in many ways have been
to the USSR what Chandigarh's Capitol was to India: a grandiloquent symbol of the consolidation of a new, technology-
oriented political order (fig. 184). Finally, we have the example
of UN world capital project (1946), in which most of the typological elements of Chandigarh's palaces appear in a first draft.

The site of Chandigarh's monumental "head" does not lack
a sense of drama: embankments of rough earth in the foreground, hills stretching into the horizon, and scattered groups
of massive mango trees (fig. 187).

The High Court of Justice is shaped like a shade-producing box (figs. 52, 193). Colossal pillars support a succession of arches, and the audience halls are inserted between the pillars like a set of pigeonholes. The Parliament, separated from the Palace of Justice by a huge open plaza, is a square structure enclosing an open court. Above it, like the funnel of a liner, sits an incurvated cylinder (the Upper Chamber) and an irregular pyramid (the Lower Chamber). A huge gutter above the facade forms a portico (fig. 195).

The administration building (the Secretariat) is a slab structure 254 meters long and 42 meters high, vertically divided into three distinct parts. A rude symphony of sunbreakers, orchestrated according to the function and size of the spaces within, articulates the facade to which the ramps are attached like the handles of an enormous tool (fig. 190).

The High Court was the first building to be completed (it was inaugurated by Nehru on March 16, 1956). With its non-bearing arches undulating from pillar to pillar this enormous box forms a vast shelter that accommodates the audience halls.[45] To the left of the center, the construction opens onto an immense hypostyle. Originally, the pillars were whitewashed; after 1962, however, they were painted green, yellow, and red to prevent them from appearing weak in comparison to the sculptural drama of the Assembly's facade on the other side of the plaza.

The vastness of the plaza, however, has the effect of isolating the very elements of the monumental whole that it was meant to unify. A 400 meter glacis separates the High Court from the Assembly so that, together with the Secretariat, the Assembly forms an autonomous group linked by a system of ramps and passerelles (fig. 191).

The Secretariat (inaugurated in 1958)[46] displays its sunbreakers alternately in uniform rows and dramatically broken patterns; from the other side of the plaza, the building has the appearance of a wounded colossus (fig. 190). Next to it, the Assembly Hall forms what is no doubt the centerpiece of this Capitoline area. The basic idea upon which it was built, that of a huge shed with the two chambers suspended from the roof, had already been formulated some years before in connection with the World Capital project.[47] The first stages of the project show a great similarity of style to the slightly earlier Palace of

Justice: the northeast and southwest facades were to be orchestrated with a row of undulating arches.[48] But as work on the
project continued, the building underwent many important
changes. First, the Upper Chamber's meeting hall took on the
shape of a cooling tower that pierces the hall's roof like a huge
chimney, while the Lower Chamber emerges from the roof as a
huge tetrahedron. A group of cooling towers at the edge of
Ahmedabad, seen from the air in June 1953, seem to have provided the inspiration for this fresh start.

The incurvated parabolic cylinder, the swept-out pyramid,
the prismatic staircase—small and narrow, ascending skyward,
from where a frail footbridge leads to the slanted roof of the High
Chamber (fig. 106)—these robust forms would have visually
crushed the elegant arches of the facade underneath if built as
they appeared on the early plans. Thus here, too, Le Corbusier
decided to make use of the engineer's arsenal: an immense gutter, supported by a series of vertical blades, forms a portico
above the main entrance. Face to face with the High Court, the
Assembly building indicates an alternative to the fifties' preference for calmly merging volumes (figs. 193, 195). As in Ronchamp, all the elements of the High Court are orchestrating a
single, although complex, melody. The Assembly, on the
other hand, like La Tourette, is based on violent contrast: its
elements are not subordinated to an organic, palpitating whole
but are juxtaposed as parts of a sculptural conglomerate of powerful, clearly distinct, geometric gestures.

Chandigarh's political symbolism[49]
Between the League of Nations and the Capitol of Chandigarh Le
Corbusier's style underwent radical modifications. But a
basic philosophical implication of his architecture remained the
same. Both in the twenties and the fifties, it was the architect's
intention to create architectural machines to serve the purposes
of government and administration with the greatest possible
efficiency. In Chandigarh's Capitol, the forms claim to be born
out of practical needs: the canopy of the High Court is a colossal
shading and cooling device, with arches—undulating from pillar to pillar—inviting the winds to ventilate the structure. But
the complicated system of sunbreakers is not only functional, it
also serves to demonstrate the essential "biological" nature of
its heat controlling function. It is a manifesto of an architectural

language created as an answer to the reality of the subtropical climate, an air-conditioning apparatus defined in structural and architectural terms, with no mechanical help.[50] And the "Forum" of the Assembly is not only a cool and shaded interior but a veritable cathedral of shade, a celebration of crepuscular relief in the midst of the heat and glare of the surrounding plains (fig. 198).

Le Corbusier's style at Chandigarh is of a strongly (but by no means exclusively) symbolic and declamatory nature. So, after all, is its underlying program inspired as it is by its political background and circumstances. At Chandigarh, the aim of government was celebration and persuasion, not merely smoothly running administration and bureaucracy. Among the symbols cast in the concrete walls and knit into the tapestries of Chandigarh's palaces, the sign of the sun determining night and day on earth plays a central role (fig. 214). It summarizes the distribution of light and darkness, heat and coolness that is the basic theme of Chandigarh's architecture, and in a way it gives this theme the irrefutability of a cosmic law. But it was not only the architecture and the society that built it that is thus placed under the sun's command: in the Assembly building Le Corbusier transfers his sun symbolism from the area of private poetic mythology into the realm of explicit political symbolism. He revives the idea of the "roi soleil." The sun sign dominates the large enamel door to the Assembly—the ceremonial gate that opens once a year for the Governor of State.

Furthermore, the larger of the two chambers of the parliament is equipped for a mysterious solar ritual to be held each year, and its sculptural envelope, the cooling tower-type volume at the center of the building, suspended in the space of the "Forum" like giant entrails, and rising above the roof like a chimney, is topped by an oblique cover. Sculptural forms, reminiscent of the observatories of Jaipur (figs. 195, 197) and of Delhi, emerge on the slanted surface as a huge, vaguely cosmological still life. Le Corbusier explains: "This 'cap' . . . will become a true physics laboratory, equipped to ensure the play of light. . . . Furthermore, the 'cork' will lend itself to possible solar festivals, reminding man once every year that he is a son of the sun."[51] It was, then, to be a cosmological sanction of earthly power, as at Abu Simbel, where a sunray reaches into

the back of the mortuary cave and touches the forehead of the
Pharoah's effigy once a year. The scientific imagery of Siwal Jai
Singh's observatories is reinstated in terms of an archaic myth.

Lutyens and the Capitol of New Delhi

Without the Imperial Capitol of New Delhi in the background,
however, Le Corbusier would never have been able to accomplish at Chandigarh what he had dreamed of ever since 1927: a
monument to the machine age, its supposedly universal values,
and its political institutions. From the beginning the Capitol
was intended as the Indian answer to the Capitol of New Delhi
with its domes and colonnades, avenues and enormous squares
glorifying the British Empire (figs. 188, 194). Photographs cannot adequately convey the spectacle of grandeur this complex
must have offered when it was first built; what its monumentality may have signified to the Indian people is another matter.
To quote Robert Byron's report in the *Architectural Review*
(1931):

The road describes a curve and embarks imperceptibly on a
gradient. Suddenly, on the right, a scape of towers and domes
is lifted from the horizon, sunlit pink and cream dancing
against the blue sky, fresh as a cup of milk, grand as Rome.
Close at hand, the foreground discloses a white arch. The motor
turns off into the arterial avenue, and skirting the low red base
of the gigantic monument, comes to a stop. The traveler heaves
a breath. Before his eyes, sloping gently upward, runs a gravel
way of such infinite perspective as to suggest the intervention
of a diminishing glass; at whose end, reared above the green
tree tops, glitters the seat of government, the eighth Delhi,
four-square upon an eminence—dome, tower, dome, tower,
dome, tower, red, pink, cream, and whitewash, gold and
flashing in the morning sun.[52]

Twenty years after Byron's visit, Le Corbusier also pays his
tribute to the work of Lutyens and Baker: "New Delhi . . . ,
the capital of Imperial India, was built more than thirty years
ago, with extreme care, great talent, and real success. The critics
may say what they like; the very act of doing something forces
respect—(at least *my* respect)."[53] In fact, as Allan Greenberg
noted, Le Corbusier's early studies for the Chandigarh skyline
could easily double as illustrations for Robert Byron's description of Lutyens's palaces and domes: "The essential ingredients
are common—the picturesque skyline of government build-

ings, the flat intervening city, and the monumental connecting axis."[54]

In an early version of the Capitol project, established after the "pathetic soliloquy," the "battle of spaces fought inside the head," described later by Le Corbusier,[55] he seems to have envisaged a complex similar in scale to Delhi's palaces and domes. Later, as the program became more specific, the size was reduced and the symmetries within the complex (particularly the axial alignment of the Assembly with the High Court) were modified. Through all the stages of its development, however, the complex remained visually dominated by the Governor's Palace (fig. 196). This building, drastically overscaled in the initial stages of its planning, was designed to "crown the Capitol"[56] similarly to the way Lutyens's Viceroy's House crowned the city of New Delhi (fig. 194). Above the roof, a huge concrete clamp grasps into the sky (an abstract "open hand," as it were), similar in sculptural presence and symbolic overtones to the grandiose St. Pauls-type dome of the Viceroy's House. But there are more analogies. The gardens of the Governor's Palace, extending toward the city and toward the rear, are organized in terms of terraces and fountains, and the access roadways in terms of depressed channels serving the building on its cross axis. Lutyens's brilliant multilevel arrangements at and surrounding the Viceroy's House must have inspired this concept.[57]

The Governor's Palace, however, was never built. Nehru regarded the building of a Governor's Palace within the Capitol area unsuitable for a democracy.[58] It must be emphasized that Nehru took a lively interest in Chandigarh's Capitol, and his interventions were both numerous and—due to the government's important subsidies—decisive. Usually he supported Le Corbusier's proposals against the objections of the local officials; despite the Punjab's desire for a red carpet in keeping with the British House of Lords, for example, Nehru backed Le Corbusier's suggestion of a green carpet in the Upper Chamber and he insisted that the architect's tapestries remain in the High Court despite the fact that they were criticized as aesthetically unacceptable in some circles.

It was, in short, its dialectical commitment to continuity as well as to innovation that made Le Corbusier's city, and above all the Capitol, a symbol of the new state in the eyes of the Indian officials. In the words of Nehru in an address at the official inauguration of Chandigarh (1953), it is "the first large expression of our creative genius, flowering on our newly earned freedom . . . , unfettered by traditions of the past . . . , reaching beyond the existing encumbrances of old towns and old traditions," and even, finally, the "temple of new India." [59]

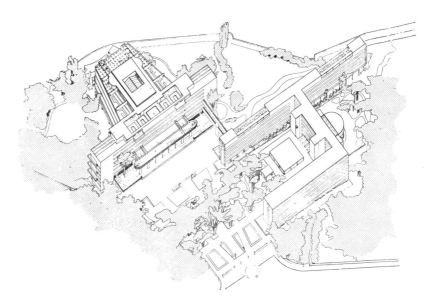

171. Le Corbusier and
Pierre Jeanneret, League of
Nations Palace, view of
project, 1927 (from *Oeuvre
complète*)

172. Hannes Meyer, League
of Nations project, 1927
(from C. Schnaidt, *Hannes
Meyer*)

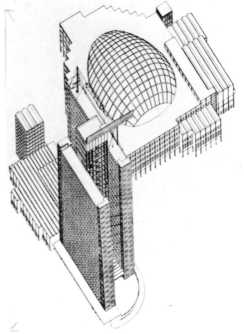

173. Le Corbusier views of
the exterior with Assembly
Hall of the League of Na-
tions Palace; presidential
pavilion (top) and interior
(bottom)

174. Helmle & Corbett, re-
construction of Solomon's
Temple, 1925 (from *Pencil
Points*, November 1925)

175. Le Corbusier, view of
the Mundaneum in Geneva
with ziggurat-shaped
museum (from *La ville
radieuse*)

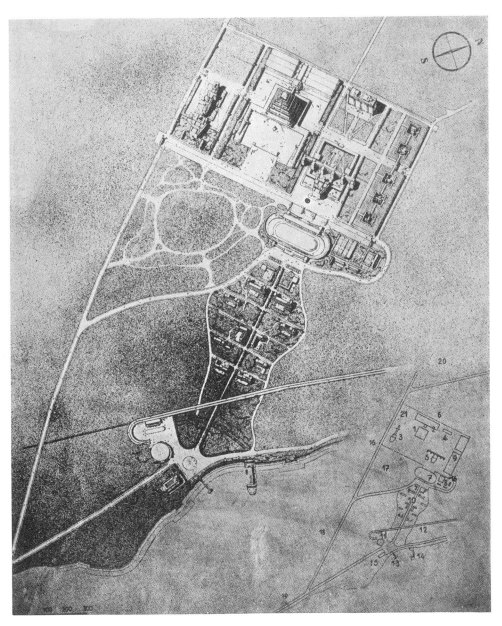

176. Le Corbusier and
Pierre Jeanneret, the Mundaneum complex in
Geneva, site view, 1929
(from *Oeuvre complète*)

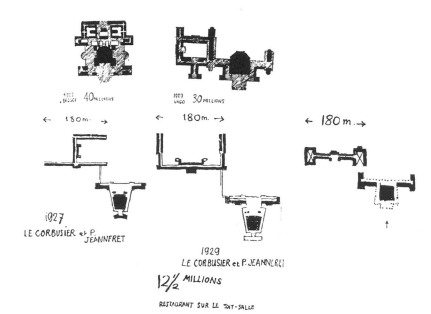

177. Comparison of projects
for the League of Nations
Palace

178. Geneva, the League of
Nations Palace as built in
1935–1936 (postcard)

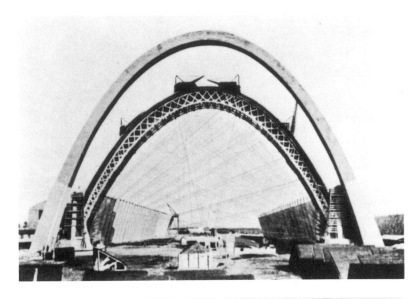

179. Eugène Freyssinet,
hangar at Orly, near Paris;
1916 (from S. Giedion,
Bauen in Frankereich)

180. Vesnin brothers, competition project for the theater at Charkov, 1930 (from
V. Quilici, *L'architettura del
costruttivismo*)

181. Le Corbusier and
Pierre Jeanneret, Soviet
Palace, 1931, schematic plan
(from *Oeuvre complète*)

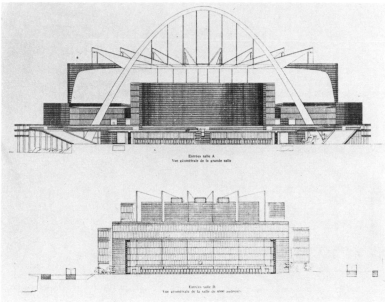

182. B. Jofan, project for a
Soviet Palace, Moscow,
1931 (from VH 101, nos.
7–8)

183. Le Corbusier and
Pierre Jeanneret, Soviet
Palace; large hall for 15,000
spectators (above) and
smaller hall for 6500 spectators (below) (from *Oeuvre
complète*)

184. Model of the Soviet
Palace project. Museum of
Modern Art, New York
(photo archives: W.
Boesiger, Zurich)

185. Le Corbusier, early
study for the UN Head-
quarters in New York, 1947
(project 23A) (from *Oeuvre
complète*)

186. UN Building in New
York (photo archives: W.
Boesiger, Zurich)

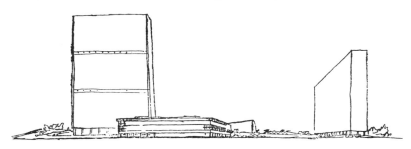

187. Le Corbusier, sketch of
Chandigarh with Capitol
complex at the city's
"head," ca. 1952 (from
Oeuvre complète)

188. New Delhi; aerial view
of the King's Way and
Capitol Buildings in the
distance (from Butler, *Sir
Edwin Lutyens*)

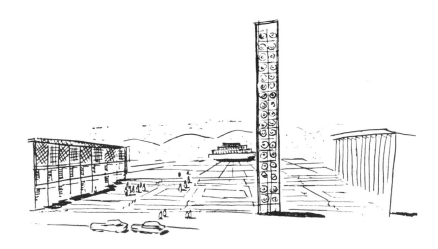

189. Matthew Nowicki, sketch of proposed capitol area in Chandigarh, with Assembly Building in the background, ca. 1950 (from N. Everson, *Chandigarh*)

190. Chandigarh; view from canopy of the High Court Building with Secretariat in the far distance (photo archives: W. Boesiger, Zurich)

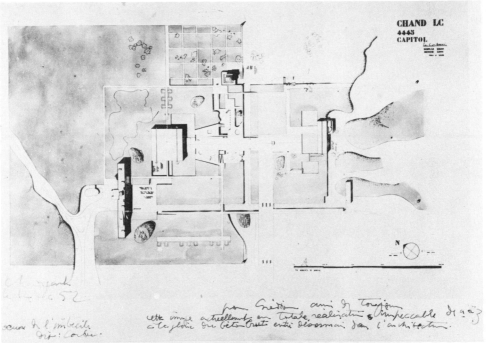

191. Chandigarh, view with mango trees from High Court toward Secretariat (left) and Assembly Building (right) (photo archives: Willy Boesiger, Zurich)

192. Le Corbusier, plan of Chandigarh's Capitol complex, 1952, with dedication for S. Giedion (courtesy CIAM, archives at the ETH, Zurich)

193. Le Corbusier, drawing
of the main facade of the
High Court Building over-
looking the Capitol Plaza
(from *Oeuvre complète*)

194. New Delhi, the Vice-
roy's Palace, 1920–1931;
architect: Sir Edwin Lut-
yens (from *Country Life*)

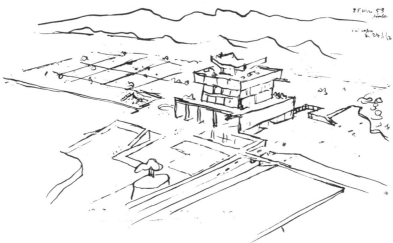

195. Chandigarh, the Assembly Building (photo: author)

196. Le Corbusier, study of proposed Palace of the Governor (from *Oeuvre complète*)

197. Jaipur, the Jantar
Mantar, astronomical ob-
servatory, built 1718–1734
(photo: author)

198. Chandigarh, Assembly
Building, interior hall
("forum") with "shell" of
the Upper Chamber (photo:
Pierre Jeanneret; archives:
Willy Boesiger, Zurich)

*"Il n'y a pas de sculpteurs
seuls, de peintres seuls, d'architects seuls. L'évènement
plastique s'accomplit dans une
forme une au service de la
poésie."*
Le Corbusier

*"There is no such thing as a
'pure' sculptor, a 'pure' painter
or a 'pure' architect. The
three-dimensional event finds
its fulfillment in an artistic
whole at the service of
poetry."*
Le Corbusier

"Synthesis" is a key concept in Le Corbusier's system of ideas.
The term appears in the opening sentence of the introduction to
the first issue of *L'Esprit Nouveau:* "There exists a new spirit: it
is a spirit of construction and synthesis guided by a clear concept."[1] This was immediately after World War I. Following
World War II, the moment for reconstruction seems to have arrived once more, and "synthèse" appears once again as a leitmotiv. On August 8, 1945, the newspaper *Volontés* published an
article entitled: "Towards a synthesis. The result of twenty
years dedicated to the search for a doctrine in the field of
building."[2]

It is clear that this concept of synthesis embraces not only
the arts but the machine age as a whole. The idea of the total
work of art, the "Gesamtkunstwerk," comprising painting and
sculpture under the aegis of architecture was only one aspect of
the problem. According to Le Corbusier, the physical environment of modern society should, in its totality, become a
"Gesamtkunstwerk" in harmony with the eternal and universal
laws of nature. The problem was to identify and organize these
laws in a way that would make them applicable to all design
problems—as Ruskin, the dominant theoretical influence in
Jeanneret's education, might have said. This search—which
later led into areas of Gestalt psychology, mathematics, and the
theory of proportions—culminated in the Modulor system
(1948).

It is interesting to note that while Le Corbusier's proportion system, the Modulor, was being established as a result of
his theoretical speculation, the terms "synthesis" and "unity"
were clearly directed again toward the arts. Thus once the Modulor had succeeded in organizing the general, ambiguous, and
utopian implications of synthesis and unity, it then became
possible to apply the words to the more practical and ordinary

problems connected with design, painting, and sculpture. Toward 1950, the idea of a "synthesis of the arts" summarized much of what an enlightened avant-garde expected from an improved culture. When the question of cooperation among the architect, painter, and sculptor was brought up at the CIAM congress in Bridgewater, England (1947),[3] Le Corbusier was most enthusiastic. In an article written a year later, he summed up his own aspirations in a single word: unity.[4]

There was certainly an element of revolt against the confusions of contemporary civilization in Le Corbusier's determination to build—a few years later—Ronchamp as a temple to the "arts," as well as in his attempts to restore architecture's long-lost commanding position in the modern environment (once again under the sign of synthesis): "Architecture is the synthesis of the major arts. Architecture is form, volume, color, acoustics, and music."[5] Compared to his earlier attempts at comprehending the machine age in its totality, this return to the traditional fine arts was not unlike a rearguard action against the assaults of such uncontrolled elements in the modern environment as electronics, advertisements, and traffic.

The Mobile Synthesis

Ronchamp epitomizes this retreat into the world of the fine arts. It also signals a breakdown of the borders that traditionally separated architecture from sculpture and sculpture from painting: the chapel is a painted sculpture on the scale of a building. Nevertheless, its amalgamation of categories did not really represent what Le Corbusier meant by synthèse des arts.

Le Corbusier's article "Unity" (1948)[6] shows that "synthesis" by no means implied a simple subordination of painting and sculpture to architecture. His problem was how to arrive at a basic consonance among the various manifestations of creativity and still allow building, painting, and sculpture to remain perfectly autonomous within the larger whole. Each of the three, he maintains, has its own poetic function and does not need the symphonic harmony of the "total work of art" for its justification.

During the twenties, Le Corbusier played with the idea of placing modern sculptures by artists like Laurens, Lipschitz, or

Brancusi at the focal centers of his monumental buildings.[7] In
the more modest scale of the home, however, a less grandiloquent approach was needed, and in 1939 he painted murals in
the house of his friend Jean Badovici at Cap Martin, choosing
locations where architecturally speaking "nothing happened"
(fig. 211).[8] This was also the case with the large mural in the
Swiss Pavilion at the Cité Universitaire, painted in 1949, which
was placed in one of the side rooms, a music and reading room,
where it does not interfere with the organization of the architectural spaces (fig. 212).

Thus the inclusion of painting in architecture did not necessarily lead to an artistic whole based upon an established
hierarchy of the arts. It was not subordination that counted,
but open, flexible combinations, a sort of "bricolage" of different art forms—a principle that is probably best illustrated
by Le Corbusier's concept of the muralnomade ("mural for
nomads")—the tapestry.[9]

Thus painting and sculpture remained accessories to architecture, and no unification of the respective formal lan-
guages was attempted, as was the case with the De Stijl movement or Russian constructivism. Painting and architecture remain autonomous fields, each with its own grammar of forms.
It is also interesting to note that Le Corbusier was always eager
to keep his activities in the different areas more or less strictly
separate. Although he adopted his pseudonym for his architecture as early as 1920, he continued to sign his paintings
with Jeanneret up until 1929. From 1923 until 1938, when his
paintings were shown for the first time at a large-scale exhibition in the Kunsthaus in Zurich, he kept quiet about his drawings and paintings since he feared—probably rightly—that an
architect who also painted would not be taken too seriously
by his colleagues or potential clients. As a result, it was only
his work in the fields of architecture and city planning that
were discussed in the first three volumes of his *Oeuvre
complète*.

The Architect/Painter

The fact that Le Corbusier left a large number of drawings, watercolors, paintings, and even sculptures in addition to his

architectural work is often regarded as a mere curiosity. To many critics, his painting was no more than a hobby, and in 1954, the large exhibition of his work at the Musée d'Art Moderne in Paris was received with mixed feelings by the Parisian press.[10] Nevertheless, Le Corbusier used to say that painting represented his visual laboratory—the field of experimentation for his architecture. "I am known only as an architect, and no one wants to recognize me as a painter, although it was through my painting that I discovered architecture."[11]

Historically, this is in a way true: as a student, he wanted to become a painter, but his master succeeded in making him an architect. Although he later referred to a work of 1918 as his "first painting," in fact he never completely abandoned his paintbrush and colors during his years at La Chaux-de-Fonds. Yet it was Ozenfant who encouraged him to paint on a regular basis.

Whereas during the purism period his "recherche plastique" as a painter had a strong scientific and experimental character and represented an official, public demonstration of a new, rational approach to art, the later work was more the result of an act of faith than a program (figs. 30–33). "A painter is determined. . . . Painting—his painting—puts him naked on the streets. Too bad!"[12]

Although Le Corbusier had for a while chosen to cultivate the image of the artist as a cool engineer of sensibility, he later came to think of his painting as a fundamentally private affair—an intimate dialogue with the drama of form and color and a struggle with the memories, fears, and joys emerging from the subconscious. It was, in a way, the revenge of the Bohemian individualist on the "homme type" of the machine age so eloquently championed in his architectural and urbanistic proposals. Although he offered his architecture and urbanism to the public as universal solutions to the supposedly universal problems of man, Le Corbusier retired into an area of privacy and seclusion through his painting; even his closest collaborators on the rue de Sèvres had no access to his studio on the rue Nungesser-et-Coli. True painting is not, he declared, meant for the general public, but only for the few who are able to recognize the adventure of their own subconscious in the painter's work.

While on the one hand, he was constantly engaged in trying to make modern architecture acceptable as a public art in
the service of the state, big business, and international organizations, when speaking of painting he displayed a fundamental
scepticism about the notion of "official" art created at the command of prelates or dictators. In a paper on "realism" he maintains that the authorities are inclined to use art as propaganda
for their own ends, while he feels that such an association "may
become either a happy or an unhappy experience for art . . .
but is by no means its destiny."[13]

The origin and development of Le Corbusier's painting, its
relationship to the intellectual and artistic circumstances of his
period and to the major currents of French painting since cubism have not yet been studied systematically. It is the painting
of an intellectual who was highly aware of Léger, Braque, and
Picasso. From the twenties on, Le Corbusier counted Léger
among his friends and owned several of his paintings; he must,
however, have been somewhat displeased at the relative indif-
ference shown by his friend to his architecture. On the other
hand, his meeting with Picasso on the building site of the
Unité d'habitation in Marseilles in 1950 was a great event. Le
Corbusier sent photographs of the meeting to several of his
friends, and he used one of them as the frontispiece of the
Oeuvre complète.[14] There is no doubt that he regarded Picasso
as the ultimate reference in the art world.

Displacement of Concepts

The concept of synthesis or unity in Le Corbusier's work refers
to the idea that the creative principles remain the same in all
areas of design and only the materials used and the functions to
be fulfilled vary. The further Le Corbusier's painting departed
from the straitjacket of purist aesthetics, the more clearly it
shows that for him the process of artistic creation was determined less by principles and programs than by a basically intu-
itive dialogue with the environment.[15] Le Corbusier's painting
was not a marginal occupation within his creative activity but
an intermediary area—a link, so to speak, between his private
and his public selves. It originated and developed in a field of
tension between everyday objects, both man-made and natural,

with all their symbolic potential, and a passion for clear-cut form with the clarity of an architectural draft. It is only possible to understand Le Corbusier's painting when it is seen as an integral factor of his artistic outlook; constantly exposed to the impulses from the sphere of the architectural work, it was trying to explore subconscious experience.

There is a clear formal kinship between some of the purist paintings and the architectural plans of the years 1925–1928. Later, under the influence of surrealism and the works of Braque, Picasso, and Léger, the analogies between Le Corbusier's pictorial patterns and architectural forms became even more striking. The impulses proceeded from painting into architecture and back again, or the other way around, and so there was a constant "displacement of concepts."[16] In other words, individual shapes or ways of organizing the surface were tried out in one area and then realized in the other. Le Corbusier himself explains how, in 1938, he adopted the proportional lines of an earlier painting (1929–1931) for the facade of his skyscraper project for Algiers.[17] There are, however, many more examples, and one is tempted to regard Le Corbusier's work as a continuous process of experimentation with formal themes, the content of which varied according to the pictorial subject matter or architectural program.

During the thirties, his obsession with wide, interwoven curves permeates not only his sketches of nudes but also his landscape drawings, some of his urbanistic projects (such as the Plan Obus), and his paintings—for example *Alma Rio 36* (figs. 199, 200). Then there are the periscope-like forms, a frequent motif in his paintings and sculptures of around 1945 (fig. 201). It is not difficult to trace their origin: in a number of figurative studies and paintings of around 1940 (when Le Corbusier was living in Ozon), he started off with the outline of a nude, emphasized certain outlines and finally arrived at a new and autonomous form. The resulting ear-like, or periscope-like, shape was the subject of his interest for years, as is demonstrated by a number of paintings.[18] Joseph Savina, a Breton cabinetmaker, often used this subject in his sculptures at Le Corbusier's suggestion. In connection with the polychrome sculpture *Ozon* (1946) (fig. 201), Le Corbusier remarked, "This type of sculpture belongs to what I call acoustic art; in other words, these forms emit and listen."[19] And it is in the chapel of Ronchamp, with its periscope-shaped shafts that absorb space and light, that this "acoustic sculpture" became an architectural theme (figs. 201, 202).

From *objets types* to *objets à réaction poétique*

Almost all the "objets types" of purism's established panoply are gathered together in the *Still Life with Stacked Plates* (1920): an open book standing upright on a table and viewed slightly from above; a pipe (seen twice), the head of which serves as the "navel" of the picture; a glass, shown partly in elevation and partly in plan; stacked plates fused into a single volume; bottles, the necks of which—like the pipes, glasses, and plates—are indicated by circles; and, finally, a guitar (fig. 32).

What is the significance of this passion for "objets types"?

In his early articles in *L'Esprit Nouveau*, Le Corbusier celebrates the grain silos, automobiles, liners, and other accessories of the machine age as materializations of pure form. In his paintings, too, the cult of ordinary objects of daily life appear first and foremost as a Platonic game with volumes in space. Here, however, it is considerably harder than it is in his Olympian discussion of the machine-age imagery to overlook the fact that these shapes are not pure forms for their own sake, but objects with specific evocative and poetic qualities derived from their use and the mechanical processes that produced them. The fact that Le Corbusier, at the time of *L'Esprit Nouveau*, was so eager to respect and even to reestablish the traditional iconography of cubist still life painting (rather than to proceed into abstraction) leads to the conclusion that this iconography must have been meaningful to him.

In the eyes of Ozenfant and Le Corbusier these glasses, plates, pipes, bottles, and guitars seem to have embodied the hard and timeless facts of everyday life (figs. 30–33, 206). By means of the pretended universality and straightforward intelligibility of its imagery, purism set out to break the "esoteric extravagance" of cubism and to lay the foundations of a new popular art. A. H. Barr is right when he notes that, in a way, the purists' goal was achieved not by their paintings but by Cassandre's brilliant posters for the French Tobacco Administration, the French railways, and the International Sleeping Car Company.[20] However, not only did purist aesthetics exert a

far-reaching influence upon the French advertising world in the
twenties, Purism itself owed much to the visual techniques
employed by the advertisements and posters of the time. As
editors of L'Esprit Nouveau, both Ozenfant and Le Corbusier
were familiar with the techniques of selling goods and services
by means of visual dramatization of the "objets" involved,
often presented in isolation on a neutral surface.[21]

The fact that the pictorial subject matter of Le Corbusier's
paintings is charged with meaning and—often ambiguous—
symbolism becomes even clearer after 1925, when stones,
shells, fruit, pinecones, ropes, and bones were introduced
into his vocabulary. Le Corbusier called them "objets à réaction
poétique." Pebbles, shells, bleached-out bones from the slaughterhouse (fig. 204), and other curiosities first appeared as slightly surrealistic knickknacks arranged on the furniture of the
Pavillon de l'Esprit Nouveau.[22] This was in 1925, the year in
which Max Ernst finished his series of plates entitled Histoire
Naturelle, reinventing, as it were, the morphology of nature on
the basis of a fantastic and surrealistic transformation of shapes
and patterns from the world of plants and animals. In his paintings of the following years, Le Corbusier increasingly played
with surprising relationships and contrasts between natural
and man-made forms, introducing a sense of "object magic"
reminiscent of Dadaism or the Italian "pittura metafisica."

Words like sky, sea, rock, street, table, bread, door, or
house conjure up the horizons of experience that were from
then on part of Le Corbusier's pictorial subject matter. "The
words of painting can only be massive, have a complete meaning and express a notion rather than a quality."[23] Thus he did
not aim at the careful reproduction of such realities but at the
evocation, by as massive as possible a signalization, of the fundamental notions which the consciousness attaches to these
realities. It was an art of signs and signals: "Signs that appeal to
old notions, settled and established in our minds, worn-out like
phrases from the catechism and uncovering a fruitful series of
automatisms."[24]

The human form

In addition to the "objets," there was another theme that com-
manded Le Corbusier's interest toward the end of the twenties: the human figure. During the thirties, it became the main

theme of his paintings. In fact, this subject had interested him
since before 1918, the official beginning of his career as a
painter. Ozenfant's comments on Jeanneret's pre-purist
endeavors were accurate although, as usual, somewhat
condescending: "He amused himself by painting a few hu-
moristic, caricatural, somewhat Viennese and extremely baroque gouaches. His preference was for brothel scenes with
fat women."[25] Naturally enough, purist morals soon put an
end to such frivolity, and Le Corbusier said later that it was
in Algiers that he discovered the beauty of the female nude
"thanks to the three-dimensional structure of certain Casbah
women under the intense and many-hued light of Algiers."[26]
Jean de Maisonseul, director of the National Museum of Fine
Arts in Algiers, showed Le Corbusier round the Casbah during
his first visit to Algiers in the spring of 1931, and he relates:

Our wanderings through the narrow streets of Algiers brought
us at the end of the day to the rue Kataroudji, where he (Le Corbusier) was struck by the beauty of a Spanish girl and a very
young Algerian girl. They led us up a narrow staircase to their
room, where Le Corbusier sketched them in the nude. I was
amazed to see that he was using the graph paper of a school
notebook and colored pencils for these very precise and realistic
drawings, which he considered poor and did not want to show.
He drew either the Spanish girl alone, or the two of them together.[27]

De Maisonseul also recalls his surprise at seeing Le Corbusier
buying postcards showing nude natives in flashy colors against
the background of an Oriental bazaar at a kiosk on the Place du
Gouvernement.
    After his return from Algiers, Le Corbusier made numer-
ous drafts on tracing paper which he then superimposed on the
original Algerian sketches, thus gradually defining the outlines
(figs. 206–208). For years, he had dreamed of a monumental
painting of three nude women, and he had made several studies from the *Women of Algiers* by Delacroix.[28] His own, final version of this group was completed in 1938, not coincidentally,
just one year after Picasso's *Guernica*, which probably gave him
the idea of working in monochrome. He projected the final
drawing on a wall of Jean Badovici's house at Cap Martin and
transcribed the black outlines on the white plaster (fig. 211).

Although the graffito at Cap Martin bears a clear relationship to the figurative scenes of Picasso's classical period, the
pictorial method owes little to Picasso and cubism and goes
back to the purist concept of "superimposed planes." In a way,
the *graffite à Cap Martin* represents a farewell to purism and its
cold, elegant idealism. The other nudes painted by Le Corbusier at this time no longer have the gracious, almost mundane air of the purist still lifes; instead they dramatize the
elementary conditions of existence: "I seek the savage, not
to find his barbarism, but to judge his wisdom. America or
Europe, peasant or fisherman."[29]

Le Corbusier's figurative work does not celebrate man as
an abstract, archaic idol in the way that Léger's does. Léger
painted heads, not faces; bodies, not individuals. In contrast,
Le Corbusier's women are by no means mechanical dolls. Faces,
hands, and feet are convulsive and exaggerated means of expression; often the face is contorted into a grin: a mask revealing a psychic abyss. Hands and feet are submitted to distortions
and convulsively twisted to become, at last, a part of the overall
ornament of the composition. A sense of parody and pathos,
despair and frantic vehemence permeates these works.

Like his architecture, Le Corbusier's painting evidences
two extremes: on the one hand, symphonic harmony of forms,
and on the other, a crowded montage of heterogeneous elements. On many of his paintings after 1930, monstrous forms
and compact heaps of stacked arms and legs, often desperately
compressed between roping and all sorts of objects, reflect a
convulsive state, a crisis.

There are more relaxed visions of existence: in the magnificent *Alma Rio 36*, painted in 1949,[30] a symphonic rhythm of
outlines and an interplay of depths and heights seem to evoke
memories of rivers, peninsulas, mountain ranges, and hills, as
if Le Corbusier were contemplating nature from very close and
from a lofty distance simultaneously (fig. 200).

A bird's eye view
As its title suggests, the painting *Alma Rio 36* refers to Le Corbusier's trip to Rio de Janeiro that he made in 1936. In addition
to architectural plans, he made many drawings on that journey,
and he recalls in particular a dinner at Copacabana where he

made sketches "since it is so pleasant to draw the beautiful shoulders of women in Rio."[31]

But the sweeping curves of the painting also recall the Corbusian projects for the urbanization of Rio (1929, 1936), not to mention the Plan Obus for Algiers (fig. 199). Such urbanistic concepts could only have been dreamed up in an airplane. The large coastal outlines of South America and Africa with their curving rivers actually became for Le Corbusier the starting point of a new urbanism intended not only for the eyes of man on the surface of the earth, but with a definite concern for the "fifth facade" to be admired from above. He describes the "lesson" of the airplane with great eloquence: "From the plane I have seen landscapes that might be termed cosmic. What an invitation to meditate, what a reminder of the earth's fundamental truths."[32] And during a flight over the Atlas Mountains in 1933 he wrote,

The flight of a plane provides a sight that teaches a lesson—a philosophy. It is not a mere sensual delight. From five feet above the ground, flowers and trees assume a proportion, a measure related to human activity, to human proportions. What is it like, in the sky, from above? It is a desert with no relation to our thousand-year-old ideas, a fatality of cosmic advents and events. . . . I can understand and measure it, but I cannot love it. I feel that I was not made for the enjoyment of this view from above. . . . The non-professional who flies (and knows nothing) is led to thought. He finds a refuge only within himself and his works. But once he is down on the ground again, his aims and intentions will have achieved a new dimension.[33]

A few years later, in 1939, Antoine de Saint-Exupéry summarizes his flight experience in the following words:

Thus we are changed into physicists, biologists, surveying these civilizations which embellish valley bottoms and sometimes, miraculously, spread out like parks when the climate is favorable. Here we are, judging mankind on a cosmic scale, observing man through our portholes, as through a microscope. Here we are rereading our history.[34]

But Saint-Exupéry also experiences the world aloft as a world unrelated to human destiny; after describing a cyclone, he adds: "It would certainly have been more of a thrill if I had told you the story of an unfairly punished child."

To both Le Corbusier and Saint-Exupéry, the view from an airplane meant alienation from nature's sensual proximity, from the direct contact with shrubs, flowers, people, daily problems, and age-old customs, while at the same time offering a kind of initiation into the cosmic laws that govern the universe. In a way, the flight experience both stimulated and confirmed Le Corbusier's paradoxical relation to reality, his obsession with absolute and universal laws that exempt the creative mind from close-up observation and empirical analysis.

Terrestrial and cosmic symbols

Le Corbusier's description of the "words" of painting, which can only be "massive, have a complete meaning and express a notion rather than a quality," does not merely indicate a surprising rapprochement of art theory and the techniques of advertising. This search for an elementary language of heraldic forms symbolizing the essential values in which a community of men is able to recognize itself and its spiritual aims was the dream of Le Corbusier's youth. It is perhaps not surprising that, at Ronchamp, Le Corbusier was struck by the evocative power of the crucifix. He relates how it was set up on the hill:

Breaking the silence of the walls, it proclaims the greatest tragedy ever to have taken place, on an Oriental hill. . . . When Bona hoisted the cross onto his shoulder and bore it through the middle of the nave behind the altar, it was a sudden moment of pathos. Even to the point that the workmen started joking so as not to be suffocated.[35]

For Chandigarh, Le Corbusier invented a whole catalogue of symbols to be cast in the concrete walls of the city's palaces and woven into the tapestries decorating its ceremonial chambers (fig. 214). The subjects were taken from his sketchbooks: the mango tree, the sacred cow, the Indian buffalo—and the Modulor man with his left arm outstretched. Hands are also present, and footprints, snakes, lightning, clouds, the sun and moon, the carriage wheel borrowed from the national arms of India, scales—the symbol of justice—and the Corbusian symbol of the sun's daily course.[36]

Many of these heraldic signs are now part of the decorative and symbolic imagery of Chandigarh's palaces. There is in turn a reasonable hope that the blown-up trademarks symbolizing

Le Corbusier's architectural mythology (that is, the sign of the Modulor, the "harmonic spiral," the "tower of shade," etc.)—a rather curious parade of devotional art planned to be displayed in a "ditch of contemplation" in the Capitol complex—will never be realized. It is even possible to detect an element of uncertainty in Le Corbusier's comments on this ritual display, for he was rarely so eager to credit one of his collaborators—in this case Jane Drew—with the original idea.[37] No doubt the most powerful sign among these monuments would have been the "monument of the open hand," for it transcends, in its evocative simplicity, the idealist abstraction of the other elements of this private Decalogue (fig. 213).

The open hand
The iconographic premises for the symbol of the open hand lay in Le Corbusier's work as a painter. In his paintings of the thirties, the human form was apt to get its hands and feet entangled—so much so that the hands tended to stand out of the pictorial context and become a sort of magic sign. A picture painted in 1930 and entitled *La main rouge*, shows the hand in an imploring gesture comparable to the prehistoric palm prints of Pech-Merle and El Castillo (fig. 209).[38] Later on in Le Corbusier's work, the hand appears sometimes convulsively knotted and sometimes in a declamatory or affirmative gesture, for example in the project for a national monument for Vaillant-Couturier (1938).[39]

On the fresco of the Swiss Pavilion in Paris, a winged female creature is placed floating above a landscape of transparent geometric and organic forms, its right wing lightly supported by a large, half open hand (fig. 212). By the side of this hand, Le Corbusier wrote: "Garder mon aile dans ta main" [Keep my wing in thy hand]—the last line of the first verse of Stephane Mallarmé's poem "Autre éventail de Mademoiselle Mallarmé."[40]

O rêveuse, pour que je plonge
Au pur délice sans chemin,
Sache, par un subtil mensonge,
Garder mon aile dans ta main.

At Chandigarh the symbolism of the hand eventually transcended the private sphere and became a public icon. Long be-

fore the construction of the city had begun, the sign of the
"open hand" had become the trademark of the town and the
values it set out to represent. The motif first appeared in a
sketch of 1948,[41] but Le Corbusier had played with the idea long
before. In 1936, he described the growth of a tree and the yearly
multiplication of its branches through the image of the open
hand: "A mathematically measured action of the branches
which open up each spring into a new open hand."[42] In fact,
the open hand can justifiably be interpreted as an ideogram of
Le Corbusier's ethos, a crystallization of his vision of the
creator as a prophet who must suffer in order to bring about the
rejuvenation of mankind. "With full hands I have received;
with full hands I give" was his caption to numerous reproductions of the *main ouverte*; and, in the final analysis, his source
was Nietzsche: "I should like to give and to share until the wise
rejoice once again in their folly and the poor in their riches."[43]

There can be no doubt that the memory of Zarathustra
served, unconsciously, as an inspiration—the lonely saint in
the woods, descended from the mountains and declaring "I love
mankind" and "What! did I speak of love! I bring a present
to mankind."[44] Zarathustra himself spoke of the open hand:
"This, in fact, is the hardest task of all: to close, out of love, the
open hand and maintain, in the act of giving, one's shame."[45]

Thus the open hand throws light upon a private, though
highly political myth: the vision of the lonely creator as saviour.
However, Le Corbusier was also eager to win acceptance for
this symbol as a metaphor of what Chandigarh, "the temple of
new India" stood for. In a letter to Nehru, he mentions the fundamental role of technology in building up a new solidarity
among men:

India was not obliged to live through the century, now past, of
the problems of the first machine age. . . .
India may value the idea of placing the symbolic and evocative sign of the open hand among the palaces that will house the
institutions and authority of the Capitol of Chandigarh at present under construction: open to receive the newly created
prosperity, open to distribute it to its people and to others. The
open hand will confirm that the second era of the machine age
has begun: the era of harmony.[46]

This commitment to technology as the premise of a new and

universal social harmony may have sounded very familiar to Indian ears, for the belief that technology would be able to create a universal brotherhood of man, to enable men to understand each other at long last, and to guarantee peace on earth once and for all is at least as old as the Victorian age that played such a great part in shaping the Indian infrastructure. The fact that technology in India in the nineteenth century turned out to be a servant not so much to the brotherhood of men but to British imperialism is another matter.

The framed view

Doors and windows are accessories of daily experience, and it is interesting to note how often they serve the spatial drama of Le Corbusier's paintings. He hardly ever depicts or even suggests a view into the far distance without framing it—as if space could only become a sensual experience if seen through the partly obstructive spectacles of a foreground.

Again, it is a principle for the organization both of pictorial and architectural space. Visually and spatially the oppressive narrowness of the Unité d'habitation's apartments "live" from the distant view that opens up from the inside. It is possible to recognize the painter in the way that Le Corbusier the architect used to arrange his windows:[47] to him, the landscape is not something that floods in from all sides and is present everywhere in the house (as is the case, for example, in Mies van der Rohe's glass architecture). He usually contrives to frame the view as he would frame a painting. He regards the landscape as an element of surprise to be measured out in small doses—a sudden vista inviting the countryside into the house, rather like setting up a painting on an easel. In a booklet about his small house on Lake Geneva, Le Corbusier states that even the most beautiful of landscapes becomes boring when it is always present:

Have you noticed that under such conditions one no longer looks at it? To make the landscape interesting, one must take the radical decision to limit it, to give it certain dimensions: to occlude the horizon by raising the walls, and to reveal it through gaps at strategic points. . . . We made a square hole in the south wall, in the interest of proportion. . . . Suddenly the wall stops and the view appears: light, space, this water and these mountains. . . . Now we have it![48]

One may, once again, think of the Villa Savoye, where the stage-set of straight and curved walls framing the solarium provides a key example for this kind of spatial manipulation (fig. 74). From the ramp approaching the solarium the eye is guided to a large rectangular opening in the eastern enclosure of the roof garden. A window, cut in the wall at the spot where the view spreads over the Seine valley—a Claude Lorrain landscape, but "real."[49] The selection and fragmentation of vistas from the roof of the Beistégui-penthouse is deliberately fancy, and here, the inspiration from surrealism, or perhaps more immediately from the pittura metafisica of Giorgio De Chirico is not to be discarded.

Yet the theme is not new. Free-standing walls limiting terrace roofs and gardens seem to have interested Le Corbusier during his Oriental trip of 1911;[50] but there are other possible references in Western architecture, for example, that of Italian Mannerism. That which characterized the Mannerist practice of the "framed view" (for example, the one-time enclosure of the Farnese gardens on the Palatine hill with its openings offering glimpses into the Forum) was also characteristic of Le Corbusier. Unlike architects like Frank Lloyd Wright or Richard Neutra, he hardly ever showed any interest in establishing a close contact with the immediate environment of lawns and shrubs. Le Corbusier preferred to keep his distance in order to achieve a total grasp of the great panoramic vision.

Even the narrow slits of Ronchamp (fig. 217) become more comprehensible when seen in the context of Le Corbusier's use of the window in his earlier buildings. It is hardly possible to ignore the pointedness of his remarks about Léger and his stained glass windows at nearby Audincourt when he states in his commentary on Ronchamp: "These are not stained glass windows: Le Corbusier regards this method of lighting as being too definitely attached to out-dated architectural concepts, and to Romanesque and Gothic art in particular."[51] The colored windows in the thick south wall of the chapel, by no means form a luminous wall as in a Gothic cathedral; they are isolated, rectangular holes that free the view to the outside. Through these "portholes," the sky and clouds penetrate the architecture, not so much as a visual background than as a poetic element, a cosmic dimension in depth.

It is no wonder that doors and windows play an important role in Le Corbusier's painting. In his *Still Life with Stacked Plates* (fig. 32), the door is depicted as open, barely visible at the rear of the room: and in later paintings, the open door becomes an essential element of spatial and poetic organization. In order to understand what the opening of a door means to Le Corbusier, it is useful to refer to his commentaries on his own buildings. In Madame de Mandrot's house (1930–1931) near Toulon, he once again considers it important to introduce the landscape into his architectural setting as an element of surprise: on the side with the most beautiful view over the plain, the walls are totally blind. "The rooms facing the view have been walled up, and a door has been put in, opening onto a terrace from which the scenery bursts in like an explosion."[52]

In the painting entitled *Léa* (1931), several objects are gathered together on a folding table (fig. 216): the magnified cross-section of a bone, the grossly simplified outlines of a guitar, and a glass. In the background is an open door, and a huge oyster floats in the shade. Le Corbusier's paintings never present a view onto a calm landscape. They never show light flooding in and transforming the interior of a room (as is often the case with Picasso's post-cubist paintings), nor do they present a dynamic articulation of space through color, as in Delaunay's *Fenêtres simultanées*. This artist was interested in depicting not a state, but dramatic action—a door or window flung violently open by a gust of wind.[53]

It is not surprising that views from windows play such an important part in Le Corbusier's perspective drawings, as in the project for the *Ferme radieuse* (fig. 215) (1934), nor does it come as a surprise to find the open window used as a poetic parable in his writings: "Let me open the window to the infinite horizons of art."[54] And finally, it is also by means of the image of a window that he circumscribes the mysterious: "Mystery is a profound opening before the soul which longs for space."[55]

Design and color

The "objets types," the sweeping curves of his nudes, the gesture of the open hand, or the spatial magic of a window intelligently cut into a wall: the Corbusian imagery pervades both his painting and his architecture. Yet the unity of his work is not only dependent on overlapping formal ideas and themes: it is also a question of method. Le Corbusier was an artist who believed in drawing and who liked to present his ideas in clearcut graphic formulas. He later quoted the words of his master L'Eplattenier, who said to the sixteen-year-old Jeanneret: "You are not gifted as a painter . . . just draw, that's enough!"[56] It could be argued that L'Eplattenier was right. In any case, Le Corbusier's obsession with drawing as *the* medium by which to see, measure, and understand his environment remained with him during his whole lifetime: "One draws in order to penetrate, and to incorporate what one sees into one's own history."[57]

Thus, when painting, he always began with a drawing and hardly ever with a combination of colors. He needed the security of a clear conceptual basis as a springboard for his imagination. In his youth, he may have read Charles Blanc's phrase: "drawing is art's male sex, color its female sex"[58]—a phrase that summarizes four centuries of academic art theory. Le Corbusier's paintings provide various illustrations of this dogma of the priority of drawing over color, for example the *Still Life with Stacked Plates* of 1920 (fig. 32). This painting exists in two versions, one of them in the La Roche Collection at the Basel Art Museum and the other at the Museum of Modern Art in New York. The composition, the *disegno*, is almost identical in both versions, but the colors and the tonality are totally different: whereas the Basel painting is dominated by cold tones—steel-blue, dark green, brown, and gray—the New York version is characterized by warm tones—light pink, yellow, and sky-blue in the background; the guitar is beige-pink, and the book is ultramarine blue. What other French painter would have thought of handling outlines and color as if they were independent phases of the creation of a painting? It is no coincidence that Le Corbusier's theoretical rationalization of this phenomenon is reminiscent of Blanc: "The idea of form comes before that of color. . . . Form is predominant, color merely one of its accessories."[59] About forty years later, Le Corbusier again describes the methodology of the pictorial process: "To make (a painting), take a canvas or board, trace the design onto it, take the color and spread it with the paintbrush. The reward for extensive preliminary work is that there is no need to search for anything on the canvas. You can express acquired ideas, you can execute."[60] And then there comes his definition of painting: "actually no more than the time required to spread a thick layer of paint."[61]

Fortunately, many among Le Corbusier's paintings are considerably more subtle than his statements about the medium. In fact, he was often seduced by the interplay of colors and shades, and his softly nuanced pastel sketches of the purist years, the pen-and-wash-tint drawings of the thirties, and many of the watercolors made in Ozon during World War II reveal him as a highly sophisticated colorist. He liked to treat the framework of the drawing and the application of the color separately. In his later years, however, he constantly quoted from his own previous oeuvre, reusing the graphic formulas of his earlier works, juxtaposing them with new color patterns, or changing and transforming them until a new form emerged—incidentally a method practised constantly by the architect. This method was the origin of the "Taureaux" series: as Le Corbusier sat in an airplane bound for India, a reproduction of a still life made between 1927 and 1940 was placed on his knees, tilted at a 90 degree angle. Le Corbusier took hold of his pen and drew what he saw, and thus bases of bottles became transformed into bulls' horns (fig. 218).[62]

Architecture in Color

In the twenties, color photography was not yet used in architectural magazines; as a result, there is a tendency to think of early modern architecture as a story in black and white. In fact, however, color was an important element for almost all the protagonists of the modern movement. During World War I, Léger and Trotsky had indulged in long discussions in Paris on the polychrome city of the future; later, Léger stated that it was possible for color to transform a home into an "elastic rectangle."[63] When Le Corbusier used color, it seems as if he wanted to add spatial elasticity to a given form. Probably influenced by the De Stijl exhibit at Léonce Rosenberg's, he used large colored surfaces in the interior of the Villa La Roche. At the workers' housing project of Pessac, color became a means of orchestrating the exteriors, with the street facades alternately

white and brown and the side facades pale green and white—
the same colors that he used in his paintings made in those
years. The idea was to "consider color as a space-bringing element";[64] colors clashing at the edge of a house annihilated its
volume and transformed it into a system of colored surfaces,
sky-blue projected the silhouette of the house into the sky,
whereas pale green blended with the spring foliage.

Two years later, in 1927, Le Corbusier sent a sample of
wallpaper to his assistant Alfred Roth in Stuttgart.[65] On the
back he had pasted other pieces of paper and color specimens as
models to be used for the polychrome facades of the two Weissenhof houses. (In the spring of 1968, the two houses were re-
painted according to the original color specifications.) Compared with the brutal elementarism of color displayed at the
same time by Bruno Taut at his house within the Weissenhof,
Le Corbusier's polychromy has a mundane, elegant, and "Parisian" touch. "Space, sky, sand, velvet"—these are a few of the
names given to the colors in his Salubra wallpaper catalogue[66]
—that is, the world of Parisian haute couture.

After 1945, Le Corbusier's use of color was different. Instead of delicate pastel shades, he now shifted to the primary
colors—red, blue, yellow, and green. But these colors were no
longer painted on the exterior walls. Raw concrete was king.
In the Unités d'habitation, the partitions of the loggias were
polychrome, and the colors scintillated like skin through a veil.
The modest whitewash, the white of the Aegean vernacular,
dominates at Ronchamp (fig. 136). One of the chapels is bathed
in glowing red, and right next to it the wall is dark violet, the
color of Lent. It is only at the Zurich Pavilion (1967) that color is
used again for the exterior, on the enameled steelplates of the
"corps de logis" (fig. 91): a kind of playing-card house, perhaps
a not inappropriate image for an exhibition pavilion.

Idea versus Craftsmanship

Beyond the problem of design and color, yet closely related to it,
there is a more general question: What is Le Corbusier's concept
of the relationship between project and realization? Does he regard the essence of architecture as a drawing board project in-

spired by the hand of genius, or does he consider it to lie in the quality of professional and artistic execution?

The problem is anything but new, and its terms were stated by Leon Battista Alberti in the fifteenth century: "It is possible to create either in thought or imagination perfect forms of buildings without paying any attention to the material."[67] Alberti considers the realization of a work of architecture as a secondary problem, as no more than the mechanical transcription of the plans into a different dimension. In fact, he himself used to control the execution of a project by means of correspondence, for example with his collaborator Bernardo Rosselino.

Le Corbusier's attitude is comparable to Alberti's: he too tends to regard architecture as a conceptual matter to be resolved in terms of a perfect plan, whereas questions of execution are of secondary, merely technical relevance. He even considers the relationship of the project to the site to be of secondary importance, and the plans for his parents' house on Lake Geneva (1924) were ready before a site had even been found. In fact, most of his projects were not bound to any particular location.

Perhaps more important is the fact that, despite the structural determinism implicit in his "five points," Le Corbusier's choice of materials turned out to have little real impact upon form, especially after 1930. The Corbusian vocabulary owes its characteristics to a certain vision of reinforced concrete and its possibilities; but, once the vocabulary had been established, it was possible for the idea of form to return to its status of relative autonomy from matters of structure and material execution. Somewhat surprisingly Le Corbusier himself states, referring to the Errazuris house in Chile, that the establishment of a clear plan and of modern aesthetics are by no means dependent on any particular materials. Thus, in Chile, free-field stone and roughly hewn tree trunks could interpret a modern space conception perfectly well.[68]

Logically, when the industrialist Edmond Wanner suggested the realization of a slice of the Corbusian villa-superblocks in glass and steel in Geneva, the shift from reinforced concrete to steel frame construction caused no architectural problem whatsoever. More recently, around 1960, Le Corbusier thought of using metal instead of reinforced concrete for the five Unités d'habitation projected for Meaux (1955–1960),[69] just for a change.

In an interesting passage on sculpture, Le Corbusier describes "a sculpture that is not modeled but assembled."[70] Here, too, it was not the surface subtleties but the correct balance of properly assembled volumes that qualified the object. Form is regarded as autonomous with respect to the techniques that bring it to life: the accidents resulting from workmanship, the grain of the wood, the brilliance of metal or the rough surface of concrete—all these might well be enlivening elements, but they are not considered to be a part of the "idea" behind a work of art. Yet the orchestral accompaniment of a melody also requires accurate control, and from 1930 on, when growing importance was attached to the chance effects of "natural" materials, Le Corbusier developed a special delight in improvising on the building site. While the lack of precision in the execution of certain Corbusian concrete buildings proved extremely irritating to most of his colleagues, Le Corbusier welcomed such marks of technical imperfection as elements of formal richness and complexity that enlivened the austerity of the whole. According to his friends in India, it seems that he was not at all dismayed when, the very day after its inauguration, the side elevation of the Supreme Court at Chandigarh seemed about to crumble, weather-beaten and full of damp. In Marseilles, far from being embarrassed by the crudeness of the concrete form-works, he played like a virtuoso with the secondary effects of the architectural epidermis—fully aware that they were secondary to the architectural idea per se. To those who questioned the bad concrete detailing, Le Corbusier would suggest that they take a look at the bark of a cherry tree, or at the rough walls of a Florentine palazzo (fig. 136).[71]

We should not forget that the image of raw concrete has its premise in both a contempt for technical perfection and craftsmanship on the one hand, and in a positive fascination in the primitive force of material that looks like a new terracotta on the other. The problem of latter-day second-hand brutalism is that the effect of primitive terracotta is lost as soon as Le Corbusier's contempt for technique and craftsmanship in the handling of raw concrete is replaced by the fetishism of technical perfection.

Le Corbusier's intellectualist emphasis on form and disregard for craftsmanship had obvious consequences, and most of his early Parisian works are today little more than ruins, except in cases where their owners lavished continuous care upon them. Long before it was finally completed, the Capitol at Chandigarh began to take the form of a landscape of heroic relics—a Paestum of the machine age as it were. It seems that Corbusier was never particularly worried by the distressing spectacle of the rapid deterioration of most of his buildings as long as one thing remained intact: the idea, the pure form, as it is preserved forever in the seven volumes of his *Oeuvre complète*.

Reproduction and the Idea of the Work of Art

Such a conceptual separation of idea and material realization in art opens up a wide range of possibilities, and it is interesting to note how many of them were in fact realized by Le Corbusier himself. The division of work between the architect-artist and "his" sculptor Joseph Savina would have been unthinkable without a theoretical framework that regarded the conception and the execution of art as two entities that were sufficiently separate to allow their being handled by different people.[72] His enthusiasm for tapestries was partly the result of his delight in seeing his *invenzioni* ("inventions") enriched by a casual effect of a realization that took place outside his orbit of control, and he was doubtlessly sensitive to the qualities of a material with a warmth that his creations generally lacked. His description of the production process that he hoped to organize for the knotting of the 576 square meters of tapestry for Chandigarh's palaces is an epic.[73] Of course, tapestries are more than just copies of drawings and paintings; as in architecture, the transposition into the new medium is a necessary stage in the realization of the artistic intention. If the "original" work of art has an "aura" that a reproduction necessarily lacks, then it might well be argued that this "aura" was, for Le Corbusier, probably not the most conclusive aspect of artistic authenticity.[74] He not

only accepted the translation of his ideas into other mediums,
he also seems to have been delighted by the surprises that resulted from such operations.

From photography to multimedia spectacles

It is thus not surprising that Le Corbusier was particularly interested in photography as a means of automatic and mechanical manipulation of reality and art; in fact, he once praised the
invention of the photographic cliché as the hinge of modern artistic culture.[75] Malraux's statement describing Picasso as a
painter of his "complete" works is almost literally applicable to
Le Corbusier—if we substitute buildings for paintings and
Boesiger for Zervos: "His final goal is not his paintings, but the
album of reproductions by Zervos, in which the breathless succession of his works is far more significant than the best single
one among them can be by itself."[76] As an editor of *L'Esprit
Nouveau*, Le Corbusier used to manipulate visual information
by tricks to clarify and dramatize the message (figs. 34, 35);
in fact, some of the photographs of the Villa Schwob in La
Chaux-de-Fonds which he published in *L'Esprit Nouveau* are so
extensively retouched that their subject was unrecognizable for
his Swiss friends (fig. 24).[77] The possibilities of reproduction
methods seem to have been a stimulus to Le Corbusier—no
less so than the surface effects of building materials that he ex-
ploited in his later works. Thus in *Oeuvre plastique*, a catalogue
of his painted works (1938), he decided to reproduce the negative of a painting, laterally reversed; the resulting inversion
of tones and shadings must have been a source of sheer joy to
the artist.[78]

  These pleasures were to become symptomatic for the art of
the sixties, and if it is true that Le Corbusier developed certain
interests analogous to those later cultivated by Rauschenberg
and Warhol, this may be partly due to the fact that both he
and the later protagonists of Pop Art had a common root in the
world of advertising and its indiscriminate use of modern
media. The Nestlé Pavilion at the Foires Commerciales in Paris
(1928; fig. 90) and the Pavillon des Temps Nouveaux at the Paris
World Fair (1937) were multimedia spectacles comparable to
the hilarious exhibition designs by contemporaries such as El
Lissitzky. It is therefore not surprising that Le Corbusier frequently used photographic enlargements in place of frescoes,

for example in the Swiss Pavilion (where he used enlargements of biological microfilms), and the Cité de Refuge (where he used details from Giotto's frescoes). As was the case later on in Pop Art, these reproductions represented originals in their own right rather than evocations of an absent original work.

When he was asked to build a pavilion for Philips at the World Fair at Brussels (1958), Le Corbusier accepted—not in order to create a piece of architecture, but in order to organize a spectacle of light and sound only barely contained in an architectural frame—a piece of "soft art," a paradigm and an anticipation of the plug-in city. The architecture itself was no more than a tent (like the Pavillon des Temps Nouveaux twenty years previously) that served as a backdrop for a breathtaking accumulation of visual and acoustic information—an "electric circus" evoking dreams and fears connected with scientific progress (fig. 219).

Marshall McLuhan would undoubtedly have something pertinent to say on the subject of the "Poème electronique";[79] in a way, this "poème," realized jointly with the composer Edgar Varèse, was to conventional film-making what Corbusier's use of concrete was to Perret's. Whereas in conventional film-making the new media of sight and sound were usually used to orchestrate traditional, conventional messages, in the "poème" they were employed to produce a new kind of spectacle unimaginable with the use of previous techniques.

Tension and Contradiction

Le Corbusier's work was a protest against the ruling state of things, and it can be defined in terms of a contradiction to the status quo. But his models of an alternative environment were not celebrations of purity and order juxtaposed to the chaos of the day-to-day world, for they themselves were embodiments of tensions and contradictions. Robert Venturi has used various examples from Le Corbusier's work to support and discuss the phenomenology of complexity and contradiction in architecture which is the subject of his seminal book.[80] Le Corbusier's early work in La Chaux-de-Fonds (fig. 20) and his use of symmetries and regulating lines in the twenties, for example in the villa at Garches (figs. 54–57) in fact served an architectural aesthetic which was more concerned with "both/and"—in the juxtaposition of crowded intricacies and rigid envelopes in fragile tension—than in simple and finite unity. Le Corbusier's whole architectural vocabulary, and not only its syntax, is based upon the simultaneous use of contrasting formal elements to engage a dialogue of forces, which frequently approaches points of rupture.

The curved partition within the rectangular box is an established theme within the Corbusian vocabulary: the possibilities of juxtaposition range from a side by side development of independent formal systems, both of which organized "their" space on "their" scale, down to various degrees of mixed uses of curves and straight surfaces as parts of *one* formal system. To a certain extent, it is possible to associate "curve" with "traffic pattern," and "box" with "residence"—as in the Villa Savoye or, on a grand scale, the Cité de Refuge (figs. 76, 127). In fact, however, a curve does not always indicate circulation or a box static space, nor are the curve and the box always the poles within the contradictory whole. In Chandigarh's Parliament Hall, the curved envelope of the Upper Chamber signals the static nucleus of the complex (fig. 106), set off against the open, fluid, yet rectangularly framed "Forum." The same is true of the curved shells of the Millowners' Association Headquarters, an anticipation of Ronchamp, set off against the Citrohan box of the envelope building.

The technique of contradiction is thus, in short, not controlled by established semantic conventions. It is interesting to observe the frequency with which importance is attached to elements connected with access and departure—porches, entrances, ramps, staircases—as challengers of the simple unity of the whole. The exaggerated frames of the porches to the Clarté flats or the baldachin entrance to the Cité de Refuge are illustrations of this (figs. 78, 126); another example is the street facade of the Millowners' building in Ahmedabad (1956–1957), where the quiet succession of slanting overhangs is abruptly interrupted by an opening, exposing, as from a wound, the entrails of the building: its stairs and ramp.

It follows almost logically that whereas for Frank Lloyd Wright and Gerrit Rietveld the problem of interior decoration was first and foremost one of scaling down the architecture to the level of furniture, Le Corbusier resorted to the technique of *bricolage*. The Thonet chair, for example, a perfectly logical companion to Corbusian architecture as far as the design theory goes, will always remain—with its commonplace implications —a quasi-surrealist objet trouvé in Le Corbusier's interiors, and the same is true of his own furniture designs.

The "fantastic" elements in the early buildings—the use of objets trouvés, for example in the Pavillon de L'Esprit Nouveau and elsewhere (fig. 39), had been both applauded as witty and invigorating and criticized as perverse and decadent,[81] and it is on this level that the object-magic of surrealism entered the stage. Usually, however, it is a friendly and edifying magic virtually devoid of any demoniac undertones—the magic of the old-fashioned vignettes that spices the architectural discourses in books like *La ville radieuse*.

Irony: History as Objet

Both as an artist and an architect, Le Corbusier wants to include the element of contrast—the clash of thesis and antithesis, of order and disorder, of seriousness and humor—as a necessary factor in the formal whole. As an observer and writer, he is extremely susceptible to the possibilities presented by unexpected confrontations and to the poetic energies that might result from unusual or grotesque situations. In his recollections of New York, he describes an Indian fancy dress ball at the Waldorf Astoria in which an elephant suddenly marched into the room. "Ladies and gentlemen, in a motley crowd dressed in silk, the gray skin of an elephant suddenly becomes a glamorous garment."[82]

In the penthouse designed for Charles de Beistégui on the Champs-Elysées (1930–1931; fig. 220),[83] the Louis XV dressers and fireplaces attached to the bright white balustrades, from the edge of which emerged the Arc de Triomphe as a colossal piece of bric-a-brac constituted an adapted surrealism, an architecture too suave to be disquieting, yet too disquieting to be rationalist. The city here, as it merged from the roof garden, appeared as a mere selection of isolated architectural "objets." It was as if only after it had been decomposed into a catalog of "objets à réaction poétique" that history could reenter the sphere of creation through the back door of irony. The monuments survived, but as mere quotations, selected and arranged with plastic wit rather than with historical consideration. This, during the twenties, was Le Corbusier's approach to the urban past—a juxtaposition of old and new rather than continuity. There was no reason why the Plan Voisin should not tolerate even occasionally an academic pastiche: "Look, how amusing, this golden dome crowning a Greek temple facade—it is the theater, the last work by M. Nénot, a member of the Institute! It does not matter whether it is genuine Renaissance or a fake . . . it is just a matter of personal taste."[84]

Whereas to Le Corbusier, the bricolage approach to history remained an ideal of urban reform, his actual realizations are on a smaller scale and limited, for example, to such things as the ironic inclusion of a heap of stones left over from a Louis XIV water spout in the outer walls of the Villa Church in Ville d'Avray.[85] Whereas in his urban renewal projects—whether for Paris, St. Dié or Bogotá—the city centers tend to disintegrate into colossal montages of new office buildings and historic relics (an idealized anticipation of trends that were just about to emerge), his real urbanistic interventions were obliged to accommodate to existing laws or, to use LeCorbusier's own term, to "respect the physiology" of a given site: the Ozenfant house and the Cité de Refuge do not stand out against their surroundings, but are forced to work with them (figs. 68, 128). And Le Corbusier knew well enough how to deal with such intricacies in an extremely elaborate fashion—even if he did continue to profess the necessity of the radical approach. Finally, in Venice, he decided to adopt an accommodating urbanistic strategy for the insertion of a modern hospital into the tissue of an old city: "if you cannot copy its skin, then you should at least respect its physiology."[86]

Le Corbusier and Surrealism

His feeling for the paradox and for visual jokes does not necessarily make Le Corbusier an architect of surrealism. In fact, in *L'art décoratif d'aujourd'hui* (1925), his attitude toward the surrealists and "the supremely elegant connection between their metaphors" would appear to be clearly ironic.[87] He does, on the other hand, see a parallel between his own work and certain aspects of surrealist art. Referring to an article by Giorgio de Chirico (from *La Révolution surréaliste*, December 1924), he insists that in both his own work and in that of the surrealists tangible objects serve as starting points of poetry: "the points of reference for all relations which have the power to move us are objects"—although he was enough of an architect and a rationalist to add: "by objects, I mean of course objects that work, or function."[88]

Although he continued to cultivate a curious mixture of reservation and condescension toward surrealism and its "gnawing doubts, indecision, and confused feelings"[89]—understandably enough in the light of his rationalist and Calvinist penchants—he was highly responsive to the surrealist technique of unexpected confrontations of functionally and organically unrelated objects. His painting of 1931 entitled *Léa* (fig. 216), in which a huge oyster is shown entering the door to be confronted with the silhouettes of the cross section of a bone and a guitar, brings forcibly to mind Lautréamont's words which have been so often quoted by the surrealists: "beautiful as the haphazard encounter between a sewing machine and an umbrella on a dissecting table."[90] Not surprisingly, Le Corbusier's own comments on such grotesque juxtapositions make them appear as the result of a wholly rational approach to visual experimentation with form and space:

For instance, when the structure of a bone occupies my mind, I try to fill a whole painting with this element and to enlarge the object in proportion to the interest it arouses. I then confront it with other figurative elements which occupy an identical surface but which seem small compared to the object depicted.[91]

Although the surrealists no doubt helped Le Corbusier to escape from the straitjacket of purist visual hygiene, they failed to bring about a philosophical conversion. The design of Le Corbusier's *Almanach d'architecture moderne* (1925), based upon classical page setting and a multitude of typographical curiosities such as Gothic lettering, hairline fancy characters, and vignettes of all kinds orchestrating the text, directly recalls the image of André Breton's magazine *Littérature* (1922–1923). It was the surrealists who discovered the dusty charm of old de-

partment store catalogues;[92] but whereas in Max Ernst's col-
lages commercial trivia are transformed into an iconography of
magic and dream, Le Corbusier returns to the mail-order house
catalog with uncompromising didacticism and edifying intention: to orchestrate and spice his architectural discourse—for
example in *La ville radieuse* (1935). Compared to the serious and
straightforward functionalist typography of books such as the
Bauhausbücher, designed by Moholy-Nagy, Le Corbusier's
books look fancy with their inclusion of grotesque imagery and
visual jokes. Perhaps, however, these techniques owe less to
surrealism itself than to one of surrealism's own sources of inspiration: the growing refinement and wit of the advertising
world of the twenties.

Nature and Geometry

The tension-contradiction motif in Le Corbusier's architecture
is primarily a problem of form. It constantly challenges—on the
level of form—the egalitarian ideal of a total, and even totalita-
rian, "harmony" that Le Corbusier persistently postulated
on the social and urbanistic levels (at least in the early years). As
we have seen, the poles of tension in each case are fixed within
the functional and formal parameter of the given project and do
not follow any semantic convention. It is, however, tempting to
isolate at least one "pair" of concepts that would appear to have
played a particularly crucial role both for Le Corbusier the architect and Le Corbusier the theoretician: the opposition of
nature and geometry.

   Nature versus geometry is a predominant formal theme in
Le Corbusier's great projects of the twenties: the sumptuous
parks spread out at the foot of the Cité d'Affaires of the Ville
Contemporaine (1922) and of the Palace of the League of Nations (1927; fig. 171) are the necessary counterparts to the "silent prisms" of the architecture itself. And at the Pavillon de
L'Esprit Nouveau, the inclusion of nature as the dialectical
counterpart of architecture is pushed to the extreme (fig. 39):
the tree becomes the "objet à réaction poétique" within the
building itself.[93]

   On the level of form, nature and geometry tend to establish
the extremes within the formal system of Le Corbusier's ar-

chitecture; the architect was set on working with tension and contrast, and there was hardly ever the sense of solidarity and conspiracy with a natural site that was so important to architects such as Neutra, Wright, or Aalto.

On the conceptual level, however, there is no fundamental opposition between nature and geometry. On the contrary, Le Corbusier constantly points to the basic analogies between biology and building. He likes to support his urbanistic theories with illustrations from old medical books, and he discusses architecture and urban planning as if they were the continuation of biology through other means. Thus the blood circulation or the digestive tract are used to serve as models for the rational organization of a city's functions (fig. 139).[94] "The introduction of the term 'biology' throws light on the subject of contemporary building. To live in a house, to work . . . to circulate, are phenomena parallel to blood circulation, the nervous system, or the respiratory system."[95]

In some cases, forms of nature seem to be almost literally translated into architecture, for instance in the Museum of Unlimited Growth, which is based on the regular spiral of a snail shell—a motif that had frequently cropped up in Le Corbusier's early studies at La Chaux-de-Fonds (fig. 101). The *Unité d'habitation* resembles a pine cone, a geometric plant designed to trap light and air (fig. 136). Thus, on the formal level, geometry frequently serves not only as an antithesis to nature but also as the mediator by which nature can be extended into the manmade environment. On the conceptual level, geometry, and mathematics in general, provide the structure through which nature, and the cosmos, can be understood and organized. To discover nature with the help of geometry and to use geometry as a cabalistic key—not only to an intellectual understanding, but also to a pantheistic experience of nature: these were the terms of Le Corbusier's beginnings. The Modulor brings them together into a system.

The Modulor

The term Modulor combines the "module" as a basic principle in building with the idea of the golden section (*section d'or*).[96] Both the module and the golden section were important issues

in the theory and practice of the architectural avant-garde—or at
least of certain factions within it. It is tempting to regard Joseph
Paxton's Crystal Palace as the birthplace of the "module" in the
architecture of the industrial age. Three years after the completion of this building (1851), Adolf Zeisig published his *Neue
Lehre von den Proportionen des menschlichen Körpers* ("New
Doctrine on the Proportions of the Human Body," Germany,
1854).[97] Zeisig's thesis was that the golden section governs
both the macrocosm and the microcosm, a theory that was to
serve as a basis for Matila Ghyka's important book on the Gold-
en Section (*Le Nombre d'Or*), published in Paris in 1931 with a
preface by the poet Paul Valéry. There can be no doubt that
Ghyka's book played an important role in Le Corbusier's coming to grips with the problem of the golden section in nature
and art.[98] Gradually, the elements of Western thought on the
subject of proportion were rediscovered and examined in the
light of modern requirements. Apparently without any immediate knowledge of Fibonacci, the thirteenth-century math-
ematician from Pisa, Le Corbusier developed the principle of
a progression of units based upon the golden section as the
foundation of a universal system of measurement—thus reinventing the Fibonacci series. The introduction of the Fibonacci
series as a scale of measurement meant the introduction of obvious practical complications on the level of the system's application in planning and design; at the same time, it meant the
control of an extremely wide range of actual dimensions with
the help of a relatively synoptical set of units. This is why the
Fibonacci series became part of the Modulor system: as a result,
the measure unit No. 1 of the Modulor represents 1/15,000 mil-
limeters, measure unit No. 270 stands for about 40,000 kilome-
ters, whereas measure unit No. 300 corresponds to interplane-
tary dimensions. As Rudolf Wittkower has emphasized, the
system can be understood as an answer to the problem of how
the space-time conceptions of modern physics can be brought
back into the neighborhood of the arts and visualized in terms
of their theories of proportion.[99]

By 1951, when a conference entitled *De Divine Proportione*
was held in Milan, it seems to have been current practice even
among professionals to visualize the history of proportion in
terms of a tradition originating with Vitruvius and ending with

Le Corbusier. In fact, however, the Modulor is not really Vitru-
vian. Unlike the systems of proportion developed and used in
the Age of Humanism, the Modulor does not envisage an an-
thropomorphic architecture linked by analogy to the proportions of the human body, but rather an "anthropometric" organization of the environment based directly upon the space
requirements of the supposed "average" man and linked by
analogy to nature's growth patterns. The Modulor diagram attempts to establish a common denominator between human
porportions and elemental geometry: a man standing with his
left arm stretched up high and his navel halfway up the diagram
is inscribed in two superposed squares with one side measur-
ing 1.13 meters (fig. 222). The two squares thus determine the
ideal height of a room (2.26 meters). Then the golden section is
introduced into the system: starting from the lower square, a
progression of measure units diminishing according to the gold-
en section is added, thus establishing a geometric progression
from foot to navel, from navel to head, and from head to extended hand, thereby defining the "ideal measure" of the Modulor man (1.829 meters). The smallest of the three measure
units established in this first operation is subsequently chosen
as a point of departure for a further, inverted progression: the
"quasi-Fibonacci" series, diminishing toward the base and
progressing upward, thus linking the sphere of man's immediate environment to the dimensions of architecture.

   The idea was that the adoption of the Modulor would enable architecture and design to recapture their long-lost state of
harmony with nature and the universe and become a true continuation of nature into the man-made environment. The introduction to the first volume of the Modulor may present surprising reading to anyone who is familiar with the rhetorics of
mass-produced, standard uniformity that had been so important as a weapon in the days of *L'Esprit Nouveau*. According to
Le Corbusier, modern society does not need a merely arithmetic
system of modules based on the repetition of identical elements
but an "organic" numerical scale that would connect the immediate environment of man to spheres too distant to be reached
by the senses. It should not be forgotten that the Modulor
was conceived as an alternative to the official French standard
building norms as established by the AFNOR (Association

Française pour une Normalisation du Bâtiment) around 1945; and it is interesting to note that, in apparent contradiction to his earlier self-effacing admiration of the cold rationality of the engineer, Le Corbusier now frontally attacks the principles of design as they had traditionally been taught by the French "Ecole Polytechnique." In this context, he praises the foot, yard, and inch as units of measurement derived from the human body and rooted in customs and popular myths. The emancipation of the natural sciences and the introduction of the decimal system in the aftermath of the French Revolution seems to him to be almost a sacrilege. The metric system, he feels, had "displaced, even perverted" architecture.[100] Thus part of the Modulor's task was to attempt a synthesis of the Anglo-Saxon and the metric systems of measurement.

In short, Le Corbusier reacts to the alarming triumph of rationalism effected by the technocrats and the bureaucrats of the postwar boom by a retreat into a universe of anti-technological, vitalist, and organicist beliefs—a romantic escape into nature. Although he does not specifically refer to John Ruskin in the Modulor, it could be argued that the whole book is an attempt at rewriting Ruskin's *Seven Lamps of Architecture* (1849) for the twentieth-century reader—by no means an unrealistic thought when one considers Ruskin's fundamental impact upon Le Corbusier's origins. And although he does not specifically mention J. N. L. Durand—with whose *Précis des Leçons d'Architecture données à l'Ecole Polytechnique* he was probably not familiar—the Modulor nevertheless represents a broadside attack on the principles underlying Durand's "lessons" that had such a far-reaching impact on French architectural culture.

Whether or not the Modulor is really a useful tool for the practice of architecture is a question that will continue to be answered in different ways. Those who expect it to be a "language of proportions which makes the bad difficult and the good easy" (Albert Einstein)[101] will continue to be disappointed; those who use it as a tool for the dimensioning of spaces, partitions, windows, furniture, etc., may continue to find it helpful. While even an incompetent application of the classical orders will guarantee a certain degree of architectural rigor to a facade, even the most systematic application of the Modulor can easily result in visual disorder. For although the Modulor is capable of organizing parts, it can never control the composition of an architectural whole.

What makes it interesting in the final result is not its pretended functionalism but its conceptual role "as a Romantic variation of the Pythagorean philosophy," as Rudolf Arnheim puts it.[102] With its undoubted mathematical and logical inconsistencies, the Modulor survives as a dream rather than a program—as the transcription of a system of numbers, both poetic and scientific, whose purpose is to visualize a world too complex to be seen and understood without it. It is not surprising that Le Corbusier, who never learned to read music although his mother and brother were musicians, likes to compare his system of proportions to music: "Pythagoras solved the problem when he took two supports capable of combining security and diversity: on the one hand, the human ear—the human capacity for hearing (and not that of wolves, lions or dogs)—and on the other hand numbers, that is, mathematics (and its combinations), which were born of the universe."[103]

There is no need to insist that the promise of the Modulor "to be always harmonious, diverse and elegant instead of being banal, monotonous and graceless"[104] has not been fulfilled by post-Corbusian architecture. The rediscovery of music and biology, nature and simplicity have resulted in new and questionable forms of vitalist escapes—not to mention the boom of provincial brutalisms that followed Le Corbusier's retreat into the virtues of existential nakedness. The "human scale" of the Modulor has become a cliché in the architecture of prosperity—like, some time previously, the "crystals of shining glass" that dominated the Ville Contemporaine. What has remained is the system as such—and its poetic consistency—synthesis and utopia of an animated architecture.

199. Le Corbusier and
Pierre Jeanneret, Plan Obus
for Algiers, 1931 (from
Oeuvre complète)

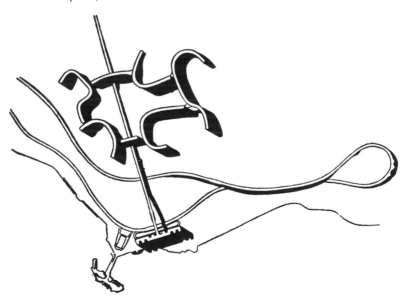

200. Le Corbusier, *Alma Rio
36*, oil on canvas, 1949.
Collection Heidi Weber,
Zurich (photo courtesy of
Heidi Weber, Zurich)

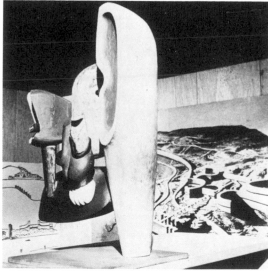

201. Joseph Savina and Le
Corbusier, *Ozon*, poly-
chrome sculpture in wood,
ca. 1946 (from *Le Corbusier*,
catalog, Lyons, 1956)

202. Ronchamp, pilgrimage
chapel "Notre-Dame du
Haut," 1951–1955; view of
outdoor altar (photo ar-
chives: Willy Boesiger,
Zurich)

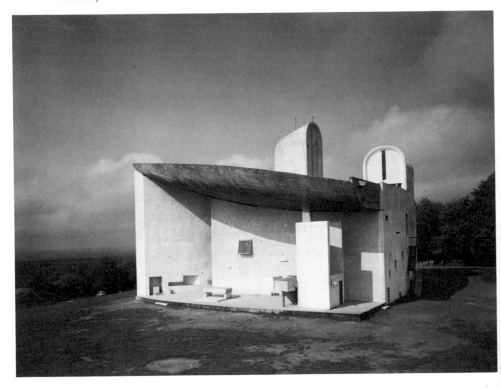

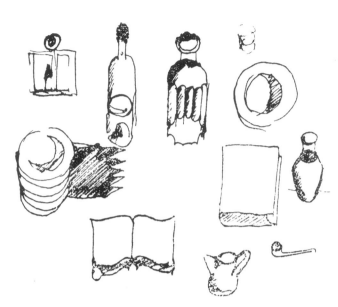

203. Ch.-E. Jeanneret,
"Modest pictorial themes,"
1917–1927 (from Le Cor-
busier, *Oeuvre plastique*)

204. Le Corbusier, study of
a shell (from *Architecture
d'Aujourd'hui*, 1937)

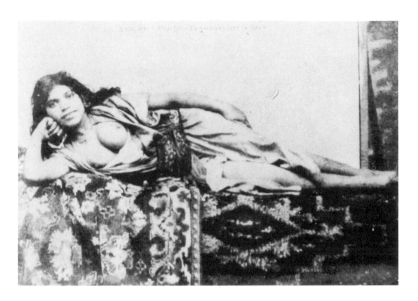

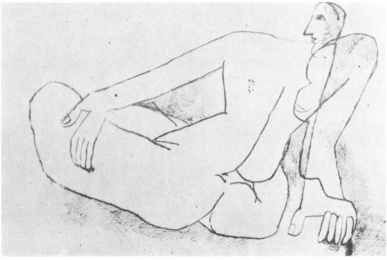

205. A North African girl at her siesta; postcard from Tangier

206–208. Algerian studies for a monumental mural, ca. 1931. Private collection, Milan (from Samir Rafi, *Revue d'histoire et de civilisation du Maghreb*)

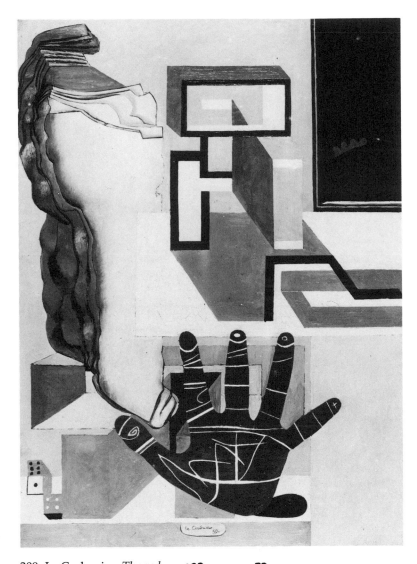

209. Le Corbusier, *The red hand*, oil on canvas, 1930. Collection Heidi Weber, Zurich (photo courtesy of Heidi Weber, Zurich)

210. Egyptian hieroglyph for the divine RA (from S. Giedion, *The Eternal Present*)

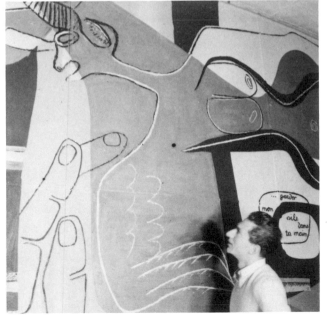

211. Le Corbusier "graffite à Cap Martin," mural in the ground floor terrace of Jean Badovici's house, ca. 1938 (recently destroyed) (from *Oeuvre complète*)

212. Le Corbusier, detail of the fresco in the lobby of the Fondation Suisse in Paris, 1949 (photo archives: Willy Boesiger, Zurich)

213. Le Corbusier, sketch
for the monument of the
open hand in Chandigarh's
Capitol complex, ca. 1952
(from *Oeuvre complète*)

214. Le Corbusier, various
symbols to be reproduced
in sunken reliefs and
tapestries throughout the
buildings of Chandigarh's
Capitol (from *Oeuvre complète*)

215. Le Corbusier and
Pierre Jeanneret, "radiant
farm" project, 1934; per-
spective view from inside
out (from *Oeuvre complète*)

216. Le Corbusier, *Léa*, oil
on canvas, 1931 (photo
courtesy of Heidi Weber,
Zurich)

217. Ronchamp, pilgrimage chapel; the windows of the South wall (photo: Hubmann, Vienna; archives: Willy Boesiger, Zurich)

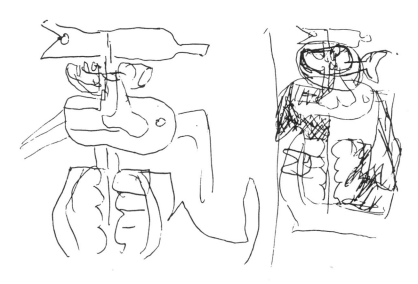

218. Le Corbusier, sketch after an earlier still life (of 1927/1940) turned 90 degrees; 1951 (a and b); (c) sketch of "taureau" (=bull), resulting from the turned-around still life motif; 1951 (from *Creation is a Patient Search*)

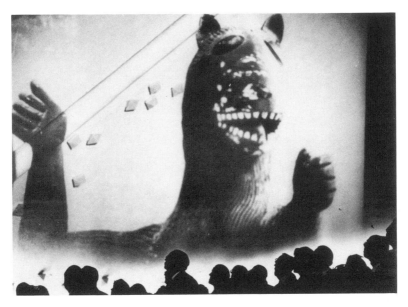

219. Le Corbusier, Philips
Pavilion at World's Fair in
Brussels, 1958; interior
during spectacle (from *Creation is a Patient Search*)

220. Le Corbusier and
Pierre Jeanneret, roof
apartment for M. Beistégui
at Champs Elysées, Paris;
1931 (from *Oeuvre complète*)

221. Le Corbusier and
Pierre Jeannert, Beistégui
apartment, 1931 (from
Plaisir de France)

222. Le Corbusier, the
Modulor, 1948 (from *Le
Modulor*)

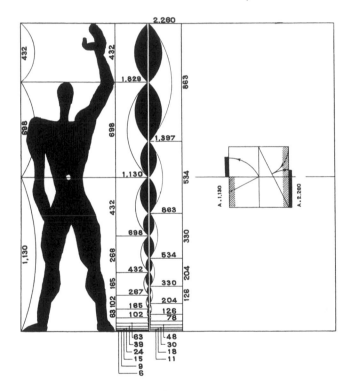

Notes

Notes to Chapter 1

1. Jean Petit, *Le Corbusier parle* (Paris, 1967), p. 13. The most comprehensive biographical information on the architect's youth, based upon the architect's own recollections, is still to be found in Maximilien Gauthier, *Le Corbusier ou l'architecture au service de l'homme* (Paris, 1944). For additional details see also Jean Petit, *Le Corbusier lui-même* (Geneva, 1970), pp. 21–48. There also exists a gramophone record of an interview taped in 1964 by Hugues Dessalle (*Réalisations sonores*, Paris, 1965). But there is hardly a book by Le Corbusier without some interesting remarks concerning his early experiences in La Chaux-de-Fonds (cf. the following notes). This chapter is deeply indebted to the personal reminiscences of Albert Jeanneret, Léon Perin and J.-P. de Montmollin.

2. Le Corbusier, *L'atelier de la recherche patiente* (Paris, 1960), p. 19; (Eng. ed. *Creation is a Patient Search*).

3. Le Corbusier has juxtaposed this phrase to the exhortation of the "Dame-Royne de Quinte-Essence" in the fifth book of Rabelais's works: "seulement vous ramente faire ce que faictes"; see Le Corbusier's preface to W. Boesiger and H. Girsberger, eds., *Le Corbusier 1910–1965* (Zurich, 1967), p. 6.

4. Le Corbusier occasionally recalled his former competence as an engraver, such as the time he told J. Petit in 1962: "You know, without that outdated and slightly ridiculous watch I had done when I was fifteen, Corbu would not be what he is today–in all modesty." In Petit, *Le Corbusier parle* p. 14, Charles-Edouard seems to have been a precocious child; he had begun to attend school at the unusually early age of four. At thirteen he had taken the entrance examination for the local school of Arts and Crafts, and although three days were allotted for the purpose, his papers were turned in by the evening of the first day.

5. Born in 1874, L'Eplattenier taught design at the school beginning in 1898. Most of his paintings, frescoes, and large sculptures came after his resignation as director of the school in 1914. In 1946 a fall from the cliffs of the Doubs River caused his death. For a good survey of his work see *Charles L'Eplattenier, 1874–1946* (exhibition catalog), (La Chaux-de-Fonds, 1974).

6. On the Cours Supérieur and the Nouvelle Section of the Art School founded in 1911 see also Patricia M. Sekler in *Charles L'Eplattenier*, appendix.

7. Julius Meier-Graefe, *Entwicklungsgeschichte der modernen Kunst* (Munich, 1927), p. 640. For the general European context compare Nikolaus Pevsner, *Pioneers of Modern Design from William Morris to Walter Gropius* (London, 1936): (New York, 1949), p. 45 and passim; as well as Pevsner, *The Origins of Modern Architecture and Design* (London, 1968), especially ch. 2, 3.

8. This Egyptian touch is not a new phenomenon in the arts of the period. Thinking of the style of the German pavilion at the International Exposition of Decorative Arts at Turin, 1902, Julius Meier-Graefe said

of the architect Peter Behrens, "He used to speak of the work of Rameses II as if he were talking about the work of an older and more venerable colleague." "Peter Behrens—Düsseldorf," *Die Kunst*, vol. 12 (Munich, 1905), pp. 381 ff.

9. Le Corbusier, *L'art décoratif d'aujourd'hui* (Paris, 1925), pp. 134, 136, 138. Ruskin's impact upon Charles-Edouard Jeanneret's education has been studied by Patricia M. Sekler, *The Early Drawings of Charles Edouard Jeanneret (Le Corbusier), 1902–1908* (New York, 1978).

10. J. Petit, *Le Corbusier parle*, p. 12. In *Modulor 2* (Paris, 1955) (Eng. ed., Cambridge, Mass., 1958; 1968) he refers to the "catastrophe of geological ruptures," p. 25.

11. Le Corbusier, *L'art décoratif*, pp. 197–200.

12. Ibid., pp. 198 ff.

13. Charles Blanc, *Grammaire des arts du dessin*, 4th ed. (Paris, 1881), p. 68.

14. Ibid., p. 305.

15. The first documentation on these early buildings was compiled by E. Chavanne and M. Laville, "Les premières constructions de Le Corbusier en Suisse" (thesis, ETH, Zurich, n.d.), partly published in *Werk* 50(1963):483–488; but a stylistic analysis of these works is still badly needed.

16. See, for example, Le Corbusier's introduction to *Oeuvre complète 1910–1929*, p. 10.

17. Compare especially Le Corbusier, *L'atelier de la recherche patiente* p. 26; *L'architecture d'aujourd'hui* (1948) (special issue on Le Corbusier); Maurice Besset, *Qui était Le Corbusier* (Eng. ed. *Who was Le Corbusier*) (Geneva, 1968), p. 12 and passim.

18. Compare *Le Corbusier, ou l'architecture au service de l'homme*, p. 23. *La Bohème* was performed at the Opera in Vienna on January 15 and February 10, 1908.

19. The Villa Stotzer was published as Chapallaz's work in the *Schweizerische Bauzeitung* (1908) 52:88 ff.

20. In his introduction to *Oeuvre complète 1910–1929*, Le Corbusier recalls the buildings of Paris that impressed him most after his arrival in 1908. See also S. Giedion, *Bauen in Frankreich. Eisen, Eisenbeton* (Leipzig, 1928). On Henri Sauvage, see also Maurice Culot and Lise Grenier, eds., *Henri Sauvage, 1873–1932* (exhibition catalog), Brussels and Paris, 1976.

21. Eugène Grasset, *Mèthode de composition ornementale* (Paris, 1905).

22. Petit, *Le Corbusier lui-même* (Paris, 1970), p. 30.

23. On the Perret brothers, see Peter Collins, *Concrete, The Vision of a New Architecture* (London, 1959).

24. See Giedion, *Space, Time and Architecture*, 5th ed., (1974), p. 330 for an interior view of Perret's studio.

25. See Le Corbusier, *L'art décoratif*, pp. 201–209.

26. Paul Turner, "The Beginnings of Le Corbusier's Education, 1902–1907," *The Art Bulletin* (June 1971):214–224. Turner's thesis has since been published in extenso as a book (New York, 1978).

27. The importance of Nietzsche has been correctly stressed by Turner, "Le Corbusier's Education," and even more (perhaps too much) so by Charles Jencks, in *Le Corbusier and the Tragic View of Architecture* (Cambridge, Mass., 1974), especially pp. 170–182.

28. This letter, dated November 22, 1908, was first published in the *Gazette de Lausanne*, Sept. 4–5, 1965; see also Petit, *Le Corbusier lui-même*, pp. 34–36; and Charles Jencks' comments in *Le Corbusier and the Tragic View of Architecture*, pp. 22–27.

29. See J. M. Nussbaum, "Quand Le Corbusier menait une petite guerre politico-artistique pour la Nouvelle Section de l'Ecole d'Art," *L'Impartial* (local newspaper), October 12, 1957.

30. Petit, *Le Corbusier lui-même*, p. 30.

31. Letter from L. Mies van der Rohe to the author.

32. Charles-Edouard Jeanneret, *Etude sur le mouvement d'art décoratif en Allemagne* (La Chaux-de-Fonds, 1912).

33. Ibid., p. 74.

34. *Le Voyage d'Orient. Fini d'écrire à Naples le 10 octobre 1911 par Charles-Edouard Jeanneret, relu le 17 juillet 1965, 24 rue Nungesser-et-Coli par Le Corbusier* (Paris, 1966). Part of this text was published in the *Almanach d'architecture moderne* (November 1925):55–71. A summary of the trip, beautifully illustrated, is given in Le Corbusier, *L'art décoratif*, pp. 209–217.

35. Le Corbusier, *L'art décoratif*, p. 212.

36. *Voyage d'Orient*, pp. 11–12; 32.

37. Ibid., p. 67.

38. Ibid., p. 76.

39. Ibid., p. 120; he is polemicizing here against Théophile Gautier's description of Turkish houses as poultry coops.

40. Ibid., p. 151.

41. Ibid., p. 165.

42. Ibid., p. 168.

43. Ibid., p. 153. It would be interesting to know more about the possible literary models for the *Voyage d'Orient*. The genre of these travel notes seem to owe something to the writings of William Ritter, a traveler, painter, and art critic from Neuchâtel (1867–1955), while—as M. Steinmann has suggested to the author—the celebration of the Parthenon recalls Théophile Gautier's travel notes.

44. Le Corbusier, *L'art décoratif*, p. 217.

45. Gauthier, *Le Corbusier ou l'architecture au service de l'homme*, pp. 34 ff.

46. *Nouvelle Section de l'Ecole d'Art* (prospectus), (La Chaux-de-Fonds, 1912).

47. *Un mouvement d'art à la Chaux-de-Fonds—à propos de la Nouvelle Section de l'Ecole d'Art, La Chaux-de-Fonds* (n.d., 1914).

48. Among his early colleagues Georges Aubert seems to have been the only one to remain a close friend of Le Corbusier. A professor of art at Lausanne, Aubert painted two frescoes in Le Corbusier's apartment block "Clarté" in Geneva (1954). He died in 1961. See Le Corbusier's moving letter to his ill friend—which arrived after Aubert's death; reproduced in Ernest Genton, *Présence de Georges Aubert* (Lausanne, 1966). Aubert's frescoes in the Clarté flats have recently been removed.

49. The Villa Jeanneret-Perret and the best among Jeanneret's immediately following designs are now illustrated in Petit, *Le Corbusier luimême*, pp. 45–47 and in Jencks, *Le Corbusier and the Tragic View of Architecture*, figs. 13–21; but their place within the architecture of the period has not been seriously studied yet.

50. On Behrens's early work cf. the beautiful monograph by Fritz Hoeber, *Peter Behrens* (Munich, 1913). While in Behrens's studio, Jeanneret seems to have been working on the project of the Cuno-house in Hagen-Eppenhausen, but he was also familiar with Behrens's other contemporary house designs, as his own later projects show. In any case, he visited Karl Ernst Osthaus's well-known artist colony at Eppenhausen, and refers to it briefly (and mistaking Bremen for Hagen) in *Le Modulor* (Boulogne s. Seine, n.d., 1948), p. 26.

51. The importance of Max Dubois (born 1884) for Jeanneret's own formation in structural engineering has been studied by Joyce Lowman, "Corb as Structural Rationalist," *The Architectural Review* (October 1976):229–233.

52. Garnier's two volumes, *Travaux pour la ville de Lyon* and *Une cité industrielle* (n.d., 1918) had been ready for publication years before they actually appeared. On other influences on Jeanneret's housing projects and on the relationship of Jeanneret's and Garnier's, see also Brian B. Taylor, *Le Corbusier at Pessac* (exhibition catalogue), (Cambridge, Mass., and Paris, 1972), pp. 2 ff. Le Corbusier's own comments on the Domino idea in *Oeuvre complète 1910–1929*, pp. 23–26, and in *Précisions sur un état présent de l'architecture* (Paris, 1930), pp. 93–95. For a brilliant analysis of the Domino system see Paul Turner, "The Intellectual Formation of Le Corbusier," in Russell Walden, ed., *The Open Hand* (Cambridge, Mass., 1977), pp. 32–38.

53. J. Caron (pseudonym of Amédée Ozenfant), "Une villa de Le Corbusier 1916," *L'Esprit Nouveau*, Paris, 1920, pp. 679–704. In this publication Le Corbusier declines all responsibility for the interior arrangement. Problems in respecting the budget have caused Jeanneret's eventual decision to leave La Chaux-de-Fonds. Compare J. Schwob, "Il n'a pas son diplôme d'architecte," *Gazette de Lausanne*, September 4–5,

1965, and Maurice Favre, "Le Corbusier in an Unpublished Dossier and a Little-Known Novel," in Russell Walden, ed., *The Open Hand* pp. 96–112.

54. Compare Reyner Banham, *Theory and Design in the First Machine Age* (London, 1960), pp. 220–221.

55. *Schweizerische Bauzeitung* (1912), pp. 148–150; 165–167; 178; and plates 33 and 34. In the preface for *Oeuvre complète 1910–1929*, Le Corbusier recalls having seen the work of Wright in a magazine in 1913.

56. Among Wright's houses published in the *SBZ* and showing certain similarities with the Villa Schwob one notes the two-story living room of the Thomas P. Hardy house in Racine, Wisconsin and the arrangement of the side wings in the country houses for D. D. Martin. But—as Othmar Birkner has shown more recently—there also exist more immediate sources for the two-story living room, such as the Villa Ed. Rudolph-Schwarzenbach in Zurich, by Robert Curjel and Karl Moser (1903–1904); Othmar Birkner, *Bauen und Wohnen in der Schweiz, 1850–1920* (Zurich, 1975), pp. 74–76.

57. The strongly projecting cornice may also have been influenced by Henri Sauvage's well-known setback apartment block in Paris, rue Vavin (1911) as B. B. Taylor indicates (*Le Corbusier at Pessac*, p. 3; compare plates 10; 11).

Notes to Chapter 2

1. He was to stay there for 17 years, until 1933 when he moved to his new apartment at the rue Nungesser-et-Coli. From 1919 to 1925 his brother Albert lived at the same address.

2. See Taylor, *Le Corbusier et Pessac* (original, complete French version of *Le Corbusier at Pessac*), p. 23; see also Le Corbusier's own recollections in Petit, *Le Corbusier parle*, pp. 51 ff.

3. Born in Saint-Quentin in 1886, Amédée Ozenfant began painting in 1903. He studied at the Ecole Quentin de La Tour under Matisse, and then at the Académie de la Palette, side by side with Dunoyer de Segonzac and Roger de la Fresnaye. In 1924, he opened his own academy with Léger. Later he headed a school of painting in New York, where he died in 1967. His book *Journey through Life* (New York, 1939), and especially his *Mémoires* published in French (Paris, 1968) are most important for any understanding of the cultural and artistic climate of Paris during the 1920s and 1930s.

4. *Aujourd'hui*, no. 51:14.

5. A. Ozenfant and Ch.-E. Jeanneret, *Après le cubisme* (Paris, 1917), pp. 31 ff. Many of the following thoughts on purism were first exposed in S. von Moos, "Der Purismus in der Malerei Le Corbusiers," *Werk* 10 (1966):413–420.

6. Ozenfant and Le Corbusier, *Après le cubisme*, pp. 58 ff.

7. Ibid., p. 16.

8. Ibid., p. 29. Judgments like these coincide almost literally with those made by Ozenfant a few years earlier in his magazine *L'Elan*.

9. Ibid., p. 18.

10. Later in his career Le Corbusier was anxious to emphasize that the term was Ozenfant's and not his, for as he said, he came to detest "isms" over the years. See his account of the story in *Art d'Aujourd'hui* no. 7 (1950). On the evolution of theories and architecture of this period see Reyner Banham, *Theory and Design in the First Machine Age* (London, 1960), still the best general study on the subject. However, the section devoted to the beginning of Le Corbusier's collaboration with Ozenfant contains errors and ambiguities (pp. 207 ff). On Purist painting see also *Léger and Purist Paris* (exhibition catalog, Tate Gallery) (London, 1971), with important contributions by John Golding, "Léger and the Heroism of Modern Life," pp. 8–23, and Christopher Green, "Léger and L'Esprit Nouveau, 1912–1928," pp. 25–82. More recently, Christopher Green has devoted an important chapter on purism in his book *Léger and the Avant-Garde* (New Haven and London, 1976), pp. 202–212.

11. Ozenfant and Jeanneret, *Après le Cubisme*, p. 53.

12. For a more detailed discussion of these problems see Green (note 10). Gino Severini's important study *Du cubisme au classicisme* appeared in 1921 and Jean Cocteau's *Rappel à l'ordre* appeared in 1925.

13. Carrà's monograph on Giotto appeared in 1924 as a volume of the *Valori Plastici*, a series.

14. It is very likely that Le Corbusier knew Appia's work. Perhaps he even saw his production of *Orphée* and *L'Annonce faite à Marie* performed in 1913 in Hellerau at Jacques Dalcroze's "Bildungsanstalt," where Le Corbusier's brother was then working. According to the annual *Bulletin* of the Ecole d'Art at La Chaux-de-Fonds, Jeanneret left for Dresden at this time to see a Building exhibition there. It can be assumed that he took advantage of the trip to visit Tessenow, who was living in Hellerau and whom he had met three years before.

15. *Aujourd'hui*, no. 51:14.

16. In an article published in 1950 Le Corbusier blames Ozenfant for having falsified dates and captions in an article on purism written by Maurice Raynal for *L'Esprit Nouveau 7*. Compare *Art d'aujourd'hui* no. 7 (1950).

17. *Aujourd'hui*, no. 51:15.

18. *Art d'aujourd'hui*, no. 7 (1950).

19. Le Corbusier-Saugnier, *Vers une architecture*, Paris, 1922 (Eng. ed. *Towards a New Architecture*), p. 9.

20. Later he made it clear, moreover, that these "personal ideas" were Ozenfant's; see *Art d'aujourd'hui*, no. 7.

21. For an early account of Ozenfant's work as a painter compare Jean Cassou, "Amédée Ozenfant," *Cahiers d'art* no. 10 (1928):437 ff.

22. Franz Meyer, "Die Schenkungen Raoul La Roche an das Kunstmuseum," *Jahresbericht 1963 der öffentlichen Kunstsammlung Basel*, pp. 55–70.

23. Two versions of the painting exist.

24. As has been noted by James Thrall Soby, "Le Corbusier the Painter," ed. Stamo Papadaki, *Le Corbusier Architect, Painter, Writer* (New York, 1948).

25. This may sound unorthodox compared to the "Copernican" role attributed to cubism as a key to modern space conception by S. Giedion in *Space, Time and Architecture* 5th ed., pp. 429–450 and passim. This view has been challenged from various points of view; compare Carlo L. Ragghianti, "Architettura moderna e cubismo," *ZODIAC* 9:18 ff.; Colin Rowe and R. Slutzky, "Transparency, Literal and Phenomenal," *Perspecta* 8 (1964):45–54.

26. See Gauthier, *Le Corbusier ou l'architecture au service de l'homme*, pp. 44 ff; on Paul Dermée see Carola Giedion-Welcker, *Poètes à l'écart* (Zurich, 1947), pp. 191–197. *L'Esprit Nouveau* has been the subject of various studies in recent years, but a systematic inquiry is still badly needed. See in the meantime R. Gabetti and C. Olmo, *Le Corbusier e 'L'Esprit Nouveau'* (Turin, 1975), and the special issue of *Parametro* on L'Esprit Nouveau, September–October 1976.

27. Reprinted as a booklet, Paris, 1946. Banham, *Theory and Design*, pp. 208 ff. refers to writings of August Choisy and Jean Cocteau where the term "esprit nouveau" seems to crop up as well. But the actual source is no doubt Apollinaire.

28. *L'Esprit Nouveau*, pp. 38–48.

29. Ibid., pp. 90–95.

30. *Aujourd'hui* no. 51:15. According to Jean Petit, *Le Corbusier lui-même*, p. 24, Lecorbésier was the name of a Belgian ancestor in Mrs. Jeanneret's (Le Corbusier's mother's) family.

31. But in *L'Esprit Nouveau*, he used other pseudonyms as well. The names of Vauvrecy and Fayet seem to have been used by both Ozenfant and Jeanneret. Occasionally, Le Corbusier wrote under the name of Paul Boulard: several of these articles, relating to exhibitions, art books or to events in the Paris art world are of great historic interest.

32. However, the articles do not appear in quite the chronological order of their first publication. Most of them have been revised. Significantly, the book does not include the reports given on the prefabricated "Maison Voisin" (*L'Esprit Nouveau*, pp. 211–215) or the "Maisons en série" (A. Perret, *L'Esprit Nouveau*, pp. 1956 ff.) These examples, while making an important point on prefabrication, somehow compromise Le Corbusier's vision of geometric purification through mass production. The first edition of *Vers une architecture* was signed Le Corbusier–Saugnier. For the second edition, Le Corbusier had the name Saugnier deleted and dedicated the book to Ozenfant, thereby removing any misunderstanding about his authorship.

33. *Vers une architecture*, p. 5. The passage recalls Anatole de Baudot, who in *Architecture, passé et présent* (published posthumously in 1916), had drawn attention to the work of engineers in similar terms. See Peter Collins, *Changing Ideals in Modern Architecture* (Montreal, 1965; reprinted ed., 1967), p. 164.

34. Walter Gropius, "Die Entwicklung moderner Industriebaukunst," *Werkbund-Jahrbuch,* (1913), pp. 17–22. Gropius recalled having given Le Corbusier in 1923, at the time of their first meeting at the Café des Deux Magots, the originals of these photographs published in *Vers une architecture* (compare *Aujourd'hui* no. 51:108). But all of them had already appeared in October 1920 in the first issue of *L'Esprit Nouveau.* Le Corbusier and Ozenfant had taken them from the *Werkbund-Jahrbuch* and retouched certain details that did not suit the point they wanted to make.

35. Le Corbusier, *Vers une architecture*, p. 16.

36. Ibid., p. 19.

37. In *L'Esprit Nouveau*, p. 198, he had even a photograph of Gropius's Fagus factory at Alfeld.

38. Le Corbusier, *Vers une architecture*, p. 56.

39. See Le Corbusier, *Modulor* (Paris, 1948), p. 27. (Eng. ed., Cambridge, Mass., 1958; 1968): "A book brought him certainty: some pages from Auguste Choisy."

40. Le Corbusier, *Vers une architecture*, p. 80.

41. Le Corbusier, *Vers une architecture*, p. 105.

42. Ibid., pp. 119–140.

43. Banham, *Theory and Design*, p. 246.

44. "Le retour à la belle tradition latine," as Charles-Edouard Jeanneret put it in his *Etude sur le mouvement d'art décoratif en Allemagne* (La Chaux-de-Fonds, 1912), p. 44.

45. Le Corbusier is, however, conscious of the fact that engineering forms are influenced by aesthetic considerations and that mere utilitarianism doesn't lead to beauty; see Le Corbusier, *Vers une architecture*, p. 7.

46. Some examples of neoclassicists' interest in pure geometry are discussed in Le Corbusier, *Urbanisme* (Paris, 1925), pp. 35 ff.

47. "Architecture d'époque machiniste," *Journal de Psychologie Normale et de Pathologie* (Paris, 1926):325–350; (facsimile reprint, Turin, 1975). See the discussion in Banham, *Theory and Design*, pp. 257–263.

48. Le Corbusier, *Vers une architecture*, pp. 73; 83 and passim.

49. Hans Sedlmayr, *Verlust der Mitte* (Salzburg, 1948), pp. 60 ff. On the role of the machine in architectural thinking see P. Collins, "The Mechanical Analogy," *Changing Ideals*, pp. 159–166; obviously, the machine was a conceptual "analogon" to phenomena in physics, poli-

tics, and economics well before theoreticians like Horatio Greenough, James Fergusson, or Viollet-le-Duc of the nineteenth century discovered it for their own use.

50. Le Corbusier, *Vers une architecture*, pp. 123, 145, 165.

51. Le Corbusier, *Oeuvre complète 1910–1929*, p. 8.

52. Letter dated June 10, 1931, in A. Sartoris, *Gli elementi dell'architettura funzionale* (Milan, 1931; 3rd ed., 1941).

53. See the catalog of the exhibition and Paul Léon, ed., *Rapport général de l'exposition internationale des arts décoratifs et industriels modernes, Paris, 1925* (Paris, 1928), and more recently, Yvonne Brunhammer, *1925. Exposition internationale des arts décoratifs et industriels modernes. Sources et conséquences* (exhibition catalog), (Paris, 1976).

54. "Un homme poli, vivant dans ce temps-ci," *Les arts décoratifs modernes*, special issue of *Vient de paraître* (1925):108.

55. Sigfried Giedion, *Mechanization takes Command*, (New York, 1947), pp. 499. Difficulties in securing the funds had caused delays in the pavilion's realization. In fact, P. A. Emery who worked on the project, claims that building was started only the night before the Exhibition's official opening. Thus the pavilion site had to be protected during construction by a fence. This requirement was later dramatized by Le Corbusier and Giedion as another proof of the establishment's distrust in modernity. For Le Corbusier's version of the story cf. his *Almanach d'architecture moderne*, (Paris, 1925) and "Brève histoire de nos tribulations," in the Le Corbusier issue of *L'Architecture d'Aujourd'hui*, pp. 59–67, and *Oeuvre complète 1910–1929*, pp. 98–100.

In order to work on the pavilion and on the "Plan Voisin" that was to be presented within, in 1924, Le Corbusier rented the space at 35, rue de Sèvres that was later to become his permanent business address. It was the second floor of one wing of a defunct convent, then used as a grocer's storeroom. Compare *The New Yorker*, April 24–May 3, 1937.

56. Quoted from Giedion, *Mechanization takes Command*, p. 492. For an interesting visual documentation and analysis of Le Corbusier's furniture designs see Maurizio Di Puolo, Marcello Fagiolo, and Maria Luisa Madonna, *'La machine à s'asseoir'* (catalog), Rome, 1976, and Renato De Fusco, *Le Corbusier designer. I mobili del 1929*, Milan, 1976.

57. "A polemical work of only local interest," as Banham claims (*Theory and Design*, p. 248). Le Corbusier seems to have felt differently; compare the lengthy discussion of the book in Gauthier's authorized biography, *Le Corbusier ou l'architecture au service de l'homme*, pp. 72–85.

58. Adolf Loos, *Sämtliche Schriften* I (Vienna-Munich, 1962), pp. 15 ff.

59. George Besson, "La décoration intérieure et les ensembles mobiliers," special issue of *Vient de paraître* (1925), p. 165.

Notes to Chapter 3

1. See Peter Collins, *Concrete. The Vision of a New Architecture* (London, 1959).

2. On Pierre Jeanneret, see *L'Architecture d'aujourd'hui*, February–March 1968, p. v. A monograph by Jacqueline Vauthier is to be published shortly.

3. Le Corbusier, *Oeuvre complète 1910–1929*, p. 128. The "five points" were first published in Alfred Roth, *Zwei Wohnhäuser von Le Corbusier und Pierre Jeanneret* (Stuttgart, 1927; reprinted Stuttgart, 1977). Earlier versions of the famous diagrams had appeared in the *Journal de Psychologie Normale*, 1926 (reprinted Turin, 1975).

4. In Le Corbusier, *Vers une architecture* (Paris, 1925), p. 45, such an early plan for an elevated city is dated 1915. In *L'Esprit Nouveau*, however, this same plan is signed "Le Corbusier–Saugnier"—which postpones its date to around 1920 (p. 468).

5. The most outstanding examples are the setback developments in Oued-Ouchaia, North Africa (1933–1934, not built); see Le Corbusier, *Oeuvre complète, 1929–1934*, p. 165, and the "Unité d'habitation" in Nantes-Rézé (1952–1954), partly built above water.

6. Le Corbusier, *Précisions*, pp. 50 ff.

7. See Othmar Birkner, *Bauen und Wohnen in der Schweiz, 1850–1920* (Zurich, 1975), pp. 74–76.

8. Again, I am not sure about the date. In Le Corbusier, *Oeuvre complète 1910–1929*, pp. 27 ff, the project is dated 1916; according to Le Corbusier, *L'atelier de la recherche patiente* (Paris, 1960), p. 45, it would be 1921. A number of interesting early sketches of houses with planted roof gardens is kept in the legacy of William Ritter to the Bibliothèque de La Chaux-de-Fonds.

9. Le Corbusier, *Une petite maison* (Zurich, 1954), p. 45. For the terrace garden of his own apartment, Rue Nungesser-et-Coli, see Le Corbusier, *Oeuvre complète 1938–1946*, pp. 140 ff. Concerning the flat roof, see also Le Corbusier, *Almanach d'architecture moderne*, p. 89.

10. Le Corbusier, *Une petite maison*, p. 50.

11. Giedion, *Space, Time and Architecture*, 5th ed., p. 525.

12. Le Corbusier, *Oeuvre complète 1910–1929*, p. 26.

13. At Stuttgart, the corridor servicing the living room follows the standards of the "Compagnie Internationale des Wagons-Lits," a fact that seems to have made circulation difficult for some of the more corpulent Swabian visitors. See Le Corbusier, *Oeuvre complète 1910–1929*, p. 150. A later example for the use of sliding partitions is the project of an apartment house (1928–1929) in *Oeuvre complète 1910–1929*, p. 184.

14. Namely the factory building at the Werkbund-exhibition in Cologne, that Ch. -E. Jeanneret visited in July 1914. See Le Corbusier, *Quand les cathédrales étaient blanches* (Paris, 1937; Eng. ed., New York, 1947) p. 107. In *Précisions*, Le Corbusier gives his opinion of Gropius's building (p. 57).

15. Le Corbusier, *Précisions*, p. 57. See also Le Corbusier, *Almanach d'architecture moderne*, pp. 95 ff. where Le Corbusier gives a humorous account of a petty quarrel with Perret concerning this matter.

16. Compare Bryan B. Taylor, *Le Corbusier at Pessac* (Cambridge, Mass., 1972), pp. 1 ff.

17. Compare for instance André Luçat's studio-houses at the Villa Seurat and the rue de Belvédère in Paris. For Banham's discussion see *Theory and Design in the First Machine Age*, pp. 252 ff.

18. Le Corbusier, *Oeuvre complète 1910–1929*, p. 31. The fellow diner was not Pierre Jeanneret as reported in Boesiger and Girsberger, *Le Corbusier, 1910–1965*, p. 25, but Ozenfant. See also *Aujourd'hui*, no. 51:15. The restaurant is still standing at 32 rue Godot-de-Mauroy, with its loft spiral staircase intact; its name is now "Le Mauroy."

19. That the type was proposed by Le Corbusier for artists' studios comes as no surprise; see *Oeuvre complète 1910–1929*, p. 54.

20. Le Corbusier, *Oeuvre complète 1910–1929*, pp. 87–91 (Villa Meyer); see also pp. 204 ff. for the curious project for "Mr. X." in Brussels.

21. It was not, therefore, a coincidence that Le Corbusier published the "five points" on this occasion. The houses were built in three months (March–July 1927) under the direction of Alfred Roth. Besides Roth's brochure, previously cited (note 3), see volume 2 of *Stuttgarter Beiträge: die Weissenhof Siedlung* (Stuttgart, 1968), published by Jürgen Joedicke.

22. Le Corbusier, *Oeuvre complète 1910–1929*, pp. 48 ff. Alterations have made this house almost unrecognizable. The role of axial symmetry and its modifications had already been recognized by Henry-Russell Hitchcock and Philip Johnson as a fundamental aspect of the International Style in *The International Style* (New York, 1932; reprinted 1966), pp. 56–168.

23. W. Gropius, *Internationale Architektur* (Munich, 1925).

24. Le Corbusier, *Oeuvre complète 1910–1929*, pp. 140–149. Preliminary studies for the Villa Stein-de Monzie were the subject of an exhibition at the Museum of Modern Art, New York, Winter 1970–1971; they are reproduced in color in *Domus*, April 1971, pp. 3–9. For a contemporary appraisal of the villa cf. S. Giedion, "Le problème du luxe dans l'architecture moderne—à propos d'une nouvelle construction à Garches de Le Corbusier et Pierre Jeanneret," *Cahiers d'art* (1928): 254–256. The villa was built for Gabrielle de Monzie, and Michael Stein, brother of Gertrude Stein. In the 1930s it was bought by a Norwegian, whose primary reason for buying seems to have been the villa's nearness to the golf course at St. Cloud; *The New Yorker* (April 26, 1947):45. In spite of slight changes (the interior and front facade, for example), this house is in fairly good shape today.

25. S. Giedion, *Bauen in Frankreich*, p. 106.

26. Le Corbusier, *Oeuvre complète 1910–1929*, p. 144.

27. See Colin Rowe, "The Mathematics of the Ideal Villa," *Architectural Review* (March 1947); reprinted in C. Rowe, *The Mathematics of the Ideal Villa and Other Essays* (MIT Press: Cambridge, Mass., 1976), pp. 1–28.

28. The subtlety with which the main entrance is balanced against the somewhat narrower and lower set service entrance can only be appreciated on old photographs; on the site, small changes have distorted the original proportions.

29. See also in this context the interesting graphic analysis of the "transparent" character of the garden facade in B. Hoesli's commentary on the article by Rowe and Slutzky ("Transparency, literal and phenomenal," *Perspecta* 8 (1964):45–54), *Transparenz* (Basel, 1968), pp. 49 ff.

30. Le Corbusier, *Oeuvre complète 1910–1929*, pp. 158 ff. The spelling of the proprietor's name as Plainex in *Oeuvre complète* is incorrect. Except for a few details, the house is intact.

31. Compare Ludwig Münz and Gustav Künstler, *Der Architekt Adolf Loos* (Vienna, 1964), pp. 83–91, and Marc Emery, *Un siècle d'architecture moderne en France, 1850–1950* (Paris, 1970), p. 99.

32. The Moller house in Vienna; see L. Münz and G. Künstler, *Der Architekt Adolf Loos*, pp. 128–134.

33. A framed white plane already characterizes the street facade of the Villa Schwob at La Chaux-de-Fonds. Colin Rowe has interpreted this as a "mannerist" motif. Compare "Mannerism and Modern Architecture," *Architectural Review* (1950):289–299 (reprinted 1976; see note 27).

34. S. Giedion, *Bauen in Frankreich*, p. 92, note 1.

35. Ibid., p. 98.

36. See Theo van Doesburg, *Neue Schweizer Rundschau* (1929), p. 536.

37. Le Corbusier wrote on this exhibition in the May 1923 issue of *L'Esprit Nouveau*.

38. A good comparison between De Stijl and Le Corbusier is given by Bruno Zevi, *Poetica dell'architettura neoplastica* (Milan, 1953) especially p. 48. See also the new revised edition of this book (Milan, 1974).

39. S. Giedion, *Bauen in Frankreich*, p. 85.

40. Le Corbusier, *Oeuvre complète 1910–1929*, p. 87. The staircase treated "hors d'oeuvre," independently from the building to which it is attached, is a great theme of French architecture ever since Fontainebleau. Cf. André Chastel's article in *Essays in the History of Architecture presented to Rudolf Wittkower* (London, 1967), pp. 74–80.

41. Le Corbusier, *Oeuvre complète 1910–1929*, pp. 48 ff.

42. There are precedents, however, in Sant Elia's "case a gradinate" and in Henri Sauvage's apartment house at the rue Vavin, where the setback arrangement of the apartments had made it necessary to articulate the vertical connections as independent bodies. See S. von Moos, "Aspekte der neuen Architektur in Paris, 1915–1932," *Werk* 2 (1965):51–56.

43. Le Corbusier, *Oeuvre complète 1910–1929*, p. 88.

44. Ibid., p. 201.

45. Le Corbusier, *Oeuvre complète 1929–1934*, pp. 200 ff.

46. Another significant project in this context is the Olivetti electronics center near Milan (1961–1965, not built); compare *Aujourd'hui*, no. 51:88 ff. The final plan is given in W. Boesiger and H. Girsberger, *Le Corbusier, 1910–1965*, pp. 169–175.

47. Ozenfant claims the honor of having been Le Corbusier's first client and of sharing the responsibility for the project. See Ozenfant, *Mémoires 1886–1962*, pp. 126 ff.

48. Had it touched the floor, it would have broken. See Le Corbusier, *Oeuvre complète 1929–1934*, pp. 53–57. The apartment was completely transformed in the early sixties.

49. Illustrated in Le Corbusier, *Oeuvre complète 1910–1929*, p. 158.

50. Ibid., p. 59.

51. Ibid., pp. 70 ff.

52. S. Giedion, "Das neue Haus. Bermerkungen zu Le Corbusiers (und Pierre Jeannerets) Haus La Roche in Auteuil," *Das Kunstblatt* (April, 1926):153–157. Compare also Le Corbusier, *Oeuvre complète 1910–1929*, pp. 60–68. Up until recently the villa was inhabited by its original owner and so has remained in perfect shape. Today it houses the Fondation Le Corbusier.

53. Interview taped in *Réalisations sonores*, Hugues Dessalle, Paris, 1965.

54. In S. Giedion, "Das neue Haus. Bemerkungen zu Le Corbusiers (und P. Jeannerets) Haus Laroche [sic!] in Auteuil," *Das Kunstblatt* (April, 1926):155.

55. Vincent Scully, *The Shingle Style Today. The Historian's Revenge* (New York, 1975), p. 23.

56. See also in this context the project for the French Embassy in Brazil, W. Boesiger and H. Girsberger, *Le Corbusier 1910–1965*, pp. 162–163.

57. Le Corbusier, *Oeuvre complète 1910–1929*, p. 192.

58. W. Boesiger and H. Girsberger, *Le Corbusier 1910–1965*, p. 221. A building whose different levels are served mainly by ramps occurs in Le Corbusier's work as early as 1917, in his project for slaughterhouses in Garchizy, Challuy. Here the idea is motivated by the program itself (i.e., the necessity to move carriages from one floor to another). For illustrations see Taylor, *Le Corbusier at Pessac, 1914–1928*, p. 13.

59. Le Corbusier, *Oeuvre complète 1929–1934*, pp. 22–31; and *Précisions*, pp. 136 ff. Giedion's first comments are in *Cahiers d'Art* no. 4 (1930):205–215. During World War II the villa served as a warehouse for fodder, and it was in very bad shape when André Malraux, then Minister of Cultural Affairs, delcared it a historic monument. It has been restored since, with questionable accuracy, but the site is forever obstructed by the new lycée de Poissy in the villa's immediate neigh-

borhood. A comprehensive study of this landmark and the different
stages of its project is at present under preparation by Tim Benton.

60. Le Corbusier, *Précisions*, p. 50.

61. See Boesiger and Girsberger, *Le Corbusier 1910–1965*, p. 221.

62. Le Corbusier, *Vers une Architecture*, p. 142. On the Fiat building
see also Marco Pozzetto, *La Fiat-Lingotto. Un architettura torinese
d'avanguardia* (Turin, 1975).

63. In both cases, pedestrian access (with stores and ticket offices)
were located below these ramps. It is not surprising that during his
first visit to the US in 1935, Le Corbusier was impressed by the approach ramps to New York's Grand Central Station; compare *Quand
les Cathédrales étaient blanches* (re-ed. 1965), p. 90; Eng. tr. *When the
Cathedrals were White* (New York, 1964), pp. 78 ff. (but the English
translation gives—unadmittedly—a reduced version of the book).

64. S. Giedion, *Space, Time and Architecture*, 5th ed., p. 529.

65. Le Corbusier, *Oeuvre compléte 1929–1934*, p. 24.

66. Le Corbusier, *Oeuvre compléte 1910–1929*, p. 60.

67. Hans Sedlmayr, *Verlust der Mitte* (Salzburg, 1948).

68. Le Corbusier, *Une petite maison*, pp. 9–11.

69. Le Corbusier, *Précisions*, p. 139.

70. Unpublished letter dated July 15, 1949 (preserved in the Fueter
legate at the Schweizerisches Institut für Kunstwissenschaft, Zurich).
See the plan in Le Corbusier, *Oeuvre complète 1946–1952*, 2nd ed.
(Zurich, 1955), pp. 64–66. I should at least mention here Kauffmann's
fascinating, yet questionable thesis according to which Le Corbusier's
interest in elementary geometry is linked to the architecture of the Age
of Reason, especially Ledoux and Boullée. Compare Emil Kauffmann,
Von Ledoux bis Le Corbusier (Vienna, 1932); Adolf Max Vogt, *Der Kugel-
bau um 1800 und die heutige Architektur* (Zurich, 1962); and Adolf Max
Vogt, *Boullées Newton-Deukmal. Zentralbau und Kugelidee* (Basel, 1969),
pp. 377 ff.

71. This interest, in turn, seems to have been stimulated by Le Corbusier himself. For the "Pavillon de l'Esprit Nouveau" he had already
used partition panels of pressed straw. He submitted the method to
Wanner who was especially interested in the possibilities of dry assembly. See Le Corbusier, *Oeuvre complète 1910–1929*, pp. 180–183;
and *Oeuvre complète 1929–1934*, pp. 66–71.

72. See Le Corbusier, *Oeuvre complète 1929–1934*, pp. 66–109.

73. The prefabricated steel elements of the Zurich pavilion are based
on the Renault studies; and they also recall the framing of Frantz Jourdain's Samaritaine department store in Paris—much admired by Le
Corbusier around 1909.

74. See Kenneth Frampton, "Maison de verre," *Arena* (April, 1966);
and S. von Moos, *Werk* 2 (1965):51–56 (where the principal references

on Pierre Chareau are listed). For a more recent and very complete documentation compare Frampton's article in *Perspecta* 12 (1969):77–126.

75. K. Frampton, "Maison de verre," p. 262.

76. I am indebted to the late Mme. Dalsace for this interesting detail, and also for her generous permission to visit her house.

77. In *Plans* 12 (February, 1932):40.

78. Le Corbusier, *Quand les cathédrales étaient blanches*, p. 26.

79. Ibid., pp. 27 ff.

80. Le Corbusier, *Précisions*, p. 210. See also R. Banham, *The Architecture of the Well-Tempered Environment*, (London, 1969), which documents and discusses the influence of environmental management on modern architecture.

81. See Le Corbusier, *Oeuvre complète 1938–1946*, pp. 103–113.

82. *Aujourd'hui*, no. 51:30 ff.

83. Le Corbusier, *Oeuvre complète 1934–1938*, pp. 78–81; *Oeuvre complète 1938–1946*, pp. 80–90; and *My Work*, pp. 111; 122 ff.

84. Even the UN building in New York should have been equipped with sunbreakers, as Le Corbusier insisted long after having lost control over this campaign. See his letter to Senator Warren Austin, reprinted in *Architecture d'Aujourd'hui* (Dec. 1950–Jan. 1951):IX.

85. *Aujourd'hui*, no. 51:51.

86. See in particular the project for the skyscraper on the Cap de la Marine in Algiers (1938) and the main facade of the Secretariat at Chandigarh twenty years later. Le Corbusier, *Oeuvre complète 1938–1946*, pp. 480–65, and *Oeuvre complète 1952–1957*, pp. 96–106.

87. Le Corbusier, *Le Modulor* (Paris, 1948), p. 224; (Eng. ed. Cambridge, Mass., 1958); where Le Corbusier uses this double concept but in a sense that is not directed at form only. See also Le Corbusier, *Oeuvre complète 1910–1929*, p. 30, and Peter Serenyi's discussion of "Le Corbusier's Changing Attitude towards Form,"*Journal of the Society of Architectural Historians*, XXIV (March, 1965):15ff.

88. Speaking of the docks at Casablanca, he emphasized that Perret returned to the same type of roof construction in the church of Raincy; cf. Le Corbusier, *Une maison—un palais*, p. 44.

89. Le Corbusier, *Oeuvre complète 1929–1934*, pp. 147–153, 178–185.

90. Ibid., pp. 186–191; and "Village coopératif," *Oeuvre complète 1934–1938*, pp. 104–115.

91. Le Corbusier, *Oeuvre complète 1929–1934*, pp. 125–130. Completely transformed and furnished with wrought-iron gates, the building is unrecognizable today.

92. Le Corbusier, *Oeuvre complète 1952–1957*, pp. 114–131.

93. Le Corbusier, *Oeuvre complète 1952–1957*, pp. 114–131.

94. See Reyner Banham, *Brutalismus in der Architektur*, (Stuttgart, 1966), (Eng. ed. London, 1966), pp. 85–124.

95. Maurice Besset, *Neue Französische Architektur*, (Teufen, 1967), p. 27. Compare Le Corbusier, *Oeuvre complète 1946–1952*, 2nd ed. (Zurich, 1955), pp. 32–35, 54–61.

96. For sketches see Le Corbusier, *Oeuvre complète 1957–1965*, p. 104; see also ibid., p. 69.

97. Le Corbusier, *Oeuvre complète 1910–1929*, p. 176.

98. Le Corbusier, *Oeuvre complète 1952–1957*, pp. 134–143. In the first plan for the Villa Shodan, intended at that time for M. Hutheesing, Le Corbusier suggested a fragile concrete parasol that looks like late Durrell-Sone. See Le Corbusier, *Oeuvre complète 1946–1952*.

99. Le Corbusier, *Textes et dessins pour Ronchamp* (Paris, 1965).

100. Le Corbusier, *Oeuvre complète 1957–1965*, pp. 22–31. The execution was directed, essentially, by the Parisian architects Tavès and Rebutato. For a more detailed discussion of the building cf. S. von Moos, "Der Corbusier-Pavillon," *Neue Zürcher Zeitung* (July 16, 1967).

101. Le Corbusier, *Oeuvre complète 1934–1938*, pp. 172–173.

102. Le Corbusier, *Oeuvre complète 1910–1929*, p. 174.

103. Le Corbusier, *Oeuvre complète 1946–1952*, pp. 67–71.

104. Ibid., pp. 28–31. For a good discussion of the Sainte Baume project cf. Anton Henze, *Le Corbusier* (Berlin, 1957), pp. 58–60.

105. Le Corbusier, *Précisions*, pp. 132 ff.

106. Le Corbusier, *Oeuvre complète 1910–1929*, pp. 144–153.

107. Le Corbusier, *Oeuvre complète 1929–1934*, pp. 144–153.

108. Le Corbusier, *Oeuvre complète 1934–1938*, p. 131.

109. Le Corbusier, *Oeuvre complète 8, The Last Works*, pp. 102–111.

110. Le Corbusier, *Oeuvre complète 1952–1957*, pp. 158–167 (Ahmedabad) and pp. 168–173 (Tokyo). On the Museum in Chandigarh see *Oeuvre complète 8, The Last Works*, pp. 92–101.

111. W. Boesiger and H. Girsberger, *Le Corbusier, 1910–1965*, pp. 176–183. It seems unlikely that the project will ever be executed.

112. *Il Gazettino*, (April 12, 1965). See also Sylvain Zegel, "Le Corbusier's' explique à bâtons rompus," *Le Figaro Littéraire* (April 15–21, 1965).

113. Le Corbusier, *Vers une Architecture*, pp. 220 ff.

114. Le Corbusier, *Oeuvre complète 1929–1934*, pp. 72 ff. The spiral-type was actually developed earlier, in connection with the ziggurat-shaped museum at the never-built Mundaneum in Geneva; compare Le Corbusier, *Oeuvre complète 1910–1929*, pp. 190–194. There is, on the

other hand, at least one of Le Corbusier's museum projects where the spiral-type has been abandoned (i.e., the project for the Museum of Modern Art in Paris, 1935); see Le Corbusier, *Oeuvre complète 1934–1938*, pp. 82–89.

115. Le Corbusier, *Oeuvre complète 1929–1934*, p. 72.

116. Le Corbusier, *Quand les cathédrales étaient blanches*, p. 21.

117. Le Corbusier, *Oeuvre complète 1934–1938*, pp. 90–97; and *Des canons, des munitions? Merci! Des logis, s.v.p.* (Paris, 1939), pp. 98–103.

118. Le Corbusier, *Oeuvre complète 1957–1965*, pp. 130–136. Also in 1956, Le Corbusier was called to Baghdad for the construction of a stadium to hold 55,000 people (see *My Work*, p. 191), but this was never built.

119. *Plans*, 8, pp. 92–108.

120. The church was not yet built at the time this manuscript was completed.

121. Karl Ledergerber, *Kunst und Religion in der Verwandlung* (Cologne, 1961).

122. Le Corbusier, *Textes et dessins pour Ronchamp*, p. 25 (dedication speech, June 25, 1955).

123. Alan Colquhoun, "Displacement of Concepts," *Architectural Design* (April, 1972):236. See also idem., "Typology and Design Method," *Meaning in Architecture*, eds. C. Jencks and G. Baird (London, 1969), pp. 267–277; the article to which this chapter owes its title.

Notes to Chapter 4

1. Compare Anatole Kopp, *Ville et révolution* (Paris, 1967); Eng. ed., *Town and Revolution* (New York, 1970), pp. 115–159. A. Gradov, *Gorod i byt. Perspektivy razvitiia sistemy i tipov obshchestbennykh zdanii* (Moscow, 1968). The present chapter is based on my article "Wohnkollektiv, Hospiz und Dampfer," *archithese* 12 (1974):30–41.

2. Quoted after Adolf M. Vogt, *Russische und französische Revolutionsarchitektur, 1917, 1789* (Cologne, 1974), p. 46.

3. Compare Walter Gropius, "Die Soziologischen Grundlagen der Minimalwohnung" (1928), reprinted in English in idem, *Scope of Total Architecture*, (New York, 1943: ed., 1966), pp. 91–102.

4. See for example, Hannes Meyer, "Der Architekt im Klassenkampf," in Hans Schmidt and Hannes Meyer, *Schweizer Städtebauer bei den Sowjets* (Basel, n.d., 1932?), pp. 26 ff.

5. Sigfried Giedion, *Befreites Wohnen* (Zurich, 1929), Fig. 57.

6. A. M. Couturier, O. P., *Se garder libre. Journal (1947–1954)*, (Paris, 1962), p. 64. Compare Le Corbusier, *Précisions*, p. 91. The following discussion owes much to Peter Serenyi's article on "Le Corbusier, Fourier and the Monastery of Ema," *Art Bulletin* XLIX (1967):277–286.

7. Niccolò Acciauoli, a banker and Florentine statesman who had made his fortune in Naples, founded the Certosa in 1341: "and if the soul is immortal, as M. Chancellour says, mine will be happy for it." Compare G. Gaye, *Carteggio inedito d'artisti dei secoli XIV, XV, XVI* (Florence, 1839).

8. Ch.-E. Jeanneret, *Etude sur le mouvement d'art décoratif en Allemagne*, p. 50. The visit seems to have taken place around Christmas 1910, when Jeanneret visited his brother Albert who stayed at the "Insitut." See, in this context, Ch.-E. Jeanneret's extensive comments on monastic life on Mount Athos in *Voyage d'Orient*, pp. 124–152.

9. Le Corbusier, *Précisions*, p. 260 ff.

10. Le Corbusier, *Urbanisme* (Paris, 1925), pp. 205 ff.; idem, *Précisions*, p. 99, (and passim); idem, *La ville radieuse* (Paris, 1933: ed., 1964; reprinted 1978), pp. 115 ff.

11. In his Plan Voisin, Le Corbusier offers two versions of "immeuble-villas": the housing blocks on the "cellular principle" (built around rectangular courtyards) and those with "setbacks" ("à redents"). Compare Le Corbusier, *Urbanisme*, passim.

12. Le Corbusier, *Oeuvre complète 1910–1929*, p. 69. On Pessac see ibid., pp. 78–86; *L'Architecture vivante*, Autumn 1927; and B. B. Taylor's excellent study, *Le Corbusier at Pessac* (Cambridge, Mass., 1972) (illustrations in *Le Corbusier at Pessac, 1914–1928* (Paris, 1972)). More references below.

13. Le Corbusier, *Oeuvre complète 1910–1929*, p. 78.

14. Compare Taylor, *Le Corbusier at Pessac*, pp. 5 ff.

15. This is rightly emphasized by André Corboz, in "Encore Pessac," *archithese* 1 (1972):27–36. A sociological analysis of the transformations that Pessac has undergone since its completion has been undertaken by Philippe Boudon, *Lived-in Architecture: Le Corbusier's Pessac Revisited* (MIT Press: Cambridge, Mass., 1972).

16. Edgar Wedepohl, "Die Weissenhofsiedlung der Werkbundausstellung 'Die Wohnung,' " *Wasmuth's Monatshefte für Baukunst, XI* (1927):391–402. See also Hans Hildebrandt's remarks on the cultural (rather than the natural) roots of the "human needs" served by this architecture in the introduction to A. Roth's book *Zwei Haäuser* (Stuttgart, 1927).

17. Hénard's term, however, is "boulevard à redans." He gives two versions of this type: the "boulevard à redans" with alternating rectangular blocks and squares along the boulevard; and the "boulevard à redans triangulaires." It is perhaps no coincidence that Le Corbusier's perspective renderings closely follow the layout of Hénard's. See also chapter 5, note 8.

18. In a caption to a rendering of the Pavillon de l'Esprit Nouveau in *Urbanisme* (*The City of Tomorrow*, p. 230) Le Corbusier refers to M. de Monzie, Minister in the Cabinet, who seems to have said: "In my capacity as a representative of the Government, I wish to testify to the

interest it takes in all efforts such as this; no government can afford to ignore the work that is being done here."

19. For the apartment house at Porte Molitor (rue Nungesser-et-Coli) see Le Corbusier, *Oeuvre complète, 1929–34*, pp. 144–154; for the Clarté flats, ibid., pp. 66–71.

20. Le Corbusier, *Oeuvre complète 1910–1929*, p. 181. More details are given in the "Ilot insalubre" project of 1937, *Oeuvre complète 1934–1948*, pp. 48–54.

21. On these Russian projects see again A. Kopp, *Town and Revolution* (Eng. ed. New York, 1970).

22. Le Corbusier, "Commentaires relatifs à Moscou et à la Ville Verte," unpublished ms. 1930, Fondation Le Corbusier, Paris.

23. Le Corbusier, *Oeuvre complète, 1929–34*, pp. 74–89. On the circumstances of the commission (first rejected by Le Corbusier and Pierre Jeanneret on the grounds of their bad experiences with the Swiss), see also Jacques Gubler, *Nationalisme et internationalisme dans l'architecture moderne de la Suisse* (Lausanne, 1975), pp. 223 ff.

24. See Reyner Banham, *The Architecture of the Well-Tempered Environment* (London, 1969), pp. 153 ff.; on the symbolism of the building and its impact on post World War II architecture cf. William Curtis, "L'université, la ville et l'habitat collectif," *archithese* 14 (1975):29–36.

25. Zurich-Hardturmstrasse; compare Le Corbusier *Oeuvre complète, 1929–34*, pp. 200 ff.; Zürichhorn, ibid., pp. 94–96. For Vesnin's project see A. Kopp, *Town and Revolution*, p. 169.

26. Le Corbusier, "Programme d'une activité possible de l'Armée du Salut en relation avec la Loi Loucheur," unpublished ms. (n.d., 1929); Fondation Le Corbusier.

27. Le Corbusier, *Sur les quatre routes* (Paris, 1941; reprinted ed., Paris, 1970), p. 256.

28. Le Corbusier, *Oeuvre complète 1910–29*, pp. 124 ff.

29. Letter by Albin Peyron to Le Corbusier, September 12, 1928 (unpublished). Fondation Le Corbusier.

30. Quoted by Le Corbusier in an unpublished manuscript "L'usine du bien: la Cité du Refuge" (ca. 1930). Fondation Le Corbusier.

31. See Peter Serenyi, "*Fourier, Le Corbusier and the Monastery of Ema*," p. 285.

32. Le Corbusier, *Oeuvre complète 1929–1934*, pp. 97–109. A critical analysis of the building is at present being prepared by Brian B. Taylor.

33. See letter by Albin Peyron to Le Corbusier, September 12, 1928 (unpublished). Fondation Le Corbusier.

34. See Giedion, *Space, Time and Architecture*, 5th printing, pp. 834 ff. No wonder that in 1950 Van Tijen approvingly wrote of Le Corbusier's Unité; compare "De hoeden af!" (Lift your hats!) "Le Corbusier in Marseille," *Forum*, no. 9 (1950):334–350.

35. Le Corbusier had been his protégé before the war.

36. Le Corbusier, *Oeuvre complète, 1938–1946*, pp. 172–193; *Oeuvre complète 1946–1952*, pp. 186–223; see also Le Corbusier, "Unité d'habitation de Marseille," *Le Point* XXXVIII (Nov. 1950). For detail plans compare especially J. Petit, "Des unités d'habitation 1960 en séries," *Zodiac* 7, pp. 39–49.

37. See *La Dépêche du Midi*, September 28, 1952.

38. A few years later, now as mayor of the small town of Firminy (southwest of Lyon), Claudius-Petit commissioned Le Corbusier to design another Unité, plus a church and a youth center.

39. See Leonardo Benevolo, *The Origins of Modern Town Planning* (Cambridge, Mass., 1971) especially pp. 56 ff. Fourier's *Traité de l'association domestique-agricole* is published in vol. IV of his *Oeuvres complètes* (Paris, 1841). The influence of Fourierist ideas upon Le Corbusier has been studied by P. Serenyi, "Le Corbusier, Fourier and the Monastery of Ema," *The Art Bulletin* (1967):277–286.

40. E. Owen Greening, "The Co-operative Traveller Abroad," *Social Solutions*, no. 6, 1886; quoted after Benevolo, *The Origins of Modern Town Planning*, p. 66.

41. Compare Le Corbusier, *Manière de penser l'urbanisme*, p. 44; "L'Unité d'habitation de Marseilles," *Le Point*, November 1950. I cannot quite agree with P. Serenyi when he suggests that "Ch. E. Jeanneret had undoubtedly studied the writings of Fourier first-hand after having been exposed to his ideas by Tony Garnier in 1908." (Compare P. Serenyi, "Fourier, Le Corbusier and the Monastery of Ema," p. 283.) There is no direct evidence for such an early "initiation" to Fourier and Fourierism.

42. Le Corbusier, *La ville radieuse* (Paris, 1933), p. 59. But see also his critical remarks on the design of the "Normandie," *When the Cathedrals were White*, p. 93.

43. On the nautical symbolism of Le Corbusier's architecture, cf. especially Peter Collins, *Changing Ideals in Modern Architecture* (Montreal, 1965; reprinted ed. 1967), pp. 162 ff.; P. Serenyi, "Le Corbusier, Fourier, and the Monastery of Ema"; Adolf M. Vogt, *Russische und französische Revolutionsarchitektur*, pp. 161 ff. That the symbolism of Le Corbusier's domestic architecture refers to the world of consumption and not of production has been noted by Norbert Huse in *Neues Bauen 1918–1933* (Munich, 1975), p. 77. I have discussed the nautical theme in my inaugural lecture at the University of Berne, "Das Schiff—eine Metapher der modernen Architektur," partly reprinted in *Neue Zürcher Zeitung*, August 23/24, 1975.

44. See Le Corbusier, *Oeuvre complète, 1946–1952*, p. 190.

45. Leonardo Benevolo, *History of Modern Architecture*, vol. 2 (Cambridge, Mass., 1972), p. 732.

46. On the shopping street, see Lewis Mumford's verdict in "The Marseilles Folly," *The Highway and the City* (New York, 1963), pp. 53–66.

When Mumford visited the Unité in 1958, no shops had been opened yet, for trivial reasons. Rather than lease the space, the government wanted the prospective shopkeepers to buy property on the eleventh floor. It took some time until a reasonable number of small enterprises settled there. Today (I last visited the Unité in 1974), not all spaces are occupied, but the situation is as lively as on a small village main street.

47. Le Corbusier, *Oeuvre complète 1946–1952*, p. 190.

48. Open, indeed, to a "plurality of approaches," compare Charles Jencks, *Modern Movements in Architecture* (New York, 1973), pp. 11–26.

49. He discusses the drawbacks of the narrow apartment-type; yet he stresses, among other significant advantages, the good sonic isolation and the well thought-out dimensions of the apartments. Compare Paul Chombart-de-Lauwe, *Famille et habitation. Un essai d'observation expérimentale* (Paris, 1960). Photos and plans in Le Corbusier *Oeuvre complète 1952–1957*, pp. 180–190.

50. Le Corbusier, *Oeuvre complète 1957–1965*, pp. 212–217.

51. Ibid., pp. 32–53; Jean Petit, *Un couvent de Le Corbusier* (Paris, 1961); A. Henze and B. Moosbrugger, *La Tourette, Le Corbusier's erster Klosterbau* (Starnberg, 1963); C. Rowe, "Dominican Monastery of La Tourette," *The Architectural Review* (June 1961):400–410. The student hostel referred to above is the "Maison du Brésil" ("House of Brazil") at the Cité universitaire in Paris, 1957–1959 (together with Lucio Costa). *Oeuvre complète 1957–1965*, pp. 192–199.

52. See the interesting correspondence between A. Couturier and Le Corbusier on the subject of Le Thoronet in J. Petit, *Un Couvent de Le Corbusier*. On the abbey itself, see W. Braunfels, *Abendländische Klosterbaukunst* (Cologne, 1969), pp. 138 ff.

53. La Tourette, planned and built as a school, does not anymore serve its original purpose, but is used mainly for summer schools and courses organized by the Dominican order. As a result of the student revolt in 1968, the order sends its future members to state universities for their education.

54. The rhythm of the lamellas follows harmonic laws, after calculations made by the composer Yannis Xenakis, then a collaborator of Le Corbusier.

Notes to Chapter 5

1. For a good presentation and discussion of the principal English and American criticism of Le Corbusier's urban theory see Norma Evenson, "Le Corbusier's Critics." *Le Corbusier: The Machine and the Grand Design* (New York, 1969), pp. 120–122. Today, one would have to add, among others, Robert Goodman, *After the Planners* (New York, 1971).

2. An early paper by Charles Edouard Jeanneret on urbanism at La Chaux-de-Fonds, written in Munich in 1910, seems to be lost; compare Jean Petit, *Le Corbusier lui-même* (Paris, 1961), p. 38. For a discussion of

Le Corbusier's early involvement in problems of housing see Brian B.
Taylor, *Le Corbusier at Pessac* (Cambridge, Mass., 1972).

3. Le Corbusier, *L'atelier de la recherche patiente* (Paris, 1960), pp.
62–64; the statement obviously represents a slightly dramatized version of what he actually may have said; see also *Oeuvre complète 1910–
1929*, 6th ed. (Zurich, 1956), p. 135.

4. Le Corbusier, *Urbanisme* (Paris, 1925), p. 135.

5. Ibid., p. 158.

6. For a discussion of *Urbanisme*, see Maximilien Gauthier, *Le Corbusier ou l'architecture au service de l'homme* (Paris, 1944), pp. 86–107
and Reyner Banham, *Theory and Design in the First Machine Age* (London, 1960), pp. 248–256.

7. Le Corbusier, *Urbanisme*, pp. 97–133.

8. The importance of Hénard as a premise and source for Le Corbusier's urbanistic concepts has been correctly emphasized by Peter
Serenyi in his review of the original edition of this book in *Journal of
the Society of Architectural Historians* (1971): 255–259. For Hénard see
Peter M. Wolf, *Eugène Hénard and the Beginnings of Urbanism in Paris,
1900–1914* (New York, 1968), (with complete bibliography).

9. Le Corbusier, *Urbanisme*, p. 265.

10. Le Corbusier, *Urbanisme*, p. 272. Le Corbusier suggests here, in
other words, to treat the important monuments of the past as "objets
trouvés" or—to quote his own term—as "objets à réaction poétique"
within the vast open spaces of the new, green city. A similarly selective
and "ironical" approach to the urban past has been suggested by Frank
Lloyd Wright in *An Organic Architecture. The Architecture of Democracy*
(London, 1939); the cultural and ideological implications of this approach have been discussed by Manfredo Tafuri in *Teorie e storia
dell'architettura*, 2nd ed. (Bari, 1970), pp. 68 ff.

11. Le Corbusier, *Urbanisme*, p. 273.

12. Ibid.

13. *L'Esprit Nouveau* 4 (January 1921):465 ff.

14. See Jean Labadié, "Les cathédrales de la cité moderne," *L'Illustration* (August 1922):131–135.

15. In *Vers une architecture*, p. 44, Le Corbusier refers to an interview
given by Perret to the newspaper *L'Intransigeant*, where Perret explains his project and the function of the bridges. Le Corbusier, however, considers these bridges (and other aspects of the project) as a
"futurisme dangereux." Perret, in turn, some time later elaborated a
project based on Corbusian cruciform towers; see *Science et vie* (1 December 1925), quoted in Le Corbusier, *Almanach d'architecture moderne*
(Paris, 1926), p. 97.

16. Compare *Urbanisme* and *L'art décoratif d'aujourd'hui* (Paris, 1925),
where Le Corbusier published several photographs of early American
skyscrapers; there are none, however, by Sullivan.

17. Compare Ebenezer Howard, *Tomorrow: a Peaceful Path to Real Reform* (London, 1898); 2nd ed. entitled *The Garden Cities of Tomorrow* (London, 1902). Brian B. Taylor has discussed the influence of the English garden city movement upon Le Corbusier's own early work, in *Le Corbusier at Pessac*.

18. Le Corbusier, *Urbanisme*, pp. 157–169.

19. Ibid., p. 165.

20. Ibid., pp. 192 ff., and passim.

21. Ibid., pp. 60, 71.

22. Ibid., p. 176.

23. See *Oeuvre complète 1910–1929*, pp. 76, 92–97, and passim.

24. Le Corbusier, *Urbanisme*, p. 3.

25. Le Corbusier, *Quand les cathédrales étaient blanches* (Paris, 1937; ed. 1965), p. 58. However, as Maurice Besset has shown (*Qui était Le Corbusier?* (Geneva, 1968), p. 151) Le Corbusier's attitude toward the city as a picturesque sequence of grandiose "vistas" is influenced by Sitte; this attitude is documented in almost all of his early urbanistic studies. His despise for Sitte's theory (see *Der Städtebau* (Vienna, 1889)) may partly be the result of the total deformation it had undergone in the French version of *Der Städtebau*; compare George R. Collins and Chr. Crasemann Collins, *Camillo Sitte and the Birth of Modern City Planning* (London, 1965), pp. 63–72; 145.

26. Le Corbusier, *Urbanisme*, pp. 5–11; 77–86.

27. Ibid., p. 255; compare his later comments on Haussmann in *La Ville radieuse* (Paris, 1933), p. 209.

28. Le Corbusier, *Quand les cathédrales étaient blanches* (re-ed., Paris, 1965), p. 59.

29. Ibid., p. 60.

30. Le Corbusier, *Urbanisme*, p. 169.

31. P. Girardet, "Le règne de la vitesse," *Mercure de France* (1923); quoted in Le Corbusier, *Urbanisme*, p. 182.

32. See Le Corbusier, *Oeuvre complète 1910–1929*, pp. 129 ff.

33. Le Corbusier, *Urbanisme*, p. 113.

34. The most famous are in the Institut de France, Ms. B., fol. 36 r.; fol. 16 r.; fol. 37 v. These sketches have often intrigued modern architects and planners; cf. e. g., their discussion in Alberto Sartoris, *Léonard architecte* (Paris, 1952).

35. See Peter M. Wolf, *Eugène Hénard*, pp. 49–60; Hénard's plan is illustrated in *Urbanisme* on p. 111. For the American background, Le Corbusier seems to have used books like Werner Hegemann, *Amerikanische Architektur und Stadtbaukunst* (Berlin, 1925). An illustration on p. 53 in this book reappears in *Urbanisme* on p. 144.

36. Le Corbusier, *Urbanisme*, p. 65. For a discussion of Le Corbusier's vision of uniformity in architecture see S. von Moos, ". . . de l'uniformité dans le détail. Notiz zur 'Monotonie' bei Le Corbusier," *werk. archithese* 1 (1977):37–40. The Laugier quotation is from his *Observations sur L'architecture* (The Hague, 1765), pp. 312 ff.

37. Le Corbusier, *Urbanisme*, p. 63.

38. Ibid., pp. 146–148.

39. Ibid., p. 270.

40. Ibid., pp. 275 ff.

41. Le Corbusier, *Oeuvre complète 1910–1929*, p. 111.

42. Le Corbusier, *Urbanisme*, p. 280.

43. For examples see Vincent Scully, *American Architecture and Urbanism* (New York, 1969; 2nd. ed., 1971), pp. 166–169.

44. See the various volumes of the *Oeuvre complète* and N. Evenson, *Le Corbusier*, figs. 16–25.

45. Le Corbusier, *Vers une architecture*, p. 243.

46. Le Corbusier, *Urbanisme*, pp. 203–212.

47. The ideology of collective happiness which underlies Le Corbusier's strategy has been the subject of numerous and often acute comments; see, for instance, Pierre Francastel, *Art et technique* (Paris, 1956; ed. 1962), p. 42: "Chacun a sa place . . . ; et tout le monde est heureux, éperdument. Les hommes, régenérés, fondent de gratitude pour ceux qui leur ont préparé leurs cadres. . . ."

48. See especially Alexander von Senger's polemics: *Krisis der Architektur* (Zurich, 1928); *Die Brandfackel Moskaus* (Zurich, 1931). Some Marxist critics, however, at an early date analysed and criticized the identification of modern architecture with communism and the identification of academism with political reaction as a "false" problem; compare the recently published article by Max Raphael, "Das Sowjetpalais. Eine marxistische Kritik an einer reaktionären Architektur" (written 1933–34), Max Raphael, *Für eine demokratische Architektur*, ed. J. Held (Frankfurt, 1976).

49. See Le Corbusier, *Précisions*, pp. 238 ff.; no wonder that the equally hilly site of São Paulo generated an analogous proposal (ibid.).

50. Ibid., p. 244.

51. Ibid.

52. In 1931, France was to celebrate the centennial of the French colonial takeover of North Africa.

53. Le Corbusier, *Oeuvre complète 1929–1934*, pp. 174–176. That Algiers should be regarded as the capital city of Africa was a much cherished idea in official French circles, especially in the aftermath of the centennial celebrations. Compare Jean-Pierre Faure, *Alger capitale* (Paris, 1933).

54. Willy Boesiger, ed., *Le Corbusier 1910–1965*, p. 327; *Oeuvre complète 1929–1934*, pp. 175 ff. I am grateful to Pierre A. Emery for his recollections of Le Corbusier's early visits to Algiers. For a brilliant discussion of the plan's ideological significance, see Manfredo Tafuri, *Progetto e utopia* (Bari, 1973), pp. 115–124, with useful references.

55. See Marco Pozzetto, *La Fiat-Lingotto. Un' architettura torinese d'avanguardia* (Turin, 1975).

56. Le Corbusier, *Oeuvre complète, 1929–1934*, p. 202 (from a newspaper interview, 1934).

57. Namely the reprint of an article by A. von Senger entitled "L'architecture en péril," first published May 5, 1934, in *La Libre Parole* (Neuchâtel) then reprinted in *Travaux Nord-Africains*, June 4, 1942. For Le Corbusier's reaction to von Senger's polemics see *Entretien avec les étudiants des écoles d'architecture* (Paris, 1951).

58. In his *Poésie sur Alger* Le Corbusier adds a rather improbable detail: the Mayor of Algiers, he says, wanted to have him arrested.

59. Le Corbusier, *Oeuvre complète 1938–1946*, pp. 44–65; *L'atelier de la recherche patiente*, pp. 146 ff.

60. A detailed study of the Centrosoyuz is at present being prepared by Charlotte Benton.

61. The best study of Le Corbusier's relations with Russia is by Giorgio Ciucci, "Le Corbusier e Wright in URSS," *Socialismo, città, architettura, URSS 1917–1937*, ed. M. Tafuri (Rome, 1972), pp. 171–193.

62. Compare Le Corbusier, *Sur les 4 routes* (Paris, 1941); *La maison des hommes* (Paris, 1942), pp. 41; 45; *Oeuvre complète 1938–1946*, pp. 72–75.

63. See Vincent Scully, *American Architecture and Urbanism*, p. 170.

64. See Philip Johnson and H. R. Hitchcock, *The International Style* (New York, 1932).

65. *The New York Times*, Jan. 3, 1932, "Magazine Section."

66. See Le Corbusier, *Quand les cathédrales étaient blanches*, p. 61 (Eng. ed. *When the Cathedrals Were White*); the incident is reported by the *New York Herald Tribune*, October 22, 1935. But the *New York Times* of the same day reported that "Of New York in particular Mr. Le Corbusier was not able to speak, having seen the city so far only from the ship's deck and hurrying taxicabs."

67. Le Corbusier, *Quand les cathédrales étaient blanches*, p. 52.

68. Ibid.

69. See William Curtis, "Le Corbusier, Manhattan et le rêve de la ville radieuse," *archithese* 17 (Metropolis I), pp. 23–28. In numbers 17, 18, and 20 of *archithese* the reaction of other European architects to New York are discussed.

70. Le Corbusier, *Quand les cathédrales étaient blanches*, p. 7.

71. See in particular H. I. Brock "Le Corbusier Scans Gotham Towers.

The French Architect, on a Tour, Finds the City Violently Alive, a Wilderness of Experiment Toward a New Order," *New York Times*, November 3, 1935.

72. See Le Corbusier, *Oeuvre complète 1934–1938*, pp. 74–77.

73. See Knud Bastlund, *José Luis Sert* (Zurich-New York, 1967), pp. 28–34.

74. For plans for Antwerp, see Le Corbusier, *Oeuvre complète 1929–1934*, pp. 156–159; for Hellocourt, Le Corbusier, *Oeuvre complète 1934–1938*, pp. 36 ff.

75. The history of the CIAM has been outlined by S. Giedion in *Space, Time and Architecture*, 5th ed., pp. 696–706. For a more encompassing study on Le Corbusier's role in the CIAM see Pier Giorgio Gerosa, *Urbanistica e mobilità. L'opera urbanistica de Le Corbusier e il significato della mobilità* (Basel and Stuttgart, 1978). Further investigations, notably by Martin Steinmann and Hilo Hilpert are currently underway.

76. After Sibyl Moholy, *Moholy-Nagy. Experiment in Totality* 2nd ed. (Cambridge, Mass., 1969), p. 93.

77. CIAM-France, *La Charte d'Athènes, avec un discours liminaire de Jean Giraudoux* (Paris, 1943). Martin Steinmann, "Neuer Blick auf die Charte d'Athènes," *archithese* 1 (1972): 37–46.

78. Le Corbusier, *Urbanisme*, p. 159.

79. For more details see *L'atelier de la recherche patiente*, p. 115.

80. Le Corbusier, *Oeuvre complète 1938–1946*, pp. 94–99.

81. J. Petit, *Le Corbusier lui-même*, p. 87.

82. Le Corbusier, *Oeuvre complète*, vols. 5–8, passim; Norma Evenson, *Chandigarh* (Berkeley, 1966), (with bibliography up to 1966); Sten Nilsson, *The New Capitals of India, Pakistan and Bangladesh* (Lund, 1973). For a more detailed discussion of Chandigarh in its political context see my essay on "The Politics of the Open Hand," *The Open Hand*, ed. Russell Walden (Cambridge, Mass., 1977); pp. 412–457.

83. A good recent introduction to Gandhi's political thinking is given by Francis G. Hutchins, *Spontaneous Revolution. The Quit India Movement* (Delhi, 1971). For a collection of Gandhi's writings on economics see M. K. Gandhi, *Economic and Industrial Life and Relations* ed. V. B. Kher, 3 vols. (Ahmedabad, 1957).

84. Varma, incidentally, happened to be in the US while the Punjab was split—and while there he gathered first hand information on planning and urbanization. Compare C. Rand, "City on a Tilting Plain," *The New Yorker*, April 30, 1955; and especially Evenson, *Chandigarh*, pp. 6–11 (with more references).

85. This estimation of the building costs is from Rand, "City on a Tilting plain," On Nowicki, see Evenson, *Chandigarh*, pp. 19–24.

86. See Maxwell Fry's report, "A Discursive Commentary," *Architect's*

Yearbook 6 (London, 1955): 40 ff., and his article in *The Open Hand*, pp. 350–363.

87. See Evenson, *Chandigarh*, pp. 31 ff. The decision to move the British administration from Calcutta to Delhi had been taken in 1911, and it was then that a planning committee was appointed, consisting of Captain Swinton (formerly the chairman of the London County Council), J. A. Brodie and Sir E. L. Lutyens. It produced the plan of New Delhi. The palaces at the Capitol are by Sir Edwin Lutyens (viceroy's house) and Sir Herbert Baker (secretariats). Compare Robert Byron, "New Delhi," *The Architectural Review* (January 1931):1 ff.; A. S. Butler et al. *The Architecture of Sir Edwin Lutyens*, 3 vols. (London and New York, 1950), vol. 2.

88. Evenson, *Chandigarh*, pp. 64–67.

89. G. Jawaharlal Nehru, *Speeches* (New Delhi, 1958), vol. 3, pp. 25 ff. (at the occasion of the opening of a factory); pp. 466 ff. (on slums).

90. For Le Corbusier's explanations of this see Le Corbusier, *Modulor* 2 (Boulogne s. Seine, 1955), pp. 187 ff.

91. Le Corbusier, *Quand les cathédrales étaient blanches* (Paris, 1937; re-ed. 1965), p. 215; see also ibid., p. 222: "il faut le bon plan, le plan totalitaire symphonique, qui réponde aux besoins collectifs et assure le bonheur individuel . . . ici est le rôle tout puissant et bienfaisant de l'autorité: autorité père de famille."

92. Le Corbusier, *Précisions*, p. 187. See also Le Corbusier, *Une maison, un palais* (Paris, 1928), p. 228: "Colbert?—Qu'il surgisse le nouveau Colbert! . . . un homme de sang froid, mais un homme qui croit. —Un homme pétri de son temps!" Or the letter to the Governor of Algiers (14 December 1932): "Aujourd'hui, on ne peut rêver qu'à un homme, c'est à Colbert. Agir, entreprendre, réaliser." In Le Corbusier, *La Ville radieuse* (Paris, 1933), p. 249.

    Le Corbusier's political philosophy has been discussed by Pierre Francastel, *Art et technique au XIXe et XXe siècles* (Paris, 1956); re-ed. 1962), pp. 37–47; Peter Serenyi, "Le Corbusier, Fourier and the Monastery of Ema," *The Art Bulletin* (1967): 277–286; Heide Berndt, *Das Gesellschaftsbild bei Stadtplanern* (Stuttgart, 1968), p. 70 ff.; cf. also, more recently, Charles Jencks's observations in *Le Corbusier and the Tragic View of Architecture* (London and Cambridge, Mass., 1973), pp. 17 ff.; pp. 110–133; Manfredo Tafuri, *Progetto e utopia* (Bari, 1973), pp. 115–124 and passim; Norbert Huse, *Le Corbusier in Selbstzeugnissen und Bilddokumenten* (Hamburg, 1976).

93. Le Corbusier, *Précisions*, p. 15. Le Corbusier's attitude to colonialism has been documented and discussed by M. Fagiolo, *Le Corbusier 1930, I progetti per Algeri e l'America Latina* (mimeographed ms.) (Milan, 1973).

94. Le Corbusier, *Prècisions*, p. 201.

95. Mulkraj Anand, "Conversation with Le Corbusier," ed. Santosh Kumar, *Le Corbusier. 80th Birthday Anniversary Issue* (Bombay: International Cultural Organization 1967), pp. 11–14.

Notes to Chapter 6

1. The following description of the League of Nations controversy is based upon Le Corbusier's own account, see *Oeuvre complète 1910–1929*, pp. 160–173 (and below, note 3). S. Giedion's recollections in *Space, Time and Architecture*, pp. 530–538. For a more recent account of the principal facts, see Alfred Roth, *Begegnungen mit Pionieren* (Basel and Stuttgart, 1973), pp. 52–57; and Martin Steinmann, "Der Völkerbundspalast: eine 'chronique scandaleuse,' " *werk.archithese* 23–24 (1978):28–31.

2. The architects were Nénot (France) and his partner Flegenheimer (Geneva); Broggi, Vaccaro, Franzi (Italy); Camille Lefèbvre (France). On the League of Nations Palace as built, see S. von Moos, " 'Kasino der Naionen,' " *werk.archithese* 23–24 (1978):32–36.

3. In Paris, the project was defended by Christian Zervos in *Cahiers d'Art*, especially 2, (1928):84–88. Compare Le Corbusier's "file" on this affair: *Une maison—un palais* (Paris, 1928).

4. *Requête de MM. Le Corbusier et Pierre Jeanneret à M. le Président du Conseil de la Société des Nations* (Paris, 1931).

5. See Claude Schnaidt, *Hannes Meyer, Bauten, Projekte und Schriften* (Teufen, 1965), pp. 23–27, and John Ritter, "World Parliament: The League of Nations Competition, 1926," *Architectural Review* (July 1964):17–23.

6. Kenneth Frampton, "The Humanist vs. the Utilitarian Ideal," *Architectural Design* 38 (1968):134–136.

7. A picture of the Grand Palais is published in Le Corbusier, *Une maison—un palais* (Paris, 1928), p. 172. Peter Serenyi first noted this relationship in his review of the German edition of this present work, *JSAH* 3 (1971):258.

8. See Le Corbusier, *Oeuvre complète 1910–1929*, p. 173, where Le Corbusier compares his project to the executed building by Broggi, Nénot, and Flegenheimer.

9. See Le Corbusier's enthusiastic comments on Gustave Lyon as an acoustics expert in "La salle Pleyel—une preuve de l'évolution architecturale," *Cahiers d'Art* 2 (February 1928):89 ff.

10. Le Corbusier, *Précisions*, p. 60. For an interesting, yet different interpretation of the formal principles determining the spatial sequence of the various parts of the building, cf. Colin Rowe and Robert Slutzky, "Transparency," pp. 45, 54.

11. Quoted from Le Corbusier, *Oeuvre complète 1910–1929*, pp. 190–197, 214; see also Paul Otlet and Le Corbusier, *Mundaneum* (Brussels, 1928); Le Corbusier, "Un projet de centre mondial à Genève," *Cahiers d'Art* (1928):307–311.

12. See "Dr. John Wesley Kelcher's Restoration of King Solomon's Temple and Citadel, Helmle & Corbett Architects," *Pencil Points* VI (November 1925):69–86. In 1926, the reconstruction was shown in Berlin in the context of a presentation of recent American architecture;

cf. *Ausstellung neuer amerikanischer Baukunst,* January 1926 (catalog), (Akademie der Künste: Berlin, 1926). That the Mundaneum owes something to Babylonian architecture had first been noted by Marcello Fagiolo in "La nuova Babilonia secondo Le Corbusier," *Notiziario Arte Contemporanea* (May 1974):15–17.

13. On the impact of the idea of "New Babylon" in America, see Rosemarie Haag-Bletter and Cervin Robinson, *Skyscraper Style. Art Déco New York* (New York, 1975), pp. 11–12; Manfredo Tafuri, " 'Neu-Babylon.' Das New York der Zwanzigerjahre und die Suche nach dem Amerikanismus," *archithese* 20 (1976):12–24.

14. See especially Karel Teige's critique: "Mundaneum," the Czech magazine *Stavba* 7 (1928–1929):145–155, and Le Corbusier's reply, written for *Stavba* but published in *Mousaion* and reprinted (in French) in *Le Corbusier et Pierre Jeanneret,* special issue of *L'Architecture d'Aujourd'hui* (1936):38–61. Both articles have been republished in English by George Baird, "Architecture and Politics: A Polemical Dispute," *Oppositions* 4 (1974): 79–108.

15. See U. E. Chowdhury, "Le Corbusier in Chandigarh, Creator and Generator," *Architectural Design* (October 1965): 504–513.

16. In the course of its realization, the original project had undergone various modifications, and the building was inaugurated only in 1935. See Le Corbusier, *Oeuvre complète 1910–1929,* pp. 206–213; *Oeuvre complète 1929–1934,* pp. 34–41; *Précisions,* pp. 58 ff. Charlotte Benton is at present preparing a detailed study of this building.

17. See the second project in Le Corbusier, *Oeuvre complète 1910–1929,* p. 208–209; his comments are in *Précisions,* pp. 47–48 and passim.

18. Le Corbusier, *Oeuvre complète 1929–1934,* pp. 123–137; on the competition itself and the projects submitted to the jury. Compare Giorgio Ciucci, "Concours pour le Palais des Soviets," *VH 101,* no. 7–8 (Spring 1972):113–134.

19. Le Corbusier, *Oeuvre complète 1929–1934,* p. 130.

20. Ibid., p. 135.

21. Only a few years before S. Giedion, encouraged by Le Corbusier, had published a choice of important works by Freyssinet in Giedion, *Bauen in Frankreich.*

22. For a good documentation see V. De Feo, *URSS architettura 1917–1936* (Rome, 1963), pp. 133; 182, and idem., "Architecture at théatre: concours pour un théatre d'état à Charkov—1930," *VH 101,* no. 7–8 (Spring 1972):89–110.

23. Le Corbusier, *Oeuvre complète 1929–1934,* p. 13.

24. *UN Headquarters, op. cit.,* p. 70.

25. Ibid., p. 20.

26. Ibid., p. 68.

27. See Le Corbusier, *Quand les cathédrales étaient blanches.*

28. After his visit to the PSFS building in Philadelphia (1936) he had ironically suggested to George Howe to contact him in case of another commission of comparable bulk. See Geoffrey Hellman, "From Within to Without," (part 2) *The New Yorker*, May 3, 1947, p. 38.

29. Le Corbusier, *Oeuvre complète 1946–1962*, pp. 37–39.

30. Reasons for this choice are given in G. Hellman, "From Within to Without," (part 1) *The New Yorker*, April 24, 1948, p. 35.

31. Peter Blake, *Le Corbusier* (Harmondsworth and Baltimore, 1960; ed. 1966), pp. 130 ff.

32. He later declined all responsibility for the building's realization; see *L'atelier*, p. 151 and *Oeuvre complète 1946–1952*, p. 39.

33. See Giedion, *Space, Time and Architecture*, p. 566.

34. Le Corbusier, *Aujourd'hui* 51:108.

35. See in this context the important book by P. Régamey, *Art Sacré au XXe siècle* (Paris, 1952).

36. Le Corbusier, *Oeuvre complète 1946–1952*, pp. 24–36; Compare A. Henze, *Le Corbusier* (Berlin, 1957), pp. 58 ff.

37. Le Corbusier and Jean Petit, *Le livre de Ronchamp*, (Paris, 1961).

38. Le Corbusier, *Ronchamp, Carnet de la recherche patiente no. 2* (Zurich 1957), p. 7.

39. Le Corbusier, *Oeuvre complète 1946–1952*, p. 72. Views and plans of Ronchamp: ibid., pp. 72–84; *Oeuvre complète 1952–1957*, pp. 16–43; Le Corbusier, *Textes et dessins pour Ronchamp* (Paris, 1955); Anton Henze, *Ronchamp. Le Corbusiers erster Kirchenbau* (Recklinghausen, 1956).

40. N. Pevsner, *An Outline of European Architecture*, 7th ed. (Harmondsworth, 1963), p. 429. See also James Stirling, "Le Corbusier's Chapel and the Crisis of Rationalism," *The Architectural Review* (March, 1965):155–161. For a brilliant ideological critique of Ronchamp, see Giulio C. Argan, "La Chiesa di Ronchamp," *Progetto e Destino* (Milan, 1965), pp. 237–243.

41. Giedion, *Architektur und Gemeinschaft* (Eng. ed. *Architecture you and me*) (Hamburg, 1956), pp. 118 ff.

42. Karl Ledergerber, *Kunst und Religion in der Verwandlung* (Cologne, 1966), p. 127.

43. On the Capitol Complex see Le Corbusier, *Oeuvre complète 1946–1952*, pp. 112–159; *Oeuvre complète 1952–1957*, pp. 50–113; *Oeuvre complète 1957–1965*, pp. 58–115; and Norma Evenson, *Chandigarh*, pp. 71–89.

44. In 1966, the Punjab was divided into two separate Indian states, Punjab and Haryana, with the result that the capital became, to quote the *New York Times* a "two-headed, three-tongued administrative and political monstrosity." See J. Anthony Lukas, "Le Corbusier's 'Organic City' in Punjab Faces Political Surgery," *New York Times*, June 27, 1966.

45. An extension building designed in 1962, accommodates more audience rooms behind the Palace.

46. Le Corbusier's first project for the Secretariat had foreseen a skyscraper; see Le Corbusier, *Oeuvre complète 1946–1952*, pp. 118 ff; Evenson, *Chandigarh*, pp. 79 ff.

47. See *UN Headquarters*, pp. 9, 33.

48. Le Corbusier, *Oeuvre complète 1946–1952*, pp. 118–121 and *Oeuvre complète 1957–1963*, p. 78. This early stage of the Assembly Hall project exerted a far reaching influence; it reappears in projects by Oscar Niemeyer (Palace of Aurora, Brasilia) and of Philip Johnson (Sheldon Art Gallery, Lincoln, Nebraska).

49. See also, in this context, S. von Moos, "The Politics of the Open Hand," *The Open Hand*, ed. R. Walden (Cambridge, MA, 1977), pp. 412–457.

50. We are here, in fact, at the other extreme of Le Corbusier's enthusiasm for the mechanically served "house with exact respiration," advertised by him around 1930. However, in order to make work possible mechanical air-conditioning had to be provided in some of the Capitol's interiors.

51. Le Corbusier, *Oeuvre complète 1952–1957*, p. 94. However, the idea was not realized, and today, the tower contains fixed skylights, see Evenson, *Chandigarh*, p. 82.

52. Robert Byron, "New Delhi," *The Architectural Review* (January 1931):1 ff; A. S. G. Butler et al., *The Architecture of Sir Edwin Lutyens*, 3 vols. (London and New York, 1950), vol. 2.

53. Le Corbusier, *Oeuvre complète 1952–1957*, p. 50.

54. Allan Greenberg, "Lutyens' Architecture Restudied," *Perspecta* 12 (New Haven, 1969):148 ff.

55. Le Corbusier, *Modulor 2*, pp. 125–237, especially pp. 225 ff.

56. Le Corbusier, *Oeuvre complète 1952–57*, p. 102; the modifications in the scale of the Governor's Palace are described in Le Corbusier, *Modulor 2*, p. 234.

57. See Greenberg, "Lutyens' Architecture Restudied," pp. 148 ff.; Butler, *The Architecture of Sir Edwin Lutyens*, plates 135–138; 159; 160; 204–213.

58. Evenson, *Chandigarh*, p. 84.

59. Quoted in S. K. Gypta, "Chandigarh," p. 6.

Notes to Chapter 7

1. Le Corbusier, *L'Esprit Nouveau*, p. 3. A slightly later version of the definition of the "sentiment moderne" is as follows: "This modern sentiment is a spirit of geometry, a spirit of construction and of synthesis." *Urbanisme*, p. 36. The ideas underlying this chapter are elaborated

further in my more recent essay, "Le Corbusier als Maler," *Gotthard Jedlicka. Eine Gedenkschrift* (Zurich, 1974), pp. 139–156.

2. Le Corbusier, *Oeuvre complète 1938–1946*, pp. 36–71.

3. See S. Giedion, *Architektur und Gemeinschaft (Architecture you and me)*, pp. 65 ff.

4. See *Architecture d'aujourd'hui*, special issue on Le Corbusier, April 1948. The most important English publication on Le Corbusier the artist is from the same year: Stamo Papadaki, ed., *Le Corbusier. The Foundations of his World* (New York, 1948). See also *Werk* 2 (1949):50 ff.

5. Le Corbusier, *Ronchamp (Carnets de la recherche patiente)*, p. 17.

6. *Architecture d'aujourd'hui*, special issue, April 1948.

7. See Le Corbusier, *Précisions*, pp. 60 ff.

8. Le Corbusier, *Oeuvre complète 1938–1946*, pp. 158–161; *Architecture d'aujourd'hui*, p. 53.

9. Le Corbusier, *Oeuvre complète 1952–1957*, pp. 123 ff.; compare *Zodiac 7*, pp. 57 ff.

10. Christian Zervos's critique was openly polemical. "Never has a painter ignored plastic truth as much as he did, or penetrated less the secrets of art, or more misunderstood its principles; never has an artist had less understanding of a painting's composition or less knowledge of the material he manipulates." *Cahiers d'Art* I (1954):116.

11. Conversation with Savina in *Aujourd'hui*, no. 51:98.

12. Le Corbusier, *Oeuvre plastique* (Paris, 1938), preface.

13. See Le Corbusier's extremely interesting statement prepared for a conference on realism; reprinted in *selearte* (Florence: July–August 1952), pp. 10–12.

14. Le Corbusier, *Oeuvre complète 1946–1952*, p. 9.

15. See Carlo L. Ragghianti, "Le Corbusier a Firenze," *Le Corbusier*, catalog of his exhibition in Florence, 1963.

16. See Alan Colquhoun, "Displacement of Concepts," *Architectural Design* (April 1972):236. More recently, Eduard F. Sekler has studied the interactions between Le Corbusier the painter and the architect in "The Carpenter Center in Le Corbusier's Oeuvre. An Assessment," *Le Corbusier at Work*, eds. E. F. Sekler and W. Curtis (Cambridge, MA, 1978), pp. 229–258.

17. Le Corbusier, *Le Modulor* (Boulogne s. Seine, 1948), pp. 216 ff.

18. Some stages of this process are documented in Le Corbusier, *Oeuvre complète 1946–1952*, p. 231.

19. *Aujourd'hui*, no. 51:97.

20. Alfred H. Barr, *Cubism and Abstract Art* (New York, 1936), pp. 163–166.

21. I have made some utterly preliminary remarks on the relations between advertising and avant-garde art in my preface to *The Other Twenties. Themes in Art and Advertising, 1920–1930* (Cambridge, Mass., 1975) (catalog of an exhibition at the Carpenter Center for the Visual Arts, Harvard University).

22. *Le Corbusier*, catalog of his exhibition in Zurich, 1938, p. 11.

23. Le Corbusier, *Oeuvre plastique*, preface. Similar terms had been are 'plastic words'; the meaning of these plastic words is not of a descriptive nature. . . ." *L'Esprit Nouveau*, pp. 1489–1494.

24. Le Corbusier, *Oeuvre plastique*, preface.

25. *Aujourd'hui*, no. 51:14.

26. See Samir Rafi, "Le Corbusier et les femmes d'Alger," *Revue d'histoire et de civilisation du Maghreb* (Algiers, January 1968), pp. 50–61. This article is still one of the few serious pieces of research concerning Le Corbusier's painting.

27. Letter from Jean de Maisonseul to Samir Rafi, dated January 5, 1968. I am grateful to P. A. Emery for having been kind enough to let me see a copy of this letter.

28. See Rafi, "Le Corbusier et les femmes d'Alger," pp. 50–61. S. von Moos, "Cartesian Curves," *Architectural Design* (April 1972), pp. 237–239; "Le Corbusier als Maler," *Gotthard Jedlicka. Eine Gedenkschrift* (Zurich, 1974), pp. 139–156 (with comprehensive bibligraphy).

29. *L'atelier de la recherche patiente*, p. 116; after *La Ville radieuse*, 1933.

30. This painting must have meant a lot to Le Corbusier, since it hung for a long time in his living room.

31. *Le Corbusier parle*, p. 62.

32. Le Corbusier, *Précisions*, p. 4.

33. Le Corbusier, *Aircraft* (London and New York, 1937).

34. Antoine de Saint-Exupéry, *Terre des hommes* (Paris, 1939; reprinted ed. 1957), p. 72.

35. Le Corbusier, *Ronchamp*, p. 128.

36. See Le Corbusier, *Oeuvre complète 1957–1965*, pp. 111–115.

37. Le Corbusier, *Oeuvre complète 1946–1952*, p. 153; N. Evenson, *Chandigarh*, pp. 86–89.

38. On the primitive symbolism of the hand, see S. Giedion, *The Eternal Present. The beginnings of Art* (New York, 1965), pp. 93–124.

39. Le Corbusier, *Oeuvre complète 1938–1946*, pp. 10 ff. Vaillant-Couturier, a leading figure in the French Front Populaire, was mayor of Villejuif at the time the important school by André Lurcat was built.

40. A similar combination of a hand and a fabulous creature appears on the cover of *Poésie sur Alger*, 1950. Carola Giedion-Welcker suggested to me that Mallarmé is the source.

41. Le Corbusier, *Modulor II*, pp. 269–274.

42. Le Corbusier, *Quand les cathédrales étaient blanches*, p. 82.

43. Friedrich Nietzsche, *Also Sprach Zarathustra* (reprinted ed. 1975), p. 5. On the title page of his copy of Zarathustra (in French) Le Corbusier has indicated the time and place of his first reading of the book (Paris, 1908) and the passages most directly relevant for the symbolism of the open hand.

44. Ibid., pp. 6, 7.

45. Ibid., p. 87.

46. For a complete publication of this letter and a more detailed discussion of its ideological implications see S. von Moos, "The Politics of the Open Hand," *The Open Hand*, Russell Walden, ed. (Cambridge, Mass., 1977), pp. 412–457.

47. See J. Alazard and J.-P. Hébert, *De la fenêtre au pan de verre dans l'architecture de Le Corbusier* (Paris 1961), where the technical (rather than the visual) aspects of the problem are being discussed.

48. Le Corbusier, *Une petite maison*, pp. 27–31.

49. See also, in this context, his first project for the Villa Stein in Garches, published in *Domus* 497 (April 1971):3–9.

50. Le Corbusier, *L'art décoratif*, p. 214.

51. Le Corbusier, *Oeuvre complète 1952–1957*, p. 16.

52. Le Corbusier, *Oeuvre complète 1929–1934*, p. 59.

53. See in this context the painting "Je rêvais" (1934); reproduced in *Werk* 10(1966):490.

54. Le Corbusier, *Quand les cathédrales étaient blanches*, p. 234; see also p. 168.

55. Le Corbusier, *Oeuvre plastique*, preface.

56. Le Corbusier, "Purisme," *Art d'aujourd'hui*, no. 7 (1950).

57. Le Corbusier, *L'atelier de la recherche patiente*, p. 34.

58. Charles Blanc, *Grammaire des arts du dessin*, p. 21. Compare Vasari's phrase on "il disegno, padre delle tre arti nostre." The mother of the arts, however, is—according to Vasari—"L'invenzione" or "la natura." See also *Le vite de' più eccellenti pittori, scultori ed architetti*, ed. Milanesi, Florence, 1878–1906, vol. I, p. 168; II, p. 11; VII, p. 183.

59. Amédée Ozenfant and Charles Edouard Jeanneret, *Après le cubisme*, p. 57.

60. Le Corbusier, *Modulor II*, p. 293.

61. Quoted from Le Corbusier, *Von der Poesie des Bauens*, Hugo Loetscher, ed. (Zurich, 1957), p. 81.

62. See Le Corbusier, *L'atelier de la recherche patiente*, pp. 232 ff.

63. Fernand Léger, *Fonctions de la peinture* (Paris, ed. 1965), pp. 100; 124.

64. *Aujourd'hui*, no. 51; compare Le Corbusier, *Oeuvre complète 1910–1929*, p. 85.

65. See Alfred Roth, *Begegnungen mit Pionieren* (Basel and Stuttgart, 1971), pp. 34 ff.

66. *Claviers de couleurs*, catalog of Salubra wallpapers (n.d., 1930?).

67. Leon Battista Alberti, *De re aedificatoria* I, 1.

68. Le Corbusier, *Oeuvre complète 1929–1934*, pp. 48–52.

69. Le Corbusier, *L'atelier de la recherche patiente*, p. 188. The use of a metal frame for a large housing complex had first been considered by Le Corbusier in the context of his Roq et Rob project at the Côte d'Azur. The use of concrete was out of question on this site—a steep slope—where building materials could only be delivered by boat. The Meaux-system had been developed in collaboration with the Régie Renault and was based on a combined use of steel and plastic.

70. *Architecture d'aujourd'hui*, special issue on Le Corbusier (1948):57.

71. Le Corbusier, *Oeuvre complète 1946–1952*, p. 190.

72. On the "division of labor" between the two men cf. *Aujourd'hui*, no. 51:96–101.

73. See Le Corbusier, *Modulor II*, pp. 280–292.

74. Any discussion on the problem of reproduction in art will have to refer to Walter Benjamin's fundamental essay "Das Kunstwerk im Zeitalter seiner technischen Reproduzierbarkeit"; reedited as one of a series of essays published under the same title, Frankfort, 1955.

75. "The photographic cliché . . . which has provoked the direct and integral use of photography, i.e., it's automatic use, without any manual help, true revolution!" Le Corbusier, *Voyage d'Orient*, p. 123 (footnote, written in 1965).

76. André Malraux, *Le musée imaginaire* (Geneva, 1947), p. 53.

77. Le Corbusier, *L'Esprit Nouveau*, pp. 681 ff.

78. See Le Corbusier, *Oeuvre plastique*, pl. 9 ("La cruche et la lanterne"). The moonlight that seems to reflect on the still life is merely the result of a photomechanical inversion of the original painting's tones. The painting is correctly reproduced in *L'atelier de la recherche patiente*, p. 53. See also p. 230 in the same book where a detail of the fresco in the Pavillon Suisse is reproduced in negative, whereas it is reproduced correctly on the following page.

79. For a good documentation of the Philips Pavilion cf. Le Corbusier, *Le poème éléctronique (Cahiers des forces vives)* (Paris, 1958); see also *L'atelier de la recherche patiente*, p. 186.

80. Robert Venturi, *Complexity and Contradiction in Architecture* (New

York, 1966). For an interesting discussion of the contradictory nature of Le Corbusier's creation see Paul Hofer, "Griff in die Doppelwelt. Notizen zur Person Le Corbusiers," *Fundplätze, Bauplätze. Aufsätze zu Archäologie, Architektur und Städtebau* (Basel, 1970), pp. 155–160.

81. Le Corbusier, *Oeuvre complète 1929–1934*; preface.

82. Le Corbusier, *Quand les cathédrales étaient blanches*, p. 173.

83. Le Corbusier, *Oeuvre complète 1929–1934*, pp. 53–57; see also Alexander Watt, "Fantasy on the Roofs of Paris," *The Architectural Review* IV (1936):155–159.

84. Le Corbusier, *Urbanisme*, p. 114.

85. S. Giedion recalls Le Corbusier's answer to his question as to why he hadn't removed this "heap of rubble": "it has a right to existence." Compare "Il a le droit de l'existence," in *Neue Zürcher Zeitung* 11 (July 1967).

86. P. Mazar, "Il avait su devenir un architecte vénitien," *Le Figaro littéraire* (2–8 September 1965):14. (Le Corbusier memorial issue).

87. Le Corbusier, *L'art décoratif*, pp. 189 ff.

88. Ibid.

89. Le Corbusier, *Quand les cathédrales étaient blanches*, p. 166.

90. *Oeuvres complètes d'Isidore Ducasse, comte de Lautréamont* (Paris, reprinted ed. 1938), p. 362.

91. Letter by Le Corbusier to S. Giedion, quoted in *Le Corbusier*, catalog of the exhibition in Zurich, 1938, p. 12.

92. See e. g., the cover design of the magazine *Coeur à barbe* (1922).

93. Any other architect would probably have been discouraged by the fact that his site was occupied by a tree—as was the case with the Pavillon de L'Esprit Nouveau.

94. See the postscript to *Urbanisme*: "Confirmations, incitations, admonestations."

95. *Zodiac 7*, p. 53.

96. Le Corbusier, *Le Modulor. Essai sur une mesure harmonique à l'échelle humaine applicable universellement à l'architecture et à la mécanique* (Boulogne s. Seine, 1948); *Modulor II. La parole est aux usagers* (Boulogne s. Seine, 1955). The second volume is Le Corbusier's reply to the world-wide reactions generated by *Le Modulor*. For brief summaries of the Modulor system see *Oeuvre complète 1938–1946*, pp. 170 ff. and *Oeuvre complète 1946–1952*, pp. 178–184.

97. Adolf Zeisig, *Neue Lehre von den Proportionen des menschlichen Körpers* (Berlin, 1854).

98. See also Mathila Ghyka, *Esthétique des proportions dans la nature et dans les arts* (Paris, 1927), where Ghyka publishes and discusses some of Le Corbusier's proportion studies, especially the regulating lines of the Villa Stein at Garches.

99. Rudolf Wittkower, "Systems of Proportion," *The Architect's Year Book* 5 (London, 1953), pp. 9–18 (parts of this article are quoted in *Modulor II*, pp. 198–202). For a more complete analysis of the Modulor by the same author see his contribution to *Four Great Makers of Modern Architecture* (New York, 1961), pp. 196–204.

100. Le Corbusier, *Le Modulor*, p. 20.

101. See Le Corbusier, *Le Modulor*, pp. 58 ff. Paul Lester Wiener, who had accompanied Le Corbusier during his visit to Einstein at Princeton has given a slightly different version of Einstein's famous dictum. According to Wiener, Einstein said, "it is a new language of proportions which expresses the good easily and the bad only with complications." After G. Hellman's interview in *The New Yorker*, May 3, 1947, p. 47.

102. Rudolf Arnheim, "A review of Proportion," *Toward a Psychology of Art* (Berkeley and Los Angeles, 1967), pp. 102–119.

103. Le Corbusier, *Le Modulor*, p. 16.

104. Ibid. p. 109.

List of Figures

Index